The Historical Jesus
Part II

Professor Bart D. Ehrman

THE TEACHING COMPANY ®

PUBLISHED BY:

THE TEACHING COMPANY
4151 Lafayette Center Drive, Suite 100
Chantilly, Virginia 20151-1232
1-800-TEACH-12
Fax—703-378-3819
www.teach12.com

ISBN 1-56585-641-4

Bart D. Ehrman, Ph.D.

University of North Carolina at Chapel Hill

Bart Ehrman is the Bowman and Gordon Gray Professor of Religious Studies at the University of North Carolina at Chapel Hill. With degrees from Wheaton College (B.A.) and Princeton Theological Seminary (M.Div. and Ph.D., magna cum laude), he taught at Rutgers for four years before moving to UNC in 1988. During his tenure at UNC, he has garnered numerous awards and prizes, including the Students' Undergraduate Teaching Award (1993), the Ruth and Philip Hettleman Prize for Artistic and Scholarly Achievement (1994), and now the Bowman and Gordon Gray Award for excellence in teaching (1998).

With a focus on early Christianity in its Greco-Roman environment and a special expertise in textual criticism of the New Testament, Professor Ehrman has published dozens of book reviews and over 20 scholarly articles for academic journals. He has authored or edited eight books, including *Jesus: Apocalyptic Prophet of the New Millennium* (Oxford University Press, 1999); *The New Testament: A Historical Introduction to the Early Christian Writings* (Oxford, 1997; 2nd ed., 1999); *After the New Testament: A Reader in Early Christianity* (Oxford, 1999); *The New Testament and Other Early Christian Writings: A Reader* (Oxford 1998); *The Orthodox Corruption of Scripture* (Oxford, 1993); and *The Text of the New Testament in Contemporary Research* (Eerdmans, 1996). He is currently at work on a new Greek–English edition of the Apostolic Fathers for the Loeb Classical Library (Harvard University Press).

Professor Ehrman is a popular lecturer, giving numerous talks each year for such groups as the Carolina Speakers Bureau, the UNC Program for the Humanities, the Biblical Archaeology Society, various local groups, and select universities across the nation. He has served as the president of the Society of Biblical Literature, SE Region; book review editor of the *Journal of Biblical Literature*; editor of the Scholar's Press Monograph Series *The New Testament in the Greek Fathers*; and co-editor of the E.J. Brill series *New Testament Tools and Studies*. Among his administrative responsibilities, Professor Ehrman has served on the executive committee of the Southeast Council for the Study of Religion and has chaired the New Testament textual criticism section of the

Society of Biblical Religion, as well as serving as Director of Graduate Studies at the Department of Religious Studies at UNC.

Table of Contents

The Historical Jesus
Part II

The Historical Jesus

Scope:

From the late Roman Empire, through the Middle Ages, down to the Reformation, and into our own day, no institution has wielded such economic, political, and cultural power as the Christian church. And behind it all stands Jesus, a man who continues to be worshiped throughout the world, by over a billion people today. Jesus of Nazareth is undoubtedly the most important figure in the history of Western civilization.

Everyone who has even the faintest knowledge of Jesus has an opinion about him, and these opinions vary widely—not only among lay people but even among historical scholars who have given their lives to the task of reconstructing what Jesus was really like, what he really said and did. This course is designed to explain why it has proved so difficult to know about the man behind the myth and to see what kinds of conclusions modern scholars have drawn about him. The course will be taught from a strictly historical perspective; no particular theological beliefs will be either affirmed or denied.

The course will begin with a discussion of the four Gospels of the New Testament, which everyone agrees are our principal sources of knowledge about Jesus. But these books were not written as dispassionate histories for impartial observers. In addition, it appears that their authors were not eyewitnesses to the events they narrate but were writing several decades later, telling stories that they had heard—stories that had been in circulation year after year among the followers of Jesus. The first step, then, will be to determine what kinds of books the Gospels are and to ascertain how reliable their information about Jesus is. Apart from their worth as religious documents of faith, we will examine how the Gospels are useful to historians who want to know what really happened.

As we will see, the Gospels create challenges for scholars who want to know about the words and deeds of Jesus. After explicating some of these difficulties, we will consider other sources that are available, including other Gospels that did not make it into the New Testament but that nonetheless purport to narrate the life and teachings of Jesus. In addition, we will examine all the references to Jesus in every other ancient Jewish and Roman source.

After reviewing the available sources, we will examine the criteria that scholars have devised for getting behind the stories told about Jesus to ascertain what he was really like. Once we have a handle on how to approach our sources of information, we will consider the historical context of Jesus' life; our assumption is that if we fail to situate Jesus in his context, we will take him out of context and, therefore, misunderstand him. After discussing the political, social, and cultural history of first-century Palestine, we will proceed to the second major part of the course, a scholarly reconstruction of Jesus' actual words and deeds.

There we will see that the earliest sources at our disposal, including the Gospel of Mark and the lost Gospel of Q (one of the sources used by both Matthew and Luke), are probably correct in portraying Jesus as a Jewish apocalypticist, one who anticipated that God was soon going to intervene in the course of history to overthrow the forces of evil and establish his kingdom here on earth. Specifically, Jesus proclaimed that a cosmic judge from heaven, called the Son of Man, was soon to appear, and that people needed to repent, turn to God, and adhere to his own teachings in preparation. Those who did so would be rewarded with God's kingdom; those who did not would be destroyed.

The remaining lectures in the course will show how this apocalyptic message of Jesus affected his ethical teaching, his own activities, and his final days. We will see that this proclamation caused a furor in Jerusalem when Jesus went there to celebrate the Passover feast at the end of his life. Fearing that his preaching might excite the mobs, the authorities in Jerusalem had him arrested and taken out of the way, handing him over to the Roman governor, Pontius Pilate, who had him executed as a troublemaker.

The course will end, then, by considering how Jesus' followers began to modify his message after they came to believe that he had been raised by God from the dead, as they transformed the religion of Jesus (i.e., the one he preached) into the religion about Jesus.

Lecture Thirteen
Jesus and Roman Rule

Scope:

Rome ruled Palestine much as it did the other provinces of the Empire. Roman or local aristocrats were appointed to run normal operations of government; their ultimate responsibilities were to raise revenue for Rome and to keep the peace. In some ways, Rome granted favored treatment to the Jews of Palestine, but Roman rule was nonetheless felt by many to be an unbearable burden.

Jews responded to Roman rule in a variety of ways: at Passover in Jerusalem, there was a type of silent protest against foreign domination and a not-so-veiled expression of hope that God would intervene once again on behalf of his people; nonviolent resistance to Roman policies; occasionally, they engaged in acts of armed rebellion, including the Jewish War of A.D. 66–70 that left Jerusalem ruins. Throughout the period, prophets arose to speak out against Rome as God's enemies and were often killed as troublemakers.

One form of resistance ideology became prominent in the period. Called "apocalypticism" by modern scholars, this ideology claimed that the forces of evil that were currently in charge of this world and responsible for its suffering would be overthrown by God in a mighty act of judgment. This imminent event was thought to be the prelude to the appearance of God's kingdom in a utopian age preserved for God's people. We have compelling reasons for thinking that Jesus himself proclaimed some such apocalyptic views.

Outline

I. In the last lecture, we saw the importance of situating Jesus in his own historical context.

    A. Jesus was a first-century Palestinian Jew. To understand him, we need to know something about the historical and social context of Judaism in Palestine in the first-century.

    B. One consequences of foreign subjugation of Palestine included the formation of Jewish sects, which exercised some power and offered religious options for Jews living at the time.

1. The Pharisees emphasized keeping the law of God to the fullest degree possible and developed a set of oral laws to ensure this.
2. The Sadducees emphasized worshiping God in the Temple in strict accordance with the Torah, the Law of Moses.
3. The Essenes emphasized maintaining their own purity in light of the imminent apocalypse in which God would judge the world and his own people.
4. The Fourth Philosophy emphasized the Jewish homeland and their divinely appointed right and duty to reestablish Israel as a sovereign state, by force if necessary.

II. The Roman imperial authorities treated the Jews of Palestine much as they treated those in other conquered territories they ruled as provinces. Rome formed conquered lands into provinces ruled either by Roman aristocrats appointed as governors or by local aristocrats designated as client kings.

A. When Jesus was born, all of Palestine was ruled by a client king, Herod; when Jesus died, the northern part of Israel, Galilee, was ruled by one of Herod's sons, but Judea in the south was ruled by a Roman governor, Pontius Pilate.

B. Roman governors and client kings had two principal obligations to the Empire: to raise revenues and to keep the peace. Local administrators were left to do what needed to be done in view of local circumstances.
1. The Romans did not have troops all throughout the conquered territories. Most Jews in Palestine probably never saw a Roman soldier. Soldiers were stationed on the frontiers to protect against invasion.
2. In Palestine a force of soldiers was kept by the Roman governor at his residence in Caesarea on the coast, for use in case of any local disturbance. At Passover, the governor took his troops to Jerusalem to quell any potential trouble.

B. The principal burden that Jews in Palestine bore was the requirement to pay taxes to the Empire, in the form of crops and monies.
1. In monetary terms, the Roman tax burden on Jews appears to have been was average, about twelve or

thirteen percent of income to support the Roman presence in the land.

   2. These taxes were on top of taxes to support the Temple and local Jewish administration, perhaps an additional twenty percent.

   3. This may not appear exorbitant by the standards of today's highly industrialized nations; we must recall, however, that in ancient agrarian societies, most farmers did well to eke out an existence in the best of circumstances.

C. Since the days of Julius Caesar, Jews were not required to supply Rome with soldiers, nor were they required to provide direct support for Roman legions stationed nearby or marching through to the frontiers.

D. In another respect, the Jewish situation could be seen as far worse than average. Many Jews considered it blasphemous to pay taxes to support Roman administration of the land that God had given them.

III. Throughout the first century, Jews of Palestine resisted Roman rule on a number of occasions and in a number of different ways.

A. Many Jews engaged in simple silent protests against foreign rule as, for example, during the Passover festival described earlier.

   1. The festival was explicitly a commemoration of God's deliverance of Israel from an oppressive foreign power in earlier times (from Egypt under Moses).

   2. Many Jews celebrated the feast because they anticipated that God would do it again (free them from Rome under…the messiah?).

   3. Romans understood full well the political implications of the feast, which is why they brought in troops for the occasion

   4. On occasion, the Roman presence had the opposite of its desired effect. For example, in the 50s, during the reign of the procurator Cumanus, a soldier made an indecent gesture to the crowds. They picked up stones, the soldiers moved in, and—according to Josephus (who may have exaggerated the numbers) 20,000 Jews were killed in the mayhem.

B. On some occasions, a Roman administrator would offend the Jews in Palestine, and they would respond through nonviolent protest. During Jesus' lifetime, when Pilate assumed the prefectorship of Judea (A.D. 26), he set up Roman standards with the image of Caesar throughout Jerusalem. Josephus says that Jews in the city erupted in protest and staged a kind of sit-in; after five days and several failed threats of killing the lot of them, Pilate backed down.

C. A very few violent insurrections also occurred in Palestine during the first century.

    1. The most significant and disastrous one came thirty-five to forty years after Jesus' death, when Roman atrocities (e.g., the plundering of the Temple treasury) led to widespread revolt.

    2. The Romans sent in the legions from the north and quickly subjugated Galilee (Josephus, recall, was the commander of the Jewish troops). A group of Galilean Jews fled to Jerusalem and provoked a bloody civil war against the priestly aristocracy who had been in charge of the Temple and the rest of the city. Once they acquired control, these "Zealots" pressed the fight against the Romans to the end.

    3. This led to a horrifying three-year siege of Jerusalem, with massive starvation within the walls. The war ended in a bloodbath in which tens of thousands of Jews were slaughtered or enslaved, rebel leaders were crucified, much of the city was leveled, and the Temple was burned to the ground in A.D. 70.

D. A fourth form of protest involved a more obviously "religious" response. Throughout this period, we know of self-styled prophets who predicted that God would soon intervene on behalf of his people to overthrow the forces of evil that ruled them

    1. As mentioned in Josephus and briefly in Acts, less than fifteen years after Jesus' crucifixion, a prophet named Theudas publicly proclaimed that he would part the Jordan River, allowing the people to cross into Israel on dry land, an obvious reference to the traditions of Israel's exodus from Egypt. The Roman governor sent forth his troops, slaughtered Theudas and his followers, and displayed the prophet's head in Jerusalem.

2. About a decade later, another prophet arose (also mentioned in Acts), called "the Egyptian." He led a huge following (30,000 people, according to Josephus) outside of Jerusalem and predicted that he would make the "walls come tumbling down"—a clear allusion to Joshua and the Battle of Jericho. The Roman troops again were sent forth, and a huge slaughter occurred.

3. John the Baptist should probably be seen as a prophet of this sort, predicting that God would soon intervene on behalf of his people and wreak massive destruction and judgment: "Who warned you to flee from the wrath that is coming? Behold, the axe is lying at the root of the tree; every tree that does not bear fruit will be cut down and cast into the fire" (Luke 3:7, 9). He, too, was executed.

4. Other Jewish prophets arose and experienced similar fates. Roman administrators of Judea had no qualms about destroying anyone whose predictions about God's intervention gained them a large, and potentially riotous, following, especially in Jerusalem.

IV. An even more widespread response to Roman rule involved a kind of religious ideology that became popular during the period, what modern scholars call "apocalypticism." This ideology originated, probably, during the time of the Maccabean revolt, but became enormously popular among the Jews of Palestine under Roman rule.

A. This ideology may have undergirded some of the self-styled prophets I mentioned (almost certainly John the Baptist), and it was widely held among large numbers of Jews.

B. The name comes from the Greek term *apocalypsis*, which means an "unveiling" or a "revealing." Jews who subscribed to this world view maintained that God had revealed to them the future course of events, in which he was soon to overthrow the forces of evil and establish his good kingdom on earth.

C. We know about Jewish apocalyptic thought from a number of ancient sources: the Book of Daniel in the Hebrew Bible, the Dead Sea Scrolls, and numerous "apocalypses" written at the time—i.e., books that describe the course of future events as "revealed" to their authors.

D. Jewish apocalypticists subscribed to four major tenets:

    1. They maintained a view of cosmic dualism, in which there were two forces in the world—good and evil—and everyone and everything sided with one of the two forces. The present age was ruled by the forces of evil and the age to come would be ruled by the forces of good.

    2. They were completely pessimistic about the possibilities of life in the present evil age.

    3. Apocalypticists believed, though, that God would intervene in the course of history, overthrow the forces of evil, and bring in his good kingdom with a judgment of the entire world, both the living and the dead.

    4. Moreover, apocalypticists insisted that this future judgment of God against the forces of evil and the appearance of his good kingdom on earth was imminent. In the words of one famous Jewish apocalypticist: "Truly I tell you, some of you standing here will not taste death before they see the Kingdom of God come in power." These are the words of Jesus (Mark 9:1). "Truly I tell you, this generation will not pass away before all these things take place" (Mark 13:30).

E. Jesus, as presented our earliest and most historically accurate sources, seems to have adopted an apocalyptic point of view and believed that the judgment would happen in his own generation.

Essential Reading:

Ehrman, *The New Testament: A Historical Introduction*, chap. 16.

Horsley, *Jesus and the Spiral of Violence*, chaps. 1–4.

Sanders, *Judaism Practice and Belief*, chaps. 1–4.

Suggested Reading:

Collins, *Apocalyptic Imagination*.

Crossan, *The Historical Jesus*, chaps. 1–4.

Rowland, *Open Heaven*.

Questions to Consider:

1. In view of the brief description of Roman domination of the provinces given above, how does that situation (say, for Jews in Palestine) seem to be like and unlike the situation of developing countries who are under the sway of the economies and policies of major world powers today?

2. Discuss how an apocalyptic worldview might provide comfort for someone experiencing oppression and personal suffering.

Lecture Thirteen—Transcript
Jesus and Roman Rule

In the last lecture, we saw the importance of situating Jesus in his own historical context. Jesus was not confronted with the problems and concerns of the English-speaking world at the beginning of the twenty-first century; if we pretend he was, for example, by thinking that his sayings were addressed directly to our situation, then we simply take him out of context. Whenever you take something out of context, you alter its meaning.

Jesus was a first-century Palestinian Jew. To understand him, we need to know something about the historical and social context of Judaism in his day, in Palestine, in the first century. Last time, we considered some of the political history of Palestine, as a history of foreign subjugation. We looked at the consequences of this subjugation in the formation of Jewish sects within Palestine, sects that by no means comprised a majority of the Jewish population; they did, nonetheless, exercise considerable power and represented religious options for Jews living at the time.

To summarize the perspectives of these sects as simply as possible: The Pharisees emphasized keeping the law of God to the fullest degree possible, and developed a set of oral laws to assure that they did so. The Sadducees emphasized worshipping God in the temple, in strict accordance with requirements set out in the Torah, the Law of Moses found in the Hebrew Scriptures. The Essenes emphasized maintaining their own purity, in light of the imminent apocalypse, in which God would judge the world and His own people. The members of the Fourth Philosophy emphasized the Jewish homeland, and their divinely appointed right and duty to reestablish Israel as a sovereign state within it, by force if necessary. These, then, are the four major sects that we know about, that arose within Palestine under foreign subjugation. In this lecture, I'd like to move a step further, to consider some of the more explicit forms of opposition to Roman rule.

I can begin by saying a few words in more detail about what it meant for Jews in Palestine to live in one of the Roman provinces. The common view that the Jews in Palestine suffered more than anyone else in the Roman Empire is, in some respects, just not true. The Roman imperial authorities treated the Jews of Palestine much like they treated the other conquered territories that they ruled as provinces. The empire, of course, covered a large territory, eventually spreading from what is now England and Spain in the west to Syria in the east, and what is now central Europe in the north to northern Africa, including Egypt, in the south. It was a very large area. The lands that Rome conquered were formed into provinces that were ruled either by Roman aristocrats who were appointed as governors; these would be people who were among the Roman elite who had risen up through the ranks of the Roman administration and then were given a province to rule, so – many provinces were ruled by Roman aristocrats. Other provinces, though, were ruled by local aristocrats, who were designated as client kings of Rome. They were actually kings of the provinces, but they were responsible to Rome who were the ultimate authorities.

When Jesus was born, all of Palestine was ruled by a client king, Herod, Herod the Great. When Jesus died, the northern part of Israel, called Galilee, was ruled by one of Herod's sons, but Judea, in the south, was ruled by a Roman governor, Pontius Pilate. With the death of Herod the Great, the territory was divided up, so there's a difference between King Herod, in the north where Jesus himself was resident, and Pontius Pilate, the Roman governor of the south.

Both Roman governors and client kings had two principal obligations to the Empire. Their obligations were to raise revenues and to keep the peace. Rome did not have a detailed set of regulations dictating how these goals were to be accomplished. Instead, they left it up to efficient administrators to do what was needed in view of local circumstances. There weren't federal laws the way we think of today in our country—having federal laws that required how states or local municipalities might organize their affairs. There were some broad principles, but basically the local administrators, whether they were Romans or members of the local aristocracy, were given free reign so that they could raise the tax monies that Rome required, and so that they could keep the peace.

The Romans did not have troops stationed throughout the conquered territories of the various provinces, as I indicated in an earlier lecture. Most Jews in Palestine probably had never seen a Roman soldier. Soldiers, instead of being located in the interior of the provinces, were instead stationed on the frontiers. In the case of Palestine, the Roman legions were situated up in Syria, to protect against invasion from those outside of the Empire. Only when there was some kind of armed conflict within Palestine would the troops march in. In Palestine, the only troops that were present were a cohort of soldiers that were kept by the Roman governor at his residence in Caesarea, on the coast. These local troops could be used in case of a disturbance, but basically stayed with the governor. It was customary for the governor to come to Jerusalem, the capital city of Judea, at the most incendiary time of the year, the annual Passover feast. At that time, he would station his troops around the temple in order to quell any possible disturbances.

The principal burden that Jews in Palestine bore as a conquered people was the requirement to pay taxes to the Empire, like all other conquered peoples. Since the Roman economy was agrarian, taxation involved payment of crops and of monies to fund the armies and the infrastructure provided by Rome, including roads, bridges, and public buildings. In monetary terms, the Roman tax burden that the Jews appear to have borne was no worse than those of other native populations in the provinces. It's difficult to calculate exactly how much people had to pay in taxes in the ancient world because our sources are so limited on this kind of information, but most recent studies suggest that a typical Jewish farmer—most Jews worked the land—a typical Jewish farmer was evidently taxed on average something like 12 or 13 percent of his income to support the Roman presence in the land.

What has to be borne in mind of course, though, is that this came on top of taxes that Jews had to pay to support the temple in Jerusalem and the local Jewish administration. These tax burdens might have added an additional 20 percent or so to the total tax bill, so that the total taxes might have been something like a third of an average Jew's average tax bill, a third of his actual income. This may not seem exorbitant by the standards of today's highly industrialized nations. Many of us pay more than 30 percent of our income in taxes when you kind of calculate it all out, but we have to recall that in ancient agrarian societies, most farmers did well to eke out an existence in the best of circumstances. Therefore, it seemed to be quite a burden, but no more excessive than many other local peoples'.

My point is, though, that on the one hand Jews were treated like everybody else in the Empire; moreover, it needs to be conceded that in some ways, the treatment of Jews was better than that of other inhabitants of the Empire. Just in strict economic, social, and political terms, Jews were better off. Since the days of Julius Caesar, Jews were not required to supply Rome with soldiers from their ranks. Most other conquered peoples had to supply Roman armies with troops. Jews had been forgiven this responsibility since Julius Caesar, who was assassinated 40 years before Jesus was born. This was a favor to the Jews because of the help the Jews had paid to Caesar's family during some of their conflicts, especially with Egypt. There was a certain advantage to this for the Roman armies as well, since faithful Jews would refuse to serve every seventh day, and you can't really soldier very well if you're not going to fight on Saturdays. In any event, they weren't required to serve, nor were Jews required to provide direct support for Roman legions who were stationed nearby, or when they were marching through the frontiers. That was another exemption Jews had.

In one respect though, of course, the Jewish situation could be seen as far worse than other people's in the Empire, in that many Jews considered it blasphemous to pay taxes to support the Roman administration of the land that God had given them, the Jews. Nobody likes to live in a conquered territory, but Jews had a theology that God Himself had given then this land, and so having to pay taxes on land that they themselves had been given by God was blasphemous to many Jews. Therefore, in some ways, treatment of Jews was better than other people's; in another way, it was worse.

Jews reacted to the Roman administration of Palestine in a variety of ways. For many Jews, for example the aristocracy, the Roman occupation probably had its advantages. We don't hear much about this kind of Jew in our sources, but there were probably lots of Jews who found it all right that the Romans were in charge of the land. After all, the Romans did provide infrastructure, and they did provide protection from hostile nations to the east; that's all to the good. For other Jews, though, the Roman domination was intolerable, a political and religious nightmare. Throughout the first century, Jews of Palestine resisted Roman rule on a number of occasions, and in a number of different ways. I'm going to talk about five different ways that Jews resisted Roman rule. I'm not saying all Jews resisted, or that all Jews resisted in these five ways, but these are five ways that some Jews, in Palestine, resisted the domination by Rome.

First kind of Jewish resistance: Many Jews engaged in simple, silent protests against foreign rule, for example, during the Passover feast that I described in an earlier lecture. The Passover festival was explicitly a commemoration of God's deliverance of Israel from an oppressive foreign power in earlier times. The meal commemorated when Moses was raised up by God to deliver Israel from the subjection to the Egyptians. When Jews celebrated this feast, it wasn't only because they were thinking about what God had done in the past. Many Jews were celebrating the feast precisely because they anticipated that God would do something like that again, this time not in regard to the Egyptians under Moses, but against Rome, under the Messiah. Romans understood full well the political implications of the Passover feast, in other words that it's a kind of silent protest anticipating that God's going to deliver His people. That's why Romans brought in troops for the occasion; less disturbances broke out.

On occasion, the Roman presence itself had the opposite of its desired effect. There's one instance we know about from the writings of Josephus, for example, just to pick one example, during the 50s A.D., so some 25 years after Jesus was executed, under the reign of the Roman procurator Cumanus. Cumanus brought in the troops during the Passover, stationed them around the temple, and according to Josephus, one of the soldiers thought that it would be humorous to moon the crowd; so he lifted up his, whatever they would wear, and he exposed himself to the crowds down below in the temple. The crowds below didn't think this was particularly funny—this was their holy place—and in protest they picked up stones and started pelting the soldiers with stones. The messengers went off to Cumanus, who reported what was happening in the temple. He sent in reinforcements, and panic struck the crowds. According to Josephus, who may have exaggerated the number, there was a huge surge of people, and Josephus says that 20,000 Jews were killed in the mayhem that ensued.

That's the sort of thing that could happen during Passover, a silent protest. Passover in Jerusalem was a particularly tense time. We should recall that Jesus was arrested and removed from the public eye during the Passover. That's probably not insignificant.

Second kind of Jewish resistance: On some occasions, a Roman administrator would offend Jews in Palestine, and they would respond with some kind of nonviolent protest. This happened during Jesus' lifetime, when Pontius Pilate himself assumed the praefectorship of Judea in A.D. 26. When Pilate became the governor, he came into Jerusalem; he actually entered the city at night, and he had his soldiers set up standards throughout the city. These were standards that had the image of the emperor on them. These were stationed, then, throughout Jerusalem to indicate that the new governor had arrived. When Jews in the city woke up and found these standards throughout town, they erupted in protest, and staged a kind of sit-in at Pilate's palace. This sit-in lasted for five days. Finally, Pilate got fed up with it, and surrounded the Jewish people who were there protesting. He surrounded them three deep with soldiers, and ordered the soldiers to pull out their swords, and threatened to murder the lot of them. These Jews responded, according to Josephus, by flinging themselves down on the ground and saying that they'd rather have their heads cut off than to submit to this sacrilege. Pilate, realizing that this probably wasn't a good idea, then backed down and removed the standards. This is a kind of non-violent protest against Roman rule that happened during Jesus' own day.

These are two kinds of protest so far; kind of a silent protest during the Passover feasts, and other times, secondly, non-violent protests. A third kind of Jewish resistance to Roman rule involved violent insurrections in Palestine that took place during the first century. These are incidents in which Jews planned and executed armed revolt against the Romans. Violent insurrections were not everyday occurrences. That's a point I should stress; these didn't happen all the time. They happened a couple of times in the first century; the incidents, in fact, were few and far between. One of them at least, however, led to horrendously disastrous results. This came 35 or 40 years after Jesus' death. Because of Roman atrocities—the Roman governor actually plundered the treasury of the temple in Jerusalem, because he wanted to fund a project of his—because of atrocities such as the plundering of the temple, there was a widespread revolt that emerged against the Romans. To quell the revolt, Romans sent in the legions from the north, which had been stationed up in Syria, and they quickly subjugated the Galilee, the northern part of the land. This is this incident I mentioned before, where the Jewish historian Josephus, before he was a historian, was an aristocrat who had been appointed to be a general of the troops, in Galilee. This is that incident. He led the troops in Galilee, but they were quickly overrun. Josephus, as I pointed out, then surrendered.

A group of Galilean Jews, though, fled to Jerusalem, and provoked a bloody civil war within Jerusalem, in which they staged a coup against the priestly aristocracy that had been in charge of the temple. This group of Galilean Jews is known to history as the "Zealots." These Zealots took over control of the city, and once they had acquired control, they pressed the fight against the Romans to the very end. It led to a horrifying three-year siege of Jerusalem, in which the Romans surrounded the city and didn't allow any supplies to get in, which led, of course, to massive starvation. It wasn't going to end well, and it didn't end well. Finally, the Romans broke through the walls, and there was a massive slaughter. This war ended in a complete bloodbath, in which tens of thousands of Jews were killed or enslaved. The rebel leaders were crucified. They just lined the streets with crosses, and much of the city itself was leveled. The temple was burned to the ground, never again, of course, to be rebuilt.   There were, on occasions—this is the most extreme occasion—there were violent protests in addition to the silent protests and the nonviolent protests.

A fourth kind of Jewish resistance during the first century involved a more obviously, you might call it, "religious" response to Roman opposition. Throughout the first century, we know of self-styled prophets who appeared, who predicted that God would soon intervene on behalf of His people, to overthrow the forces of evil that ruled them. These people were not necessarily urging armed rebellion against the Romans; they were saying that God was going to intervene, and overthrow the Romans. Some of these prophets had large followings. None of them, for obvious reasons, was well received by the Roman authorities themselves. I'll give you a couple of examples of these Jewish prophets protesting Roman rule.

Less than 15 years after Jesus' crucifixion, there was a prophet who was named Theudas. We don't know much about this person, except for what we find in Josephus; the Book of Acts in the New Testament also mentions him. Theudas apparently was a Jewish prophet, he *was* a Jewish prophet, who apparently led a large crowd of Jews out of Jerusalem to the Jordan River. There, he publicly proclaimed that he was going to make the Jordan River part, allowing the people to cross back into Israel on the dry land. This was an obvious reference to the traditions of Israel's exodus from Egypt through the Red Sea, which Moses kind of parted—Moses parts the waters and people walk on the dry land—and then the conquest of the Promised Land, where, again, when the people enter into the Promised Land, the Jordan parts and they enter into it on dry land. This is saying Theudas is going to be the instrument through whom God once again brings back a sovereign state to the Promised Land.

The Romans knew what this was all about, and they heard about what was happening out there in the wilderness by the Jordan River, and so the Roman governor sent forth his troops. They slaughtered Theudas and his followers, and brought Theudas' head back to Jerusalem for display. Romans didn't take kindly to prophets who were predicting that God was going to bring an end to the Roman order.

About a decade later, after Theudas, another prophet arose, who is called by both Josephus and the Book of Acts simply as "the Egyptian." We don't know the name of this person; he's called "the Egyptian." "The Egyptian" led a huge following—according to Josephus, it was 30,000 people—outside of Jerusalem. He predicted that he was going to make the walls of Jerusalem come tumbling down, which again is a clear allusion to the Hebrew Bible, in this case not to the exodus from Egypt, but to the battle of Jericho, under Joshua, when they marched around the city and blew the trumpets, and the walls came tumbling down. Once again, the Romans knew what this was about, that this was a prophet predicting that God was going to do something to destroy the enemy. The Roman troops were sent out again, and a huge slaughter occurred.

Those are two examples of religious responses to Roman rule. A third example of this kind could be seen as John the Baptist, whom we know about from the New Testament, but also from Josephus. John the Baptist appears to have been a prophet of this type, predicting that God was soon going to intervene on behalf of His people, and wreak a mass of destruction and judgment, as John says in the sayings preserved in Q. "Who warned you," he says to the people who've come to hear him, "who warned you to flee from the wrath that's coming? Behold the ax that's lying at the root of the tree. Every tree that does not bear fruit will be cut down and cast into the fire." In other words, he's predicting that if people don't repent,

God is going to enter into judgment with them, and it's going to happen right away; the ax is at the root of the tree. John also, of course, was executed by the ruling authorities.

Other prophets arose and experienced similar fates. Roman administrators of Judea had no qualms about destroying anyone whose predictions that God would soon intervene on behalf of His people gained them a large and potentially riotous following, especially in Jerusalem. We should bear in mind this kind of scenario, when we start to reflect on the life of Jesus, a Jewish prophet who gets executed in Jerusalem.

Fifth and finally, an even more widespread response to Roman rule involved the kind of religious ideology that had become popular during the period. This religious ideology may have originated— probably did originate—during the Maccabean revolt, but it had become enormously popular among the Jews of Palestine under Roman rule. This is an ideology that modern scholars have called "apocalypticism." It was a view held by a number of Jews, probably by many of these prophets that I've just referred to. The term "apocalypticism" comes from the Greek word *apocalypsis*, which means a "revealing" or an "unveiling." Apocalypticists believed that God had revealed to them the future course of events, in which He was going to bring a good kingdom on earth to replace the current evil kingdom.

We know about Jewish apocalyptic thought from a number of ancient sources, such as the Book of Daniel in the Old Testament— the Hebrew Bible—and the Dead Sea Scrolls. Jewish apocalypticists appear to have subscribed to four major tenets of thought; four major tenets characterize Jewish apocalypticists. First, Jewish apocalypticists were dualists. They maintained that there were two fundamental forces of reality, the forces of good and the forces of evil. Everyone and everything sides with one of these two forces. Everyone's on the side of God or the side of Satan. You have angels on the side of God; you have demons on the side of Satan. You have life and righteousness on the side of God. You have death and sin on the side of Satan. Everything participates in one of these two forces. Moreover, the history of the world is divided into two ages. There's the present age, that's ruled by the forces of evil, and the age to come, that will be ruled by the forces of good. Two cosmic powers, two ages of the world, according to Jewish apocalypticism.

First, they're dualists. Second, they're pessimists. Jewish apocalypticists were completely pessimistic about the possibilities of life in the present evil age. It's the evil forces that are in charge now. Therefore, those who side with the good will be punished by the forces that are now in control. Moreover, these evil forces are gaining in power, so that things are going to go from being bad to being very much worse, and there's nothing anyone could do to stop it. You can't improve your lot, for these people, for example by improving technology, by throwing more money into the welfare system, by putting more teachers into the classroom, by putting more cops on the beat. You can't improve society, because it's forces of evil that are in control, and they're going to make it much worse.

Third, apocalypticists believed that God was going to intervene in history, though, and overthrow the forces of evil to bring in His good kingdom. There was going to be a future judgment day in which God would overthrow the forces of evil. When He did so, He would raise people from the dead, so that they would face judgment. There'd be a resurrection at the end of this age in which everybody would face their maker. If they'd sided with the good they'd be rewarded; if they'd sided with the evil, they'd be punished, eternally.

Fourth, apocalypticists maintained that this future judgment of God against the forces of evil and the appearances of His good kingdom on earth was an imminent event. It was going to happen right away. God's kingdom was almost here. How soon would it be? In the words of one famous Jewish apocalypticist from the first century, "Some of you standing here will not taste death before you see that the kingdom of God has come in power." These are the words of Jesus himself, Mark chapter 9, verse 1. "Truly I tell you," says Jesus, "this generation will not pass away before all of these things take place."

Jesus himself appears to have adopted an apocalyptic point of view. There were evil forces in the world, but God was soon going to intervene and overthrow them in a mighty act of judgment; He would bring, then, His good kingdom to Earth. This all was going to happen within Jesus' own generation. At least, that's the point of view of Jesus that's presented in our earliest sources, among the traditions that I think we can accept as most historically accurate, when considered in light of the three criteria that we already discussed. That's going to be the topic of our next lecture.

Lecture Fourteen
Jesus the Apocalyptic Prophet

Scope:

Now that we have examined our sources for the historical Jesus, discussed the historical criteria, and set the context for Jesus' life in first-century Palestine, we can establish what Jesus was actually like and what he said and did. The first step is to set forth the general character of Jesus' message. It appears that Jesus proclaimed an apocalyptic message, that God would soon intervene in the course of history to overthrow the forces of evil and establish his kingdom earth.

We will examine this by looking at the earliest sources at our disposal (Mark, Q, M, and L), even though it later came to be muted (Luke), altered (John), and even spurned (Thomas) and determine if the apocalyptic view of Jesus passes all three of our historical criteria.

Finally, the idea that Jesus was essentially an apocalypticist can explain *both* the beginning and the aftermath of his ministry, which clearly began with Jesus' association with an apocalyptic prophet, John the Baptist, and resulted in the establishment of apocalyptic communities of Christians throughout the Mediterranean. Jesus' ministry links the apocalyptic John and the apocalyptic Christian church.

Outline

I. The only way to know what Jesus actually taught is through the sources that survive from antiquity. Principally, these sources are the Gospels.

   A. These books must be examined critically using the various historical criteria that we have already discussed. It is not good enough to object to any reconstruction of the historical Jesus simply by citing proof texts—i.e., verses that seem to say something else. Every verse in all our sources must be examined carefully, not just to see what it says and to determine what it means, but also to establish whether it actually goes back to the life of Jesus himself.

   B. A careful examination of all the surviving evidence suggests that Jesus was a Jewish apocalypticist.

II. The view that Jesus was an apocalypticist has been dominant among scholars for most of this century.

    A. The view was first popularized by the classic *Quest of the Historical Jesus* written by Albert Schweitzer, the humanitarian and medical missionary who began his career as a philosopher, theologian, and New Testament scholar.

        1. Schweitzer's book discussed in detail all the attempts to write a life of Jesus down to his own day (1906), showing how scholars had portrayed Jesus incorrectly, because they failed to recognize that he was an apocalypticist.

        2. Schweitzer's own reconstruction of Jesus' life and teachings has, probably with justification, been called into question over the course of the past century, but his overriding points—that Jesus must be situated in his own first-century Palestinian context and that his message was apocalyptic—came to dominate scholarship.

    B. Even this broader point of view has come into question in recent times.

III. When applied to our sources for the historical Jesus, the basic rules of thumb indicate that he probably held an apocalyptic view.

    A. We know that historians prefer sources that are closest to the time of the events they narrate and that are, insofar as possible, not tendentious.

    B. In the case of Jesus, we see a clear and consistent trend when it comes to the apocalyptic materials. The earliest sources at our disposal—Q, Mark, M, and L, for example—all portray Jesus apocalyptically. Later sources, for example, John and Thomas, do *not*. This scarcely appears to be an accident.

    C. The basic point is this: throughout the earliest accounts of Jesus' words are found numerous apocalyptic predictions: a kingdom of God is soon to appear on earth, in which God will rule; the forces of evil will be overthrown, and only those who repent and follow Jesus' teachings will be allowed to enter the kingdom; judgment on all others will be brought by the Son of Man, a cosmic figure who may arrive from heaven at any time.

D. Jesus is said to have proclaimed this message in Q, Mark, M, and L—our earliest surviving sources. Consider the following examples: Mark 13:24–27, 30; Luke 17:24; 26–27, 30 (this is Q material; cf. Matt. 24:27, 37–39); Luke 12:39 (also Q; cf. Matt. 24:44); Matt. 13:40–43 (M); and Luke 21:34–36 (L).

E. Some of the most clearly apocalyptic traditions are toned down as we move further away from Jesus' life to the later Gospels.

   1. Mark was our earliest Gospel and was a source for Luke (along with Q and L). We can easily see how the earlier traditions of Mark fared later in the hands of Luke. Interestingly, some of the earlier apocalyptic emphases begin to be muted.

   2. Contrast Mark 9:1 with Luke 9:27, then consider Luke 17:21 (found only in Luke). In this later Gospel, Jesus no longer says that his disciples will see the kingdom come in power, but only that the kingdom will arrive in the ministry of Jesus himself.

   3. In Luke 17:21, Luke has Jesus say that the kingdom is "in your midst." This differs from Mark's earlier "coming with power."

   4. So, too, the high priest is no longer told that he himself will see the Son of Man arrive in judgment (Mark 14:62), but simply that the Son of Man would henceforth be in heaven (Luke 22:69).

   5. Luke does not seem to think that the coming of a real kingdom would occur in the lifetime of Jesus' companions. Evidently, because he was writing after they had died, and he knew that the end had not come. To deal with the "delay of the end," he made appropriate changes in Jesus' predictions.

F. In still later sources, the apocalyptic materials are eliminated.

   1. Thus, in the Gospel of John, the last of the canonical accounts to be written, the kingdom is not described as soon to come, but as already present to those who believe in Jesus (John 3:3, 36).

   2. In fact, the older view—that a day of judgment is coming and the dead will be resurrected at the end of the age—is debunked in view of the newer view, that in

Jesus a person can already be raised into eternal life (John 11:23–26).

G. This "de-apocalypticizing" of Jesus' message continues into the second century. The Gospel of Thomas, for example, written somewhat later than John, contains a clear attack on anyone who believes in a future kingdom here on earth (sayings 3, 18, 118).

H. If we were to tally up these data to this point, we'd have a fairly compelling subtotal. Early traditions record apocalyptic teachings on the lips of Jesus. Later traditions generally mute this emphasis; still later sources explicitly argue against it.
   1. It appears that, when the end did not arrive, Christians realized that Jesus said it would and changed his message accordingly.
   2. If scholars are to prefer the accounts of our earliest sources, then it's clear that the early Jesus is portrayed as an apocalypticist.

IV. The same results accrue if we consider the apocalyptic traditions associated with Jesus in light of the specific criteria that we've discussed: contextual credibility, dissimilarity, and independent attestation.

A. We have absolutely no trouble seeing Jesus as an apocalypticist in terms of contextual credibility.
   1. First-century Palestine had numbers of apocalyptic Jews who left writings, e.g., the Dead Sea Scrolls.
   3. Other apocalyptic Jews were written about, e.g., John the Baptist (in the New Testament accounts) and various other prophets (e.g., Theudas and the Egyptian) who were mentioned by Josephus

B. Some of the most striking apocalyptic traditions also pass the criterion of dissimilarity. I have already discussed a couple of them.
   1. Mark (8:38) talks about a cosmic judge of the earth, the Son of Man, without giving any hint that the reference is to Jesus—even though that's what the earliest Christians who transmitted the saying believed. It seems that they didn't formulate this saying, but it goes back to Jesus himself.

2. The parable of the sheep and goats in Matthew 25 indicates that, at this apocalyptic judgment, the Son of Man will judge the nations based on how they lived. Because this does not coincide with the view of Jesus' later followers—that salvation comes only on the basis of faith in Jesus, not on the basis of good works—the story was probably not formulated by Christians, but by Jesus himself.

3. Some of Jesus' key apocalyptic sayings, therefore, pass both the criteria of contextual credibility and dissimilarity.

C. Some of these sayings also pass the criterion of independent attestation.

1. Jesus is portrayed as an apocalypticist in Mark, Q, M, and L.

2. The later Gospel of Thomas argues against this portrayal. Why argue against something unless someone else subscribes to it?

3. All these sources were independent of one another and all of them, to a greater or lesser extent, especially the earlier sources, portray Jesus apocalyptically.

V. A consideration of the way Jesus' ministry began and how it ended is the key to everything that lies between.

A. There is little doubt that Jesus began his ministry by associating with, and even being baptized by, John the Baptist. The traditions are independently attested and dissimilar to what Christians would have wanted to say about Jesus.

B. John was an apocalyptic prophet in the wilderness. Jesus could have joined forces with the Pharisees, Essenes or the Fourth Philosophy, but intentionally went to John, presumably because he stood in agreement with John's apocalyptic message of the coming judgment.

C. There is also little doubt about the aftermath of Jesus' ministry. After his death, Christian communities were established throughout the Mediterranean.

1. We know about these communities because of the writings of their earliest leaders, such as the apostle Paul, whose writings clearly indicate that he believed he was

living at the end of the age and that Jesus was soon to return from heaven in judgment against the earth (1 Thess. 4:13–5:10).

2. The first communities of Christians were, in other words, thoroughly apocalyptic.

D. How can we explain that the beginning and the aftermath of Jesus' ministry were both thoroughly apocalyptic?

1. If only the beginning were apocalyptic, we could claim that Jesus associated with John but then changed his mind about his apocalyptic views. That wouldn't explain why Jesus' own followers, after his death, were hard-core apocalypticists.

2. If Jesus' later followers were apocalypticists but Jesus did not begin as one, we could say that after Jesus' death, followers changed his teachings to make them coincide with their beliefs.

3. The fact that both the beginning and the end are so clearly apocalyptic is compelling evidence that the middle—Jesus' life, which provides the continuity between John the Baptist and the early Christian communities—was also apocalyptic.

Essential Reading:

Ehrman, *Jesus: Apocalyptic Prophet*, chap. 8.

Schweitzer, *Quest of the Historical Jesus*.

Suggested Reading:

Allison, *Jesus of Nazareth.*

Sanders, *Jesus and Judaism*, chaps. 1–4.

Questions to Consider:

1. What strikes you as the strongest evidence that Jesus was an apocalypticist? Where does the evidence seem to you to be the weakest?

2. How would you counter an argument that said that Jesus was not an apocalypticist because he is not portrayed that way in the Gospel of John?

Lecture Fourteen—Transcript
Jesus the Apocalyptic Prophet

In the past two lectures, we've examined the historical context of Jesus' life as a Jew in first-century Roman Palestine. I've argued that it's important to understand not only the various kinds of social and political reactions that Jews had to their domination by Rome, but also the ideological response that modern scholars have labeled "Jewish apocalypticism."

Apocalypticists maintained that God was soon going to overthrow the evil forces of this world, in order to bring in a kingdom of peace and justice, in which He Himself would reside as king, probably through some kind of human intermediary. This kingdom of God would arrive only after a massive destruction of the governments and institutions of this evil age. People who had sided with the forces of evil that are now in control of this age would themselves enter into judgment. Those who had sided with the forces of good and had suffered as a result would be rewarded when this kingdom came. Moreover, people would be raised from the dead to face judgment, so that a person shouldn't think that they could side with the forces of evil, succeed and prosper because they're on the side of the forces that are in control, and then die and get away with it. God was going to raise people from the dead, and they were going to have to face judgment.

This imminent judgment of God—which was sometimes thought that it was about to be brought by some kind of cosmic figure from heaven, some kind of cosmic judge who would appear on the clouds of heaven as judge of the Earth—this cosmic judgment of God was soon going to happen. According to apocalypticists such as the Essene community, responsible for production of the Dead Sea Scrolls, God's final act of intervention was going to happen in the near future. It was going to happen very soon.

In this lecture, I'm going to be adducing some of the evidence that indicates that Jesus himself held to some such view, that Jesus of Nazareth, like many of his compatriots in the first century, was a Jewish apocalypticist. Before doing so, I need to reemphasize a couple of the major points of these lectures so far.

The only way to know what Jesus himself actually taught is through the sources that survive from antiquity. Principally, these sources are our four Gospels. These books must be examined critically, however, using the various historical criteria at our disposal that we've already discussed. It's not good enough to object to any reconstruction of the historical Jesus simply by citing proof texts, that is, by naming verses that seem to say something else. Every verse, in all of our sources, needs to be examined carefully, not just to see what they say or to determine what they mean, but also to establish whether they actually go back to the life of Jesus himself. A careful examination of all of the surviving evidence suggests, I think, that Jesus himself was a Jewish apocalypticist.

The view that Jesus was an apocalypticist has been dominant among scholars at least in Germany and in America for most of this century. The view was first popularized by the great classic work entitled *The Quest of the Historical Jesus*, written by Albert Schweitzer, the humanitarian and medical missionary who began his career as a philosopher, theologian, and New Testament scholar. Schweitzer wrote a number of books on the New Testament; this *Quest of the Historical Jesus* was his most famous, written in 1906.

This book discussed in detail all of the previous attempts by scholars, especially in Germany, to write a life of Jesus, down to Schweitzer's own day. In the book, Schweitzer showed how scholars had misportrayed Jesus precisely because they failed to recognize that he was an apocalypticist. Schweitzer's own specific reconstruction of Jesus' life and teachings has, probably with good justification, been called into question over the course of the past century. In fact, I don't know any New Testament scholar who thinks that the specifics of Schweitzer's reconstruction are correct. His overarching point, however, has become dominant; namely, that Jesus must be situated in his own first-century Palestinian context, and that Jesus' message was apocalyptic.

Even this broader point of view, though, has come into question in recent times. There are a number of scholars writing about Jesus today who claim that, contrary to the dominant view, Jesus was not an apocalypticist. This should come as no surprise to anyone familiar at all with the ebb and flow of scholarship. For one thing, very few people who devote their lives to studying the historical Jesus actually want to find a Jesus who seems so completely removed from our own time. Somebody who's a first-century Jewish apocalypticist just doesn't seem to relate very well to those of us living today. People, even scholars, want to find a Jesus who's more obviously relevant. Therefore, it's no wonder that scholars, who are, after all, human, want to see Jesus in some other light; for example, seeing Jesus as a neo-Marxist, or a neo-feminist, or a countercultural cynic. As I've insisted, however, historians who try to reconstruct the past are obliged to follow their own self-imposed rules. These rules include things like looking at what they call "evidence," and the evidence is rooted in ancient sources, which must be examined in critical ways. Whatever the reasons scholars may have, then, for debunking the idea that Jesus was an apocalypticist, one can always look at the sources to see whether what the scholars say is probably right or not.

I'm going to look at our sources in two basic ways in this lecture. First, I'm going to deal with the basic rules of thumb that I've talked about in an earlier lecture, of what historians like to see when reconstructing the past, and then I'm going to apply our specific criteria of contextual credibility, independent attestation, and dissimilarity to our earliest traditions about Jesus in order to show that Jesus probably was an apocalypticist.

First, I want to apply to our sources for the historical Jesus the basic rules of thumb that indicate that he probably has an apocalyptic view. As we've seen, historians give preference to sources that are closest to the times of the events that they narrate, and that insofar as possible are not tendentious. In the case of Jesus, there is a clear and consistent trend when it comes to the apocalyptic material. Our earliest sources: Q, Mark, M, and L, all portray Jesus apocalyptically. Our later sources, for example, John and Thomas, do not. This scarcely appears to be an accident. I'll not provide all of the data here, since we'll be considering lots more of it in later lectures, but I do want to make the basic point: Throughout the earliest accounts of Jesus' words are found numerous apocalyptic predictions. Jesus preaches that a kingdom of God is soon to appear, which God Himself will rule. This will be an actual kingdom here on Earth.

When this kingdom of God comes, the forces of evil will be overthrown, along with everyone who has sided with them, and only those who repent and follow Jesus' teachings will be allowed to enter this kingdom. Judgment on all others will be brought by the Son of Man, which Jesus uses as a title to refer to a cosmic figure who may arrive from heaven at any time—the Son of Man. Being a member of

Israel, according to Jesus, will not be enough to escape the coming judgment. People need instead to heed Jesus' word to return to God, and to follow His commandments before it's too late.

Jesus is said to have proclaimed this message in Q, Mark, M, and L, our earliest surviving sources. Consider the following examples. From Mark, our earliest surviving Gospel, chapter 13, verses 24 and following, Jesus says, "In those days, after that suffering, the sun will be darkened, the moon will not give its light, the stars will be falling from heaven, and the powers in the heavens will be shaken. Then they will see the Son of Man coming in clouds, with great power and glory, and then he will send out angels, and gather his elect from the four winds, from the ends of the Earth to the ends of the heaven." When is this going to happen? Verse 30: "Truly I tell you, this generation will not pass away before all of these things take place." A cosmic judgment of the Earth, and it's going to happen within Jesus' own generation.

Or consider the account from Q. Q, of course, is the sayings material found in Matthew and Luke, not found in Mark. From Q, using Luke's form, Luke chapter 17, verse 24 and following, Jesus says, "As the lightning flashes and lights up the sky from one side to the other, will the Son of Man be in his day. Just as it was in the days of Noah, so it will be in the days of the Son of Man. They were eating and drinking and marrying, and being given in marriage, until the day Noah entered the ark, and the flood came and destroyed them all." That's what it's going to be like in the days of the Son of Man. It's going to be a mass of destruction. So it will be, he goes on to say, it will be like that on the day the Son of Man is revealed.

Consider one other Q saying from Luke chapter 12, verse 39: "Know this," says Jesus, "if the owner of the house had known at what hour the thief was coming, he would not have his house be broken into. So also you must be ready, for the Son of Man is coming at an unexpected hour." Mark, Q, M, and L all have sayings like this, in which the Son of Man is soon coming in judgment on the evil forces of Earth, and people need to repent in preparation.

That's what we find in our earliest sources. What is striking is that most of the clearly apocalyptic traditions in these sources comes to be toned down as we move further away from Jesus' life in the mid-20s to the Gospel materials used near the end of the first century.

The apocalyptic emphasis gets toned down in our later traditions. Here I'll just provide one example.

I've already pointed out that Mark was our earliest Gospel, and was probably used by the Gospel of Luke, along with Q and of course L. It's relatively simple business, then, to see how the earlier traditions of Mark fared in the hands of Luke, who was using his traditions to compose his own Gospel. Interestingly, when you do this kind of comparison of Mark and Luke, you find that the earlier apocalyptic emphases of Mark begin to be muted. You can see this, for example, by comparison of specific verses. I've quoted this verse, Mark chapter 9, verse 1: "Some of you standing here won't taste death before you see the kingdom of God having come in power, the powerful appearance of the kingdom of God." Luke has the verse, but instead he words it a little differently by cutting out the end. In Luke, Jesus says, "Some of you standing here won't taste death before you see the kingdom of God."

Isn't that the same thing? Not quite. In Luke's Gospel, people do see the kingdom of God, not in its coming in power, though. They see the kingdom of God in the ministry of Jesus himself. In a verse found only in Luke, Luke chapter 17, verses 20 and 21, Jesus is talking to his opponents, the Pharisees, and he tells them—this is only Luke, it's not our earlier sources—"The kingdom of God," says Jesus in Luke, "is not coming with things that can be observed, nor will they say, 'Look here it is, or there it is,' for in fact," says Jesus, "the kingdom of God is among you." It's "among you." That's found in Luke, not found in Mark. Luke doesn't have the kingdom of God coming in power; he has the kingdom of God present. It's present among them in Jesus' own ministry. That's why, in Luke's Gospel, you have a change of what Jesus says to the high priest at his own trial.

In Mark's Gospel, the high priest asks Jesus, "Are you the Messiah, the son of the blessed?" and Jesus replies, "I am, and you shall see the Son of Man coming on the clouds of heaven." You, the high priest, will see it happen. Luke changes that. In Luke's Gospel, Jesus doesn't say, "I am the Messiah, and you will see the Son of Man coming on the clouds of heaven." Instead, he says, "I am, and from now on, the Son of Man will be seated at the right hand of power." He doesn't tell the high priest that he's going to be alive to see it happen. Why not? Luke, writing 15 years or so after Mark, does not apparently think that there was going to be an actual in-breaking of a real kingdom in the lifetime of Jesus' companions. Why didn't he think that? Evidently, because he was writing after they had died, and he knew that in fact the end had not come. To deal with the delay of the end, he made the appropriate changes in Jesus' predictions.

In still later sources after Luke, the apocalyptic materials come to be eliminated altogether. For example, in the Gospel of John, the last of our canonical accounts, the kingdom is not described as soon to come, but as already present to those who believe in Jesus; for example, John chapter 3, verse 36. In fact, John's Gospel argues against the older view, that there will be a day of judgment and a resurrection of the dead at the end of the age. John argues against this view—John chapter 11, verses 23 through 26—by maintaining that the resurrection of the dead is not a future event that's going to happen later. The resurrection happens as soon as somebody has faith in Jesus. Then a person already has eternal life, not that they'll have the kingdom when it comes (John chapter 11, verses 23 through 26).

This is what we might call the "de-apocalypticizing" of Jesus' message. As time goes on, the apocalyptic emphasis, that there's going to be an imminent appearance of the kingdom of God, gets muted by Luke, then is argued against by John, and is argued against even more strenuously even later, for example, in the second-century Gospel, the Gospel of Thomas. Here, in fact, there's a clear attack on anyone who thinks that there will be a future kingdom here on earth, in the Gospel of Thomas. For example, saying number 3, in which Jesus says, "If anyone tells you the kingdom of God will appear in the sea, well, the fish will go before you. If anyone says that the kingdom of God will come in the heavens, then the birds will come before you. Instead, the kingdom of God is among you, is within you, and outside of you." Sayings like Gospel of Thomas 3, Gospel of Thomas 113, and others, argue against an apocalyptic point of view.

If we were to tally up these data to this point, we'd have a fairly compelling subtotal. The early traditions record apocalyptic teachings on the lips of Jesus. Later traditions generally mute this emphasis, and still later sources explicitly argue against it. It appears that when the end never did arrive, Christians had to take stock of the fact that Jesus said it would, and they changed his message accordingly. You can hardly blame them.

If scholars are to prefer the accounts of our earliest sources, then it's clear that Jesus is, early on, portrayed as an apocalypticist. That's looking at our traditions according to these basic rules of thumb. I also, though, want to look at our early traditions in light of the specific criteria we've used to establish historically reliable material—contextual credibility, dissimilarity, and independent attestation.

First, contextual credibility: There's absolutely no trouble with seeing Jesus as an apocalypticist in light of his own context. We know that there were lots of apocalyptic Jews in precisely his time and place, first-century Palestine, and a number of these Jews have actually left us writings; for example, the Dead Sea Scrolls. Others of these apocalyptic Jews were written about. For example, John the Baptist in the New Testament accounts is clearly an apocalypticist. There were also various other prophets at the time who were mentioned by Josephus; for example, Theudas and "the Egyptian." In terms of contextual credibility, therefore, there's no question that Jesus could well have been an apocalypticist.

The second criterion to discuss is the criterion of dissimilarity. In fact, some of the most striking apocalyptic traditions we have do pass the criterion of dissimilarity. I've already discussed a couple of them in trying to illustrate the criterion; let me review what we saw there. There are some sayings that appear to pass the criterion, like Mark chapter 8, verse 38. In Mark 8:38 Jesus is talking about the Son of Man. It's important to remember that the early Christians thought that Jesus was the Son of Man. In fact, they have him saying all sorts of things in which he identifies himself as the Son of Man, as you would expect Christians to do, since they thought he was the Son of Man. Mark 8:38, though, seems a little different from that. Mark 8:38 talks about a cosmic judge of the earth, the Son of Man, without giving any hint at all that Jesus is actually referring to himself, even though that's what the earliest Christians who transmitted the saying believed. In Mark 8:38, Jesus says, "Whoever is ashamed of me and of my words in this adulterous and sinful generation, of that one the Son of Man will be ashamed when he comes on the clouds of heaven in the presence of the holy angels."

"Whoever is ashamed of me, of that person the Son of Man will be ashamed." There doesn't seem to be a linkage between Jesus himself and the Son of Man. He seems to be talking about somebody else. That probably means that Christians didn't formulate the saying, because it's ambiguous whom Jesus is referring to. That probably means it goes back to Jesus himself, and it's an apocalyptic saying; there's going to be a future judgment based on how people react to Jesus' own proclamation.

A second example that I gave earlier, the parable of the sheep and the goats, in Matthew chapter 25—this is a story that indicates that at the apocalyptic judgment, the Son of Man will judge the nations based on how they lived, either doing good to others in need, or ignoring their needs: People will be brought into the kingdom, because when one was hungry, they fed him, when one was thirsty, they gave him to drink, when one was naked, they clothed him, when one was in prison, they visited him. People are brought into the kingdom on the basis of the good things that they did.

Christians probably didn't make up that story, though, because Christians, after Jesus' death, thought that a person came into the kingdom not on the basis of the good deeds they did, but on the basis of their faith in Jesus' death and resurrection. Since Christians didn't make up that story, it probably goes back to Jesus, and it's a story that emphasizes that there's a future kingdom that's coming; people need to be ready for it by behaving in appropriate ways, and the kingdom will involve a judgment brought by the Son of Man. These sayings, then, appear to pass the criterion of dissimilarity.

Even more impressively, the apocalyptic materials that we have in our earliest traditions pass the criterion of independent attestation, as I've already shown when discussing our rule of thumb. Jesus is portrayed as an apocalypticist in Mark, Q, M, and L. These are all independent sources for our early traditions about Jesus. Moreover, the portrayal of Jesus as an apocalypticist is actually argued against in our later Gospel of Thomas. That's an important point, because you don't argue against something unless somebody else subscribes to it, so in a kind of ironic way, Thomas itself shows that there are people who thought that Jesus was an apocalypticist based on traditions it heard. The point is that throughout our sources that are independent of one another, we find Jesus being portrayed apocalyptically, especially in our earliest sources.

To this stage, what I've done is looked at our basic rules of thumb, which argue that the earliest materials are more likely authentic than later materials, and that the earlier sources consistently portray Jesus apocalyptically, and I've looked at our three criteria and shown that Jesus as an apocalypticist passes contextual credibility, dissimilarity, and independent attestation. These are pretty good grounds for thinking that Jesus himself taught something like other Jewish apocalypticists were teaching. In broad terms, this means that there are evil forces in control of this world that God's going to overthrow in an act of judgment, when he brings in a kingdom on Earth that will replace the evil kingdom now in power, and that this was an imminent event.

I have one other argument, though, that I want to make for Jesus being an apocalypticist, that strikes me as the most convincing argument of all. It's a consideration of the way that Jesus both began his ministry, and what happened in the aftermath of his ministry. The beginning of his ministry and the ending of his ministry, in conjunction with one another, provide a key to everything that lies in between the two. In other words, the beginning and the end are the keys to the middle of Jesus' own ministry.

How do I unpack this? There is very little doubt about how Jesus began his public ministry. Jesus began his public ministry by associating with, and even being baptized by, John the Baptist. As we saw in an earlier lecture, we don't know much about what Jesus was doing prior to his baptism by John. There's a shroud of silence over what Jesus was doing as a boy and a young man. We are certain, though, fairly as certain as we can be about anything from the life of Jesus, that he began by being baptized by John. These traditions, as we've seen, are independently attested. We have traditions of the association in Mark, in Q, and in John. Moreover, the idea of Jesus being baptized by John is dissimilar to what Christians would have wanted to say about Jesus, because it might suggest that Jesus was inferior to the one who's baptizing him, just as normally happened in early Christianity. It was thought that the one baptizing was spiritually superior to the one being baptized, so nobody would make up the story.

We've seen that John the Baptist was an apocalyptic prophet in the wilderness, as is recorded in the Q source. John says that people need to repent because the "ax is laid at the root of the tree," and every tree that doesn't bear fruit will be cut down and thrown into the fire; a judgment image, and an image of the imminence of the end, because the ax is ready to start its chopping.

John was an apocalyptic prophet. Jesus associated with him at the beginning of his ministry. I need to stress that Jesus was by no means compelled to associate with John. Jesus could just as well have joined forces with the Pharisees, or with the Essenes, or with the Fourth Philosophy. This shows that Jesus intentionally went to John, and we can only assume that it was because he stood in basic agreement with John's apocalyptic message of the coming judgment. That's how Jesus began his ministry.

On the other side of things, there's little doubt about the aftermath of Jesus' ministry. After his death, Christian communities were established throughout the Mediterranean. We know about these communities because of the writings of their earliest leaders. What were these communities like? We know, because we have writings. The first author we have is the apostle Paul, whose writings clearly indicate that Paul believed he was living at the end of the age, and that Jesus himself was soon to return from heaven in judgment against the earth. This was a firm belief of Paul's. In some of Paul's letters, like First Corinthians chapter 15, and first Thessalonians chapter 4, Paul indicates that he thinks that he himself is going to be alive when the end comes. There's a slight difference between Paul and Jesus, because Jesus talked about the Son of Man coming, and Paul talked about Jesus coming. For Paul, though, Jesus was the Son of Man, who would be the cosmic judge of the Earth, who would destroy everybody who was opposed to God, and then bring in God's kingdom. Paul's writings show us that the first communities of Christians were apocalyptic.

Here's the argument: We know that Jesus began by associating with an apocalypticist, and we know that the aftermath of Jesus' ministry was the establishment of apocalyptic Christian communities. How do we explain both phenomena? If the beginning and end are both apocalyptic, how could the middle not be?

In other words, if Jesus had begun by associating with John the Baptist, but then the later communities of Jesus were not apocalyptic in nature, you could say that Jesus started out apocalyptically, but then changed his mind, and so his followers weren't apocalyptic. Conversely, if Jesus started out associating with someone who was not an apocalypticist, but his later followers were apocalypticist, you could say that Jesus himself wasn't apocalyptic, but then his followers became apocalyptic after his death. The problem is you've got both ends of Jesus' ministry that are thoroughly apocalyptic. The fact that both the beginning and end are apocalyptic is compelling evidence, I think, that the middle itself, Jesus' own life, which provides the only continuity we have between John the Baptist and the early Christian community, was itself apocalyptic.

In conclusion, I should say that all of this evidence needs to be taken together as a cumulative kind of argument, and that when it is, it seems to me that it makes a pretty compelling case. Our earliest sources portray Jesus as an apocalypticist, who proclaimed the judgment of God was soon to come, bringing in its wake the appearance of God's own kingdom. These traditions are independently attested, some of them pass the criterion of dissimilarity, and all of them are completely credible when seen in light of Jesus' own historical context. Moreover, they alone can explain the continuity between the beginning of Jesus' ministry, his association with John the Baptist, and its aftermath, in the establishment of apocalyptic communities of faith by his followers.

Having established that Jesus was an apocalypticist, of course, is not the same thing as knowing exactly what he taught. That, then, will be our next task, to see what we can learn about the actual proclamation of Jesus, based on a critical evaluation of our earliest surviving sources.

Lecture Fifteen
The Apocalyptic Teachings of Jesus

Scope:

Jesus proclaimed that God's kingdom was coming to earth imminently. This would be a real kingdom with real rulers (the twelve disciples), a kingdom that would welcome some people but exclude others. Before the kingdom arrived, a scene of judgment would take place, in which the Son of Man, a cosmic figure from heaven, would appear to destroy God's enemies. This coming judgment would involve a massive reversal of fortunes; those who had prospered in this world through siding with evil would be taken down, but those who had suffered would be exalted. The judgment would come not to individuals, and also to institutions and governments. In particular, the Jewish Temple in Jerusalem, the heart of all Jewish worship, would be destroyed.

Outline

I. In the last lecture, we saw that, in the most general terms, Jesus can be labeled a first-century Jewish apocalypticist who taught that a kingdom of God was coming to earth.

    A. I take the summary of his preaching in Mark 1:15 (the first words he is recorded to have said in that Gospel) to be reasonably accurate and thoroughly apocalyptic: the present age is nearly up; repent now.

    B. Throughout his authentic teachings, when Jesus refers to the coming kingdom, he seems to mean an actual earthly kingdom, ruled by God. Consider the things Jesus says in early traditions found in Q:

        "Truly I say to you, in the renewed world, when the Son of Man is sitting on the throne of his glory, you [disciples] also will be seated on twelve thrones, judging the twelve tribes of Israel." (Matt. 19:28; cf. Luke 22:30)

        "And there will be weeping and gnashing of teeth when you see Abraham and Isaac and Jacob and all the prophets in the kingdom, but you are cast out; and people will come from east and west and from north and south and recline at table in the kingdom of God." (Q: Luke 13:23–29; cf. Matt. 8:11–12)

II. While the arrival of the kingdom was "good news" for Jesus' followers, it was not good news for everyone. In a mighty act of judgment, evil rulers will be toppled and punished, and the oppressed will be raised up.

A. This judgment will be universal in scope. Compare the saying in our earliest Gospel:

> "And in those days, after that affliction, the sun will grow dark and the moon will not give its light, and the stars will be falling from heaven, and the powers in the sky will be shaken; and then they will see the Son of Man coming on the clouds with great power and glory. And then he will send forth his angels and he will gather his elect from the four winds, from the end of earth to the end of heaven." (Mark 13:24–27)

B. This coming judgment is the subject of a number of Jesus' parables. Consider this one that is multiply attested in Matthew and Thomas:

> "Again, the kingdom of heaven is like a net which was thrown into the sea and gathered fish of every kind. When it was full, they hauled it ashore, and sitting down chose the good fish and put them into containers, but the bad fish they threw away. That's how it will be at the completion of the age. The angels will come and separate the evil from the midst of the righteous, and cast them into the fiery furnace. There people will weep and gnash their teeth." (Matt. 13:47–50)

B. As seen in these references, Jesus calls this coming agent of judgment, who is regularly accompanied by angels, the "Son of Man," a title deriving from a passage from the Hebrew Bible, Dan. 7:13–14.

1. In some of the sayings about the future coming of the Son of Man, Jesus does not appear to be speaking about himself. These sayings, pass the criterion of dissimilarity, because Christians would be unlikely to make up sayings in which it was unclear that Jesus himself was the future judge.

2. These sayings also pass the criterion of contextual credibility—cf. Enoch, ch. 69, a contemporaneous

Jewish apocalyptic prophecy referring to the "son of man" as an agent of God's judgment.

3. In other sayings, though, Jesus clearly does speak about himself using the term "son of man." These obviously do not pass the criterion of dissimilarity.

4. As a result, we can be reasonably sure that Jesus said that a future judge of the earth, whom he called the Son of Man, was soon to be sent from heaven as a prelude to God's kingdom.

C. Similar teachings can be found in other apocalyptic writings from the same time period (e.g., 1 Enoch 69:4; Ezra 13:1–11).

III. This coming judgment would involve a serious reversal: Those who are in power would be removed; those who are oppressed would be exalted.

A. This kind of reversal of fortune makes sense in an apocalyptic context.

"And so the one who exalts himself shall be humbled and the one who humbles himself shall be exalted; for the first shall be last and the last shall be first" (Mark 10:31; Luke 13:30).

B. This is the theme of some of Jesus' best known but least understood teachings, the Beatitudes.

1. In these teachings, notice the verb tenses, in view of Jesus' apocalyptic emphases: "Blessed are the meek, for they *shall* inherit the earth, blessed are those who hunger and thirst for righteousness, for they *shall* be satisfied, blessed are the pure in heart, for they *shall* see God." When? In the future kingdom.

2. And so, "blessed are those who are persecuted for doing what is right, for theirs is the kingdom of heaven." God's kingdom will come to those who are beaten down, poor, hungry, and persecuted.

IV. The coming judgment of God would involve not just individuals, but governments and institutions.

A. In particular, Jesus is reported in independent sources to have predicted that the grand and glorious Temple in

Jerusalem, the center of all Jewish religion, would be destroyed at the appearance of the Son of Man (Mark 13:1).

1. As we will see more fully in a later lecture, even though the Temple was ordered to be built by God and was run according to his dictates in Scripture by the leaders of his own people, Jesus taught that the institution had become corrupt and was going to be overthrown by God when the Son of Man arrived.

2. That a Jew would say such a thing about the Temple is completely credible. The prophet Jeremiah in the Hebrew Bible made a similar prediction six centuries earlier (Jeremiah 7), as did other self-styled prophets in Jesus' day, as we know from Josephus.

B. As we will see in a later lecture, this teaching in particular got Jesus into trouble with the ruling authorities.

V. Jesus maintained that the Son of Man's arrival was not some far off event to be worried about at some remote time in the future. It was imminent. It would come in his own generation (Mark 8:38–9:1; 13:30).

A. In the next lecture, we'll consider some of the ethical corollaries of Jesus' proclamation of the coming kingdom. His moral teaching was situated clearly in his apocalyptic context.

1. Jesus did not teach his ethics to show people how to live in peace for the long haul. For him, there wasn't going to be a long haul.

2. His ethical teachings are meant to show people what they need to do now to escape judgment when the Son of Man arrives and to be brought into the kingdom of God. Believers needed to be humble (Mark 9:35; 10:42–44); be like "little children" (Mark 10:14); give away all their possessions and all their attachments to earthly things, (Mark 10:25).

B. Similarly—and possibly even more strikingly—Jesus taught that it would not be the upright and religious people who are brought into the kingdom, but sinners (Matt 21:31–32; Luke 18:9–14).

1. Probably none of Jesus' teachings caused such an uproar as these. Tax collectors and prostitutes and sinners will

come into the kingdom before the righteous leaders of the Jews (Matt 21:31).

2. It is hard to know what he meant by this, but given the number of places in which Jesus urges people to repent and return to doing what God really wants, it appears that those who were exalted leaders of his people were not right before God, whereas those who humbly repented of their wicked ways were.

E. Jesus taught that people needed to repent and live in ways God wanted them to in light of the coming kingdom. In the next lecture, we'll consider more fully what that might have entailed.

Essential Reading:

Mark 10, 13; Matthew 5–7, 24–26.

Ehrman, *Jesus: Apocalyptic Prophet*, chap. 9.

Sanders, *The Historical Figure of Jesus*, chaps. 11–13.

Suggested Reading:

Chilton and Evans, *Authenticating the Words of Jesus*.

Meier, *A Marginal Jew*.

Sanders, *Jesus and Judaism*.

Questions to Consider:

1. Why have Christian readers been so reluctant to take literally Jesus' teachings about the coming Son of Man, the cosmic destruction he'll bring, and the need to give away possessions and live like slaves?

2. Read over some of the more familiar teachings of Jesus, such as the Beatitudes in Matthew 5, the Lord's Prayer in Matthew 6, and the parable of the sheep and the goats in Matthew 25, and reflect on what they would mean in an apocalyptic context.

Lecture Fifteen—Transcript
The Apocalyptic Teachings of Jesus

In the previous lecture, we began to apply the historical criteria that scholars have devised for reconstructing the life of the historical Jesus, and saw that in the most general terms, he can be labeled as a first-century Jewish apocalypticist. The apocalyptic traditions about Jesus are not only contextually credible; they're independently attested in our earliest sources, and some of them even pass the criterion of dissimilarity. Moreover, only if Jesus were an apocalypticist could we make sense of two of the most certain facts of his life—that he began his public ministry by associating with an apocalyptic prophet, John the Baptist, and that the aftermath of his life involved the establishment of apocalyptic communities by his followers. Jesus, then, appears to have taught, like so many of his contemporaries, that he was living at the end of the present evil age, but that a new age was coming, to be inaugurated by a mighty act of judgment, in which the forces of evil would be overthrown, and God's kingdom would appear on Earth.

Having established that Jesus was, in some sense, an apocalypticist does not actually tell us much about the specific things that he taught. In this lecture, we'll begin to dig a bit deeper into our sources, to try to uncover the actual apocalyptic teachings of Jesus. Because of our serious time constraints, I won't be able to engage in lengthy discussions of our historical criteria at every point to demonstrate that Jesus actually said these things that he's recorded as saying in our earliest sources. You'll be able to find a fuller analysis of these traditions in my book on the historical Jesus that's given in the reading connected with the course, and with other readings that I've suggested there. Here, for this lecture, then, I'll simply go into some of the main points.

Jesus taught that an actual kingdom of God was coming to earth. I take the summary of his preaching in Mark chapter 1, verse 15 to be reasonably accurate. These are the first words that Jesus is recorded to have said, in this, our first Gospel. Mark 1:15, Jesus says, "The time has been fulfilled. The kingdom of God is at hand. Repent and believe the good news." This is an apocalyptic image that Jesus is using: "The time has been fulfilled." The idea behind it is that this age that we live in now has a certain amount of time that's been allotted to it. That time has been fulfilled. Once this age is over, the new age will come, in which there will be a kingdom of God. The kingdom of God is at hand. It's near. It's upon us. People, then, need to prepare for the coming of this kingdom of God by turning their lives around, repenting, and believing this good news of its imminent advent.

Throughout Jesus' authentic teachings, when he refers to this "coming kingdom," he seems to mean an actual kingdom here on earth, in which God Himself will be the ruler. When Jesus talks about the kingdom of God coming, he doesn't seem to be referring to what many people today might think of as heaven. In other words, he's not talking about the place people go when they die, or he's not referring to the kingdom of God as the rule of God in your heart. He appears actually to be talking about a kingdom, a place here on earth, in which God Himself will rule, possibly through a human emissary of some type. Jesus then talks about this earthly entity of the kingdom that will arrive with a powerful act of God. There'll be actual rulers in this kingdom. People will eat and drink in this kingdom. Some people will be allowed to stay in this kingdom. Others will be forcibly removed from this kingdom. My point is that this is an actual place here on Earth that God's going to rule.

Consider some of the early traditions about Jesus found in the Q source; for example, the Q saying found in Matthew 19:28: "Truly I say to you," says Jesus, "in the renewed world, when the Son of Man is sitting on the throne of his glory, you," he's talking to the twelve disciples, "you will also be seated on twelve thrones judging the twelve tribes of Israel." The twelve disciples are going to be rulers in this future kingdom. Or consider the Q saying that's now found in Luke chapter 13 verses 23 through 29, where Jesus says, "There will be weeping and gnashing of teeth when you see Abraham and Isaac and Jacob and all the prophets in the kingdom, but you are cast out." Now he's not talking to the twelve disciples, he's talking to his opponents. "And people," he says, "will come from east and west and from north and south, and recline at table in the kingdom of God." This is going to be a place where people can eat, people can drink, people can be thrown out of. The disciples will be ruling over this kingdom.

These kinds of references are scattered throughout the tradition. Jesus, like other apocalypticists living before him and afterwards, evidently thought that God was going to extend His rule from the heavenly realm, where He resides now, down to earth, in a real, physical kingdom, here in a kind of paradisal world in which God Himself would rule His faithful.

While the arrival of the kingdom was preached by Jesus as "good news" for his followers, it wasn't good news for everyone, for this kingdom would be brought by a mighty act of judgment. You need to recall the kind of apocalyptic thinking behind this teaching of the kingdom. The present age is ruled by the forces of evil, and so those in power now are empowered by evil. When God's kingdom comes, then, those people are going to be taken out of power, and the humble are going to be exalted and given this good kingdom. Thus, it's good news for those who are humble, those who are oppressed, those who are downtrodden now. It's not good news for everybody.

There's going to be a future judgment, and the judgment is going to be universal in scope. It isn't simply gong to involve a few people. Some of Jesus' sayings indicate, in fact, that it's going to be a kind of cosmic judgment. Consider this early account we've already seen in Mark chapter 13, where Jesus says, "In those days, after that affliction, the sun will grow dark, the moon will not give its light, the stars will be falling from heaven, and the powers in the sky will be shaken, and then, then they will see the Son of Man coming on the clouds with great power and glory. Then he will send forth his angels, and he will gather his elect from the four winds, from the end of the earth to the end of the heaven." Jesus taught that there's going to be a future judgment, angels will be sent forth, the elect would be gathered together, and there'd be a kind of a cosmic destruction of the present order before this new kingdom came.

This idea that there'd be a future act of judgment is the subject of a number of Jesus' parables. There's a particularly interesting parable preserved for us in Matthew chapter 13. This is an interesting parable in part because it's multiply attested. It's found in Matthew 13; it's also attested in the Gospel of Thomas, independently of Matthew. This is sometimes called the parable of the dragnet. Matthew 13, verse 47; in this form, Jesus says, "The kingdom of heaven," which is another term for the kingdom of God, "is like a net that was thrown into the sea and caught fish of every kind. When it was full, they drew it ashore, sat down, and put the good fish in baskets, but threw out the bad. Sin it will be at the end of the age. The angels will come and separate the evil from the righteous, and throw them into the furnace of fire, where there will be weeping and gnashing of teeth."

As an anecdote on the side, there was a professor of Princeton back in the 1940s who wrote an article that claimed that he had discovered a manuscript of Matthew's Gospel that had a little marginal note after this particular parable, where Jesus says they'll be thrown into the furnace of fire; there will be weeping and gnashing of teeth, and then in this marginal note, the story was continued by a scribe. The disciples then respond to Jesus, "But master, what of those who have no teeth?" Jesus replied, "Teeth will be provided."

This is a parable of judgment, in which, at the end of the age, the Son of Man will destroy those who have sided with the forces of evil. This is a typical kind of apocalyptic image of what will happen at the end of the present age, as we've seen in these various references and other passages that we've talked about, is probably going back to the historical Jesus. Jesus refers to a coming agent of the judgment, and calls this future agent of judgment the "Son of Man." Scholars have long debated why Jesus calls this future cosmic figure the Son of Man. It's a complicated issue, in part because, as we've seen, there are a number of sayings about this man on Jesus' lips in the Gospels. Not all of the sayings about the Son of Man can be established as going back to Jesus, based on our various criteria. In a number of instances, Jesus uses the words "Son of Man" evidently just as a self-reference; "the Son of Man must go to Jerusalem and be rejected by the scribes and elders and be crucified," he says. There, he's just talking about himself.

In other passages, though, when he talks about the "Son of Man," he doesn't seem to be referring to himself, and in those passages, he talks about this cosmic figure coming on the clouds of heaven in judgment. Most scholars have been convinced for a long time, when Jesus is referring to this cosmic judge, the "Son of Man," he in fact is alluding to a passage in the Hebrew Bible, Daniel chapter 7, verses 13 and 14. In the Book of Daniel, a prophet has a vision of the future of earth, in which four kingdoms come out of the sea. They aren't portrayed as kingdoms, but as wild beasts, grotesque animals who come and wreak havoc on Earth successively, one after the other. After the fourth beast, which is the wildest and most severe, the prophet then has a vision of "one like a Son of Man, who comes on the clouds of heaven, to whom is given the glory and dominion and power forever and ever."

This "one like a Son of Man" is, in Daniel's vision, a son in contrast to these wild beasts. In other words, there'd be someone who actually comes from God, who is humanlike, as opposed to these beasts that are destroying the earth. Some apocalyptic authors took this reference to "one like a Son of Man," one who is humanlike in Daniel's prophecy, and started thinking in terms of an actual individual, a judge who would come from heaven, calling this one the "Son of Man." That seems to be the way Jesus himself is using this term, as an actual title of a future cosmic judge who's going to overthrow the wicked kingdoms of Earth. As I've shown, some of these sayings about this future coming Son of Man are ones in which Jesus appears not to be talking about himself. In other words, these sayings do pass the criterion of dissimilarity, because Christians wouldn't have been likely to have made up sayings in which it was unclear that Jesus was referring to himself as the future judge.

Thus, Jesus talks about a future coming kingdom, which will be wrought by judgment, and the judgment specifically will be brought by this one called the Son of Man. These sayings, I should emphasize, some of them not only pass the criterion of dissimilarity, they clearly pass the criterion of contextual credibility. We have other Jews from roughly the same time who are saying roughly the same thing about a future judgment. Let me read just one example from another kind of Jewish apocalyptic text that we know about, that we've known about for a long time. It's a text called 1 Enoch. Like a number of apocalyptic texts from this time period, this one is pseudonymous. The author of this book actually claims to be Enoch, who's a person from the Hebrew Bible who never died, but was taken up to heaven alive. Who better to know God's plans for the Earth than one who's actually been to heaven without ever having died?

He narrates the future plans for the Earth, and it turns out that in some passages, what he says sounds a lot like what Jesus was saying within the same time frame. Listen to this quotation from 1 Enoch chapter 69: "And the Son of Man sat on the throne of his glory and the whole judgment was given to him. And he will cause the sinners to pass away and be destroyed from the face of the Earth. Those who led astray the world will be bound in chains, and will be shut up in the assembly place of their destruction, and all their works will pass from the face of the Earth. And from then on, there will be nothing corruptible, for that Son of Man has appeared and has sat on the throne of his glory, and everything evil will pass away, and go from before him." 1 Enoch chapter 69. The passage sounds very similar to what Jesus himself was saying about a coming kingdom, brought in by judgment – to be brought by this Son of Man.

This coming judgment by the Son of Man, in Jesus' words, would involve a serious reversal of fortunes for people on Earth. Those who are empowered now will be removed from power. Remember the logic: They're in power because the evil forces have put them there. Those, though, who are oppressed now, will be exalted then. When God overthrows the powers of evil, those who have benefited from these powers, then, will be taken out of power. That's why Jesus can say that the one who exalts himself will be humbled, and the one who humbles himself will be exalted. That's why Jesus can say, "The first shall be last, and the last shall be first." Mark chapter 10, verse 31; Luke chapter 13, verse 30. These weren't simply clever one-liners that Jesus threw out. These were apocalyptic realities for him. Those who are first now actually will be last. They'll be taken down out of power. Those who are lowly now actually will be exalted. This is the theme, this reversal of fortunes that's going to come with the future judgment.

This is the theme of some of Jesus' best known, but I think probably least understood, teachings—the Beatitudes. The Beatitudes come to us from the Q source; they're incorporated in both Matthew's Gospel and in Luke's. What's important to understand about the Beatitudes, what's important to notice that people haven't noticed, is the verb tenses. Let me read some of them to you: "Blessed are the meek, for they will inherit the Earth. Blessed are those who hunger and thirst for righteousness, for they will be filled. Blessed are the merciful, for they will receive mercy. Blessed are the pure in heart, for they will see God." Notice the verb tenses. People are blessed now because of what's going to happen to them then. When are these things going to happen? Put these in the context of Jesus' apocalyptic teaching, and you can explain, then, why people who mourn now are going to be comforted then, why people who hunger and thirst for righteousness now are going to be filled then. Why? Because there's going to be a reversal of fortunes that comes when the Son of Man arrives. It's in the future kingdom that these blessings are going to take place. It's not that people should be all that happy now that they're mourning, or that they're being beat up, or that they're being persecuted, or that they have to go out and make peace when people are fighting. It's not that they're happy now. They're going to be blessed in the future kingdom. Thus, Jesus can say, "Blessed are those who are persecuted for doing what's right, for theirs is the kingdom of heaven." When the kingdom of heaven comes, they're going to be rewarded for what comes to them now. They're persecuted now because they side with the wrong side; they side with the side that's out of power. God is going to intervene and bring in His kingdom. When He does so, this kingdom is going to come precisely to those who are beaten down, poor, hungry, and persecuted. That's why these Beatitudes have the verb tenses they do.

When Jesus talked about this coming kingdom of God, he didn't refer to its implications simply for individuals. In fact, the judgment that was coming, to be brought by the Son of Man, didn't apply just to individual people. It also applied to governments and to institutions. The governments in charge now are controlled by the evil forces. It's the kingdom of God that's coming that is going to overthrow those future kingdoms. In particular, Jesus is reported in independent sources to have predicted that the grand and glorious Temple in Jerusalem would be destroyed at the appearance of the Son of Man.

We're going to talk more about the Temple in a later lecture. It was an immense structure, a beautiful structure that was at the very heart of and soul of Judaism. According to the Law of Moses in the Old Testament, the Temple was the one place where sacrifices could be made to God. Jews were commanded to perform sacrifices of animals and of foodstuffs to God, and this could only be done in the Temple that was located in Jerusalem. Devout Jews would gather there in the Temple to do what God had commanded them to do, in order to worship Him, as He gives His instructions in the Torah. The Temple itself was ordered to be built by God, and Jews built it according to the instructions that He gave in the Law of Moses.

Jesus, though, predicted that this Temple was going to be destroyed. The accounts are found throughout our sources. It's independently attested. Probably the most familiar account is Mark chapter 13. At the very beginning of Mark 13, the disciples, who've come with Jesus from Galilee—they're rural peasants, they aren't used to the kind of grandeur and glory of the big city, and they see this immense, beautiful Temple. This is a Temple whose walls stood as high as a ten-story building today, built with the best materials, large parts of it overlaid with gold, a spectacular place. The disciples look at these fantastic buildings, and Jesus says, "Truly I tell you, not one stone will be left upon another. All will be torn down." He begins, then, to talk about what's going to happen in the future apocalypse at the end of the age when the Son of Man arrives.

That a Jew would say such a thing about the Temple of God is not without precedent. In fact, it's completely credible. We have numerous instances of Jewish prophets predicting the destruction of the Temple. Jesus himself, at least in our early accounts, actually quotes a Hebrew prophet, Jeremiah, in talking about the future destruction of the Temple. Jeremiah was predicting the destruction of a temple in his own day, the first temple. He predicted the temple would be destroyed. It was destroyed. Jesus quotes his words in our earliest traditions, talking about the destruction of the Temple in his day. There were other prophets in Jesus' time who also predicted that God's Temple would be destroyed by God. It appears that, like other people including the Essenes, Jesus believed that the institution of the Temple had become corrupt, and that it would be overthrown when God entered into judgment with the world. The judgment wasn't just going to involve individuals, then, whether Jews or non-Jews; it was also going to involve governments and institutions, including the institution of the Temple, the center of all Jewish life and worship.

This was a fairly radical message, and we're going to see in a later lecture it's this particular teaching that got Jesus into trouble with the ruling authorities, who were not only in charge of the Temple and didn't much appreciate the aspersions Jesus was casting on it, but who were also the aristocratic liaisons with the Romans, and had the ear of the Roman governor, Pontius Pilate. These are the ones who end up turning Jesus over, leading up to his execution.

Jesus maintained that this coming judgment with the Son of Man was not some kind of far-off event, not to be worried about at the present, something that would take place in the remote future. Jesus was not predicting things that were going to happen 2000 years later. He was urging people to repent in his own day precisely because he thought this coming end was imminent. In fact, Jesus appears to have proclaimed that it would happen within his own generation. "Some of you standing here won't taste death before you see the kingdom of God has come in power." Precisely because Jesus thought that the end had come upon his own generation, he spent the bulk of his teaching proclaiming how people should live in preparation for the arrival of this Son of Man.

In the next lecture, I'm going to talk about some of the ethical corollaries of Jesus' proclamation of the coming kingdom. I'll spend the next lecture talking about some of the more familiar ethics of Jesus, for in fact, what I'm going to maintain is that Jesus' moral teachings are situated best in his own apocalyptic context, and they make the best sense when understood as apocalyptic teachings. Jesus didn't teach his ethics in order to show people how to live in peace and harmony for the long haul. That's maybe the reason we think about ethics, to show us how we can get along with one another for the long haul. For Jesus, there wasn't going to be a long haul. His ethical teachings are meant to show people what they need to do now in order to escape judgment when the Son of Man arrives, and so to be brought into this coming kingdom.

Since it is the humble who would be brought into the kingdom rather than the great and the mighty, Jesus' followers should be humble servants rather than exalted masters. Jesus tells his followers that "Yes, we know that the rulers of the Gentiles are great lords, but if you want to be great, you need to become the slave of others." The slave of others; that's how you become great. Why? Because there's going to be a reversal of fortunes, and those who are lowly now will be exalted then; those who are exalted now will be lowly then. Since it's the weak and the powerless who will inherit the kingdom, rather than the strong and the powerful, Jesus' followers should become like little children, rather than like mighty kings and rulers. You should become like insignificant, powerless, little kids, rather than mighty rulers. Since it's the poor and oppressed who will inherit the kingdom rather than the rich and the eminent, Jesus' followers should give away all of their possessions, all of their attachments to earthly things. They're soon going to pass away, in any event. As I'll stress again later, I think Jesus really meant it. Since those who are rich and wealthy are the ones who are going to have everything taken away in the future judgment, you shouldn't live like that. In fact, it's easier for a camel to go through the eye of a needle than it is for someone who's rich to enter into the kingdom when it arrives; Mark 10:25.

These are sayings that Jesus both said and meant. I don't think he intended that these sayings would be explained away to future readers who didn't like their implications. Similarly, and maybe even more strikingly, Jesus taught that it would not be the upright and religious people who were brought into the kingdom, but sinners. This was a teaching that has always caused offense, in Jesus' own day and even now, I suppose. It's one that people have difficulty getting a handle on. How is it that the religious people are the ones who are not going to enter into the kingdom? In fact, that is what Jesus appears to have taught. He teaches this in a number of places. For example, there's this passage in Luke chapter 18, verses 9 through 14. It's the story of the Pharisee and the tax collector, who are both praying.

Tax collectors were thought to be particularly sinful folk, not just because they were thought to be collaborators with the Romans, which they were—they're collecting taxes that are being paid to the dominating power, and so this is somewhat blasphemous—but also because tax collectors have never had a high reputation, and that means that they were widely thought to be corrupt. The way they would normally make their own income was by collecting more taxes than were required by the government, and so they were thought to have corrupted others. Jesus tells us parabolically that you have a Pharisee who's an upright person, and a tax collector, both praying. The Pharisee thanks God, says, "Thank you, that I'm not like other people. I'm not a thief, or a rogue, or an adulterer like this tax collector here. I fast twice a week; I give a tenth of my income."

The tax collector, standing far off, beats his breast and says, "God, be merciful to me, a sinner." Jesus says, "It's that one who will be returned to being right with God, not the other."

Jesus taught that it was the wicked, not the righteous, who'll be brought into the kingdom. As he says in Matthew 21 verse 31, "The prostitutes and the sinners will come into the kingdom of God before the righteous leaders of the Jews." It's somewhat hard to know what he meant by this, but given the number of places Jesus urges people to repent, and to begin doing what God really wants, it appears that Jesus thought that the exalted leaders of his own people were not right before God, where as those who humbly repented of their wicked ways were. Jesus appears, then, to have taught that people needed to repent, and live in ways that God wanted them to, in light of the coming kingdom. The next lecture will see more fully what this might have entailed for him.

In conclusion, we've seen in this lecture that sayings of Jesus preserved in our earliest sources go further to support the view that he was an apocalypticist expecting the imminent intervention of God in the affairs of the world. Jesus taught that a day of judgment was coming, in which a cosmic figure called the Son of Man would arrive in power, destroying all those who are opposed to God, even the leaders and leading institutions of the Jews, and rewarding those who had done what God had really wanted, in accordance with Jesus' own teachings. The appearance of the Son of Man was imminent, and people needed to prepare. That's why Jesus' message was so urgent. It's also why, as we'll see in a later lecture, he made his final and fatal trip to Jerusalem during the Passover feast sometime around the year 30, to bring his message to the heart of Judaism, in view of imminent danger.

Lecture Sixteen

Other Teachings of Jesus in their Apocalyptic Context

Scope:

Jesus did more, of course, than talk about the coming apocalypse. He is widely regarded as one of the greatest ethical teachers of all time. We must realize, however, that even his teachings about ethics were situated in an apocalyptic context that radically affects their meanings. Jesus did not deliver timeless truths to guide individuals in leading long and productive lives. His teachings were meant to show people how to live to enter the kingdom of God that was soon to appear.

These teachings are based on the Law of Moses, as found in the Jewish Bible. In particular, Jesus stressed the two laws to love God above all else (Deut. 6:4) and to love one's neighbor as oneself (Lev. 19:18).

Outline

I. Many people today consider Jesus to be one of the greatest ethical teachers of all time, with his stress on the law to "love your neighbor as yourself" and his formulation of the "Golden Rule" that tells us "do unto others as you would have them do unto you."

    A. Jesus' ethical teachings may have meant something quite different in his context than they do in ours.

    B. Jesus' ethical teachings, in other words, were ethics of the coming kingdom. They reflected what life would be like in the kingdom and qualified a person to enter it once it arrived.

II. It would be a mistake to think of Jesus' ethical teachings without considering their relation to the Jewish law. As we have seen, Jesus was fully Jewish in every way; he embraced the Jewish law and saw himself as a principal proponent and interpreter of that law.

    A. Recall the three major ideas of Judaism:

        1. It was monotheistic, with one Creator–God.

        2. God made a covenant with the people of Israel (Abraham, Moses).

3. The law told the Jews how to worship their God and how to live in a community of believers.

B. To be Jewish meant, in part, to embrace the law that God was believed to have given Moses, as embodied in the first five books of the Hebrew Bible, the Torah. Jesus regularly turns to the law as its interpreter throughout independently attested traditions; e.g., Mark 10:17–22; Luke 16:16 (Q = Matt. 5:18); Matt. 5:17, 19–20 (M); John 10:34–35.

C. Throughout the Gospels, Jesus constantly quotes the law and places his interpretation against the interpretations of other teachers of his day, e.g., Pharisees, Sadducees, and Essenes.

1. In contrast to Pharisees (as we'll see in a later lecture), Jesus did not think that God was concerned about scrupulous observance of every single detail of every law.

2. In contrast to Sadducees, Jesus did not think that carefully adhering to the laws of how to sacrifice in the Temple would bring a person into a right standing before God.

3. In contrast to Essenes, Jesus did not think that maintaining one's own ritual purity by separating oneself from the sinfulness of the rest of the world was ultimately what God wanted.

4. In all these disagreements, the issue was never over whether God's law, as found in the Hebrew Bible, should be kept. The question was how it should be kept and what it meant to keep it.

D. For Jesus, as for other Jewish teachers of his day, what God wanted was for his people to keep the commandments that formed the heart of his law, the commandments to love God above all else (Deut. 6:4) and to love one's neighbor as oneself (Lev. 19:18; Mark 12:28–34).

E. Even though the commandment to love is simple, it is also all encompassing. Giving oneself over to the command is necessary to enter God's kingdom, which is the ultimate goal of all existence.

1. The kingdom is to be sought after as one's most prized possession (cf. the parable of the pearl of great price; Matt. 13:45–46).

    2. Nothing else in human existence should be of any ultimate concern—not even food and clothing (Matt. 5:39–42; 6:33).

    3. Trying to live for things of this world while committing oneself totally to God would be like a slave trying to serve two masters—it can't be done (Luke 16:13).

    4. Thus, one should give up everything—all possessions and everything that binds one to this world—in light of the coming kingdom (Mark 10:17–21). Those who give up their lives in this world will gain much in the kingdom that will soon appear (Mark 10:29–31).

F. This emphasis on giving up everything for the kingdom means that Jesus was not a major proponent of what we now call "family values."

    1. In fact, he was quite unambiguous that parents, siblings, spouses, and even children were to have no importance in comparison with the kingdom (Luke 14:26).

    2. Jesus appears to have realized how divisive this teaching could be, but he claimed that he would split families up rather than keep them together (Luke 12:51–53).

    3. As with other hard saying of Jesus, these should not be explained away so that they no longer mean what they say. Instead, they should be placed in their own apocalyptic context.

G. Jesus' teachings on marriage considered in this context are different than some modern interpretations.

    1. In his society, it was unusual for a man to be unmarried (as he was). Some were ascetics, as the evidence indicates Jesus was.

    2. Jesus never taught against marriage.

    3. In Mark 12, Jesus argues with the Pharisees over bodily resurrection, showing his belief in bodily resurrection into a state of no marriage.

    4. Thus, Jesus may be saying, "don't get married" (in view of the coming judgment).

H. Jesus did not advocate a strong structure to promote a healthy society, because he thought society was diseased and soon to be destroyed.

III. Jesus "maximized" the commandment to love and "minimized" everything else in comparison.

    A. This can be seen in the so-called "antitheses" preserved now in the Sermon on the Mount in Matthew's Gospel (Matt. 5:21–48).

        1. The law says not to murder; if you really love your neighbor, though, you won't even get angry with him.

        2. The law says not to take your neighbor's wife; if you really love your neighbor, though, you won't even desire to take her.

        3. The law says to make the punishment of someone who has offended you commensurate with the offense ("an eye for an eye, a tooth for a tooth"); if you really love your neighbor, though, you will not demand a punishment at all or even take offense when he harms you ("turn the other cheek").

    B. This love of others should extend to everyone, even in the most extreme situations.

        1. Rather than seek restitution for what has been taken from you or destroyed by another (as set forth in the law), you should forgive what others owe you—so that God will forgive what you owe him (Mark 11:25; Luke 11:4).

        2. You should not condemn even the genuine shortcomings of others—lest God judge the genuine shortcomings that are yours: "judge not so that you will not be judged" (Luke 6:37).

        3. You are to love even those who are your sworn enemies, who are out to hurt and kill you (Luke 6:27; Matt. 5:43–44).

    C. In particular, Jesus was concerned that his followers love those who were underprivileged and oppressed—the impoverished, the mentally diseased, the terminally ill, the outcast, the imprisoned. These people would inherit the kingdom when it arrived.

    D. This command to love one's neighbor had its corollary in the command to love God above all else.

        1. The reason people could put the kingdom of God above all else—including food and clothing—is because God would provide all these things (Matt. 6:25–33).

    2. People can trust God as a parent to give his children what they need. All a person must do is ask (Matt. 7:7–11; Luke 11:9–11).

    3. To those who trust God (that is, have "faith") all things are possible (Mark 9:23, 11:23; Matt. 17:20), because God cares for his children and will give them whatever they ask—especially his kingdom, which is soon to come.

IV. In conclusion, the more clearly ethical teachings of Jesus—some of the greatest ethical instructions ever heard in the history of our form of civilization—are not to be removed from their apocalyptic context.

    A. Jesus gave these teachings as interpretations of the Jewish law, especially Deut. 6:4 and Lev. 19:18.

        1. Jesus, in other words, did not see himself as inventing a new system of ethics, but as explaining the Law of Moses in view of his own apocalyptic context.

        2. Those who committed themselves completely to God and their fellow humans in love would survive the coming onslaught.

Essential Reading:

Ehrman, *Jesus: Apocalyptic Prophet*, chap. 10.

Sanders, *The Historical Figure of Jesus*, chaps. 11–13.

Meier, *A Marginal Jew*.

Suggested Reading:

Allison, *Jesus of Nazareth*.

Chilton and Evans, *Authenticating the Words of Jesus*.

Questions to Consider:

1. If Jesus was so Jewish in his basic orientation and his teaching, why do you suppose the religion that later developed in his name became so emphatically anti-Jewish?

2. Discuss how the apocalyptic character of Jesus' proclamation can change one's understanding of his teachings about loving one's neighbor as oneself. Does it seem appropriate to you to reinterpret Jesus' teachings that a person should give up everything for the kingdom so that they no longer require a person to give up a single thing?

Lecture Sixteen—Transcript
Other Teachings of Jesus in their Apocalyptic Context

To this point, we've seen that Jesus is best understood as a Jewish apocalyptic prophet who predicted that the end of this evil age was imminent, that God would soon send a cosmic judge from heaven called the Son of Man, who would destroy the forces aligned against God and bring in His kingdom. This point of view is expressly found in our earliest traditions, many of which attested independently of one another. Some of these traditions pass the criterion of dissimilarity, and all of them are contextually credible.

As we saw in the last lecture, the apocalyptic thrust of Jesus' message puts a new light on the nature of his ethical teachings. In this lecture, we'll explore further some of the other familiar words of Jesus, at least those that can be established as historically authentic, and try to situate them within their own historical context.

Many people today consider Jesus to be one of the greatest ethical teachers of all time, with his stress on the law to love your neighbor as yourself, and his formulation of the Golden Rule, "Do unto others as you would have them do unto you." This stress on Jesus as an ethical teacher is true; Jesus did teach ethics, and many of his ethical teachings have come down to us today as perfect examples of how people ought to live. It's important for us to understand that the meaning of Jesus' ethical teachings may have been quite different in his own context, however, from their meaning in ours.

In our context, ethical teachings assist us in knowing how to get along with one another, so that we can build a more healthy and wholesome society, allowing us to have peace and prosperity over the long haul. As we've seen, however, for Jesus there is not going to be a long haul. The Son of Man was soon to come in judgment, and people needed to prepare for his coming by acting in ways that showed they sided with God, rather than with the forces of evil that were opposed to him. Jesus' ethical teachings, in other words, were ethics of the coming kingdom. They both reflected what life would be like in the kingdom, and qualified a person to enter into it once it arrived. In the kingdom, there would be no hatred, so people should love one another now. In the kingdom, there would be no oppression, so people ought to work for justice now. In the kingdom, there would be no war, so people should work for peace now. In the kingdom, there would be no sexism, so people should work for equality now. Only those who lived in ways that were appropriate to the kingdom would be allowed to enter into it when it arrived.

It would be a mistake to think that these ethical teachings of Jesus could be understood apart from considering them in relationship to the Jewish law, for in fact, as we've seen before, Jesus himself was fully Jewish in every way. He embraced the Jewish law, and saw himself as a principal proponent, interpreter, of that law. This is a point that I have to stress with my students, especially my graduate students, time and again—that Jesus has to be understood as himself being thoroughly Jewish. Among other things, this means that Jesus presupposed in all of his teachings ideas that were central to Judaism at his time, that virtually every Jew in his world subscribed to.

Every Jew that we know about from that world subscribed to three major ideas that put them over against the pagans of their environment and the Greco-Roman world. First, Jews, unlike their pagan neighbors, were monotheistic. They believed in one God, who was the Creator of all things. Everybody else, of course, was a polytheist, believing in many gods. Jesus, naturally, presupposed the existence of one God, and since his ministry was almost entirely dealing with Jews, he didn't go to any great lengths to try and prove that there was only one God, or to try and expound upon the nature of the oneness of God. He simply assumed that there was only one God, as did the other Jews that he spoke with.

Second, Jews in that environment believed that God, the one God, the Creator of all, had made a covenant with His people, Israel, had made an agreement or a treaty, a pact, with the people of Israel to be their God so long as they would be His people. This covenant that God had made with the people of Israel goes all the way back to the time of the Jewish ancestors. God made a covenant with Abraham that his descendants would be the people of God. He made a covenant with Moses that involved choosing the people and saving them from their slavery in exchange for them keeping His commandments.

The third aspect of Judaism, then, that Jesus presupposed, that other Jews subscribed to, was this idea of the law. The law of God was given by God to Moses, to instruct His people both how to worship, and how to live in community together. Jews accepted the idea that

God's law had been given to them as the covenant people of God, and Jesus accepted the law as well. As we'll see, it would be a completely false idea to think of Jesus as somebody who was opposed to the Law of Moses, or who tried to set up a new religion that was against the law. Jesus didn't understand himself as an opponent of the law; on the contrary, Jesus understood himself as an interpreter of the law. To be Jewish in Jesus' day meant, in part, to embrace the law that God was believed to have given to Moses, as this law was embodied in the first five books of what we think of as the Hebrew Bible, the Torah; the five books of Genesis, Exodus, Leviticus, Numbers, and Deuteronomy. These five books, of course, were in existence in Jesus' day, and these five books were seen as scriptural authority by virtually all Jews that we know about. Jesus himself appealed to this law and interpreted it throughout his teachings.

The idea that Jesus understood himself as an interpreter of the law and saw the law as important for Jewish life, as what we might think of as ethics, is attested throughout many of our traditions. In other words, the idea of Jesus as an interpreter of the law is independently attested. One of the most interesting passages found in the Gospels with respect to Jesus and the law is found in our earliest account, the Gospel of Mark, in chapter 10. This is a story that I think probably passes our various criteria, probably in some sense goes back to Jesus. It's an account in Mark chapter 10, where a man comes up to Jesus, kneels before him, and asks Jesus, "Good teacher, what must I do to inherit eternal life?" Jesus says to him, "Why do you call me good? No one is good but God alone. You know the commandments. You shall not murder; you shall not commit adultery; you shall not steal; you shall not bear false witness; you shall not defraud; honor your father and mother."

The man wants to know how to have eternal life; "How do I enter the kingdom that's coming?" Jesus tells him, "Keep the commandments." The person then responds to him by saying, "'Teacher, I've kept all of these since my youth.' Jesus, looking at him, loved him and said, 'You lack one thing. Go, sell what you own, and give the money to the poor, and you'll have treasure in heaven. Then come follow me.' When the man heard this, he was shocked and went away grieved, for he had many possessions." Then right after this is where Jesus is telling his disciples that "it is easier for a camel to go through the eye of a needle than for a rich person to enter into the kingdom of heaven." Why? Because to enter the kingdom of heaven, you have to give up everything for the sake of this coming kingdom.

I'm not sure that this entire story as it's framed in Mark goes back to Jesus. In other words, I'm not sure that if you had a video camera you would have been able to capture this on tape. I do think that the basic idea of the story, the kernel of the story, probably is historical, though, because it seems to me to pass the criterion of dissimilarity. Christians would probably not have made up a story that said, "If you want to have eternal life, all you have to do is keep the commandments, and then on top of the commandments, simply give away all of your possessions." Why? Because Christians thought that the only way to have eternal life was to believe in the resurrection of Jesus. There's nothing about belief here; simply, "Follow the commandments, give away all of your possessions, then you'll have treasures in heaven."

If Christians wouldn't have made up the story, why is it in the tradition? Probably this is a story that goes back to Jesus. It portrays Jesus as somebody who is firmly committed to the Law of Moses. What must you do to have eternal life? You keep the commandments. This teaching of Jesus is consonant with other teachings throughout the Gospels. Jesus constantly refers to the law in order to tell people how to behave, and in order to explain both the will of God and his own activities. We find these teachings in Mark, as we've just seen. We find them in Q. We find them in M. We find them in John. Matthew's Gospel, preserving a tradition in what we call M, has Jesus say that in fact a person must keep the commandments of God found in the Torah better than the scribes and the Pharisees if they want to enter into the kingdom. Jesus says, "Don't think that I came to abolish the law. I came to fulfill the law. Not one jot or tittle will pass from the law until all is fulfilled. Moreover, your righteousness must exceed that of the scribes and Pharisees."

Throughout the Gospels of the New Testament, Jesus constantly quotes the law, and gives his own interpretation of it, over against the interpretations of other teachers of his day. The disputes Jesus had with the Pharisees, Sadducees, and others, as we'll see more fully in the next lecture, were not disputes over whether somebody should be Jewish, or whether somebody should keep the law, or whether the law came from God. The disputes were about the interpretations of the law. Just as within Phariseeism, different rabbis disputed this commandment, what it meant here, what it meant there, how one should understand the law, so too Jesus entered into disputes with other Jewish teachers about legal interpretation.

In contrast to Pharisees, as we'll see more fully next time, Jesus did not think that scrupulous observance of every single detail of every law was what God was ultimately concerned about. Jesus didn't think that a person should actually break the law; in fact, as we're going to see—to the surprise of many people, in fact—there's very little evidence that Jesus himself ever did break the law, let alone that he wanted anybody else to break it. It's not that Jesus thought you should break the law, but Jesus appeared to think that it's possible to keep the law, technically speaking, without really doing what God wants. Jesus tried to show them what it was, that is, that God really wanted. In contrast to the Sadducees, Jesus evidently did not think carefully adhering to the laws of the sacrifice in the temple would bring a person into a right standing before God. In contrast to the Essenes, Jesus did not think that maintaining one's own ritual purity by separating oneself from the sinfulness of the rest of the world was ultimately what God wanted.

In all of these disagreements, the issue is never over whether God's law, as found in the Hebrew Bible, should be kept. The question was *how* it should be kept, and what it meant to keep it. For Jesus, as for other Jewish teachers of his day that we know about, because we have other sayings of other teachers preserved, what ultimately mattered was that the people of God keep the very heart of God's law—namely the commandments that one should love the Lord your God with all your heart, with all your soul, with all your strength, Deuteronomy chapter 6, verse 4, and that one should love one's neighbor as oneself, Leviticus chapter 19, verse 18. According to an ancient tradition found in Mark's Gospel, Mark chapter 12, verses 28 through 34, when a legal scholar came up to Jesus and said, "What's the greatest commandment," these are the two commandments that Jesus gave—God above all else; love your neighbor as yourself. Jesus did not invent the saying, "Love your neighbor as yourself." When he gave that teaching, he was simply quoting scripture itself, Leviticus chapter 19, verse 18. Jesus, then, like other Jewish teachers of his day, saw the "love" commandments as standing at the heart of the law. If somebody really does that, really loves God above all else, and really loves one's neighbor, then one will be fulfilling what God wants.

For Jesus, the way one loves God above all else is by committing oneself completely to him, rather than living for oneself. The way one loves one's neighbor as oneself is by becoming a servant of others, rather than seeking to exalt oneself over them. Doing these things, for Jesus, a person would fulfill the law of God. Even though the commandment to love—to love God, to love one's neighbor— even though the commandment to love is simple, for Jesus it is also all-encompassing. Giving oneself over completely to the command to love is necessary if one wants to enter into God's kingdom, which for Jesus is the ultimate goal of all human existence.

The kingdom of God, according to Jesus, is to be sought after as one's most prized possession. One in fact should give up everything one has for the sake of this coming kingdom. There's this very interesting parable in Matthew chapter 13, which has a parallel in the Gospel of Thomas, the so-called parable of the pearl of great price; very brief little parable that's intriguing. Jesus says that the kingdom of God is like a merchant who's in search of pearls, and he finds, finally, a great pearl, a perfect pearl. In order to own the pearl, then, the merchant sells everything he has, and with the proceeds, he buys the pearl. That's the end of the story.

It's a strange story, though, when you think about it. This person gives up everything he has, sells the entirety of all he has, to buy the pearl. What does he have? He's got the pearl. He's got nothing else. What good is that? Presumably, having a pearl is of some use, if you maybe can sell it to buy other things, if you can display it, or if you could do something; it's just a pearl. All he's got, but he sold everything for it. Sometimes Jesus' parables are meant to be ridiculous like that, to sound odd, or paradoxical, or to make you kind of sit up and think, "What in the world?" For Jesus, though, that's exactly right. The kingdom of God is like that. It might seem absurd, but you give up everything for it. That's how valuable it is. Nothing in human existence should be of any ultimate concern except for this coming kingdom.

As Jesus says in Matthew's version of the Sermon on the Mount, Matthew chapter 6, verse 25: "Not even what you eat or what you wear should be of any importance to you. Don't worry about your life, what you eat or what you drink, or about your body, what you wear. Is life not worth more than food, and the body more than clothing? Look at the birds of the air. They don't sow, nor gather into barns, but your heavenly father feeds them. Aren't you worth more than they are? Can you, by worrying, add a single hour to your span of life? How can you worry about clothing? Look at the lilies of the field, how they grow. They neither toil nor spin. Yet I tell you even Solomon in all his glory was not clothed like one of these. But if God so clothes the grass of the field, which is alive today, and tomorrow is thrown into the oven, will he not much more clothe you, oh you of little faith?" Then it goes on to say, "Strive above all for the kingdom of God and his righteousness, and all these other things will be given to you."

What is of ultimate importance is not what you eat, drink, or wear. What's of ultimate importance is this coming kingdom. You should abandon everything for it. Abandoning everything for it means being completely committed to God. A person cannot be committed to more than one master, as Jesus says in Luke chapter 16. You can't serve two masters; if you do you'll despise the one and love the other. You can only serve one master, and therefore you should serve God alone; or, as the same saying is said in the Gospel of Thomas—I rather like this way of putting it; this is independent of Luke—Jesus says, "It's impossible for a person for a person to mount two horses, or to stretch at the same time two bows, and impossible for a servant to serve two masters; otherwise, he'll honor the one, and serve the other contemptuously." One should then give up everything, all possessions, and everything that binds one to this world, in light of this coming kingdom. One should serve God alone, then, in anticipation that he'll give this kingdom. Those who give up their lives will gain much in the kingdom that is soon to appear.

In one story, in Mark's Gospel, we have the account of Jesus saying, "You have to give up everything," and Peter saying, "Look, we've left our homes, and our families, and our fields, our houses to follow you." Jesus replies, "Yes, everyone who's given up everything to follow me in this age will gain more fields, more houses, more family, and in the age to come, will gain eternal life." Following Jesus to enter into the kingdom means giving up everything. Once one does, one will gain more now, and one will gain eternal life then.

This business of leaving one's family in order to follow Jesus brings up another point. As odd as it might seem to us today, Jesus' emphasis on giving up everything for the kingdom probably means that Jesus was not a major proponent of what people today call "family values." In fact, Jesus was quite unambiguous, that parents, siblings, spouses, and even children were to be of no importance in comparison with this coming kingdom. As he says in both Luke and the Gospel of Thomas, a person must hate his father and mother if they're to be his disciple.

Hate father and mother? In comparison with the coming kingdom, father, mother, siblings, spouse, children, are to be of no importance. Jesus himself appears to have realized how divisive this teaching could be, but he evidently claimed that he came not in order to keep families together, but to split them up. "Don't think that I've come to bring peace. I've come to cast a sword on the Earth. Families will be divided against one another, a father against a son, a son against a father, a mother against the daughter, a daughter against the mother." And so forth. Jesus' teachings are going to split families rather than bring them together. As with the other hard sayings of Jesus, I don't think that these should be explained away so that they no longer mean what they say. Instead, they should be placed within their own apocalyptic context. For Jesus, the kingdom was so important, and so near, that people should abandon everything, even their own families and their own family commitments if necessary, in order to prepare for its arrival.

This raises a related question about what Jesus taught about marriage. It's an interesting question, to think about what did Jesus think about men and women being married together, because there's no indication that Jesus himself was married, which would be highly unusual for a Jewish man in the first century. In today's culture, if a middle-aged man is not married, the common assumption is often, "Well, he's gay." In ancient society, that wasn't the assumption at all. In the ancient society of Jesus' day, if a middle-aged man wasn't married, the assumption was, "He's ascetic," depriving himself of the pleasures of the flesh. There is good evidence that in fact Jesus was ascetic, as we've just seen. He teaches that you shouldn't be concerned about what you eat, what you drink, what you wear. Did Jesus think that you shouldn't be married?

Jesus of course never teaches against marriage, but there are some suggestions about what Jesus thought about marriage, especially in a passage found in our earliest source, Mark, in one of Jesus' conflicts with, in this case not the Pharisees, but the Sadducees. The Sadducees, as we've seen, were a group that subscribed principally to the teachings of the first five books of the Hebrew Bible, the Torah. The Sadducees, among other things, did not think that there was going to be a future resurrection of the dead. They come up to Jesus, in Mark chapter 12, and ask him why he thinks there's going to be a future resurrection. They kind of set a trap for him, a hypothetical situation. There's a man who's married, and he and his wife don't have any children. The man dies. According to the Law of Moses, if a man dies without leaving his spouse any children, and he's got a single brother, his brother is supposed to marry the woman. It turns out there were seven brothers. The first one to marry the woman, they had no children. He dies, the second one marries her, no children, he dies. Third marriage, no children, et cetera. All seven if them end up marrying this woman; they all die. Then the woman dies. When everybody's raised from the dead, whose wife is she going to be?

It's a tricky question, but Jesus deals with the question, because he believes there is going to be a future resurrection, as a good apocalypticist would believe. His reply, though, is that "You don't know the scriptures nor the power of God, because in the resurrection, there will not be marriage nor giving in marriage." People won't be married. They'll be like, he says, "the angels." Jesus appears to have believed that in the new age that's coming; there will not be marital relationships. Elsewhere, we've seen that Jesus believes his followers should begin implementing the ideals of the kingdom in the present, now. It may well be that Jesus urged his followers not only to leave their spouses, but not to get married if they could help it. That is exactly the teaching of one of his followers, the apostle Paul, in 1 Corinthians, some 25 years later, when Paul urges the Christians, if they could help it, not to get married, because the end was near, and there's no point in being married in the present age.

Jesus appears not to have advocated what we might think of today as strong family values, because he wasn't interested in a strong social structure to promote a healthy society, precisely because he thought society was diseased and was going to be destroyed. One needed to be ready for the new order, in which there'd be no marriage, no children, where everyone would be brothers and sisters of one another, and all people would be children of the one true God.

Jesus appears to have maximalized the commandment to love one another, and to have minimalized everything else in comparison. We can see this throughout Jesus' various teachings. In the Sermon on the Mount, Jesus delivers these statements that are called the "antitheses," in which he will set up a teaching of the law, and then set over against it his interpretation of the law, which show his maximalization of the teaching of love. The law says, "Don't murder." Jesus says, "If you really want to love your neighbor, you'll not only not murder your neighbor, you won't even be angry with your neighbor." The law says, "Don't take your neighbor's wife." Don't commit adultery. If you really engage in love, though, you won't just not take your neighbor's wife, you won't even want to take your neighbor's wife. You won't even lust after her. The law says that you should make the punishment of someone who has offended you commiserate with the offense. An eye for an eye, and a tooth for a tooth. If you really love your neighbor, though, you won't demand a punishment at all, or even take offense when he harms you, so if somebody hurts you, you should turn the other cheek.

This love of others should extend to everyone in the most extreme circumstances. You shouldn't seek restitution for what others have taken from you. Instead, you should forgive what others owe you. You shouldn't judge others for their genuine shortcomings. "You should judge not, lest you be judged." You should love those even who are your own sworn enemies, who are out to hurt and kill you. In particular, Jesus was concerned that his followers engaged in an act of love for those who were underprivileged and oppressed—the impoverished, the mentally diseased, the terminally ill, the outcast, the imprisoned. It was such as these, according to Jesus, who would inherit the kingdom of heaven when it arrived.

The command to love one's neighbor as oneself, of course, had a corollary in the command to love God above all else. This love of God meant anticipating His coming kingdom and putting His kingdom above everything. People could trust that God would give them this good kingdom, because God was like a good parent, a father who loved his children and would give them what they needed. That's why people could ask God for whatever they needed and God would provide it for them. This trust of God to give them what they needed as a good parent is of course Jesus' teaching about faith. Faith in God means trusting God, as you trust a good parent to give you what you need, especially this good kingdom that was coming.

In conclusion, the more clearly ethical teachings of Jesus are not to be removed from their apocalyptic context. It's true that Jesus delivered some of the great ethical instructions that have ever been heard in the history of our form of civilization. These instructions were not meant to make us better people, though, so that we could lead long and productive lives in a harmonious society. They were instead meant to prepare people for the coming kingdom, where love would reign supreme, and there would be no more hatred, oppression, or abuse.

Jesus gave these teachings as interpretations of the Jewish law. They were ultimately based on two commandments of the law that Jesus saw as encompassing all others; the commandment to love God completely, and the commandment to love one's neighbor as oneself. Jesus, in other words, did not see himself as inventing a new set of ethics, but is explaining the Law of Moses in view of his own apocalyptic context. Those who committed themselves completely to God and their fellow humans in love would survive the coming onslaught, when the Son of Man arrived from Heaven in judgment against all those who stood opposed to God and His ways.

Lecture Seventeen
The Deeds of Jesus in their Apocalyptic Context

Scope:

The previous lectures discussed some of the evidence that has led many scholars to think that Jesus was a Jewish apocalypticist. Other scholars have begun to question this view. In this lecture, I will evaluate two of the ways that such scholars have tried to explain away the early evidence for an apocalyptic understanding of Jesus. I will then discuss how the activities of Jesus that can be established as historically probable also fit well into an apocalyptic framework.

Outline

I.   Jesus' apocalyptic focus also allows us to better understand the kinds of things that he is known to have done. His deeds are established by considering the reports in the Gospels in light of the historical criteria we have established.

    A.   Before getting into this discussion of Jesus' deeds, I want to stress that simply citing some verses and drawing conclusions are not adequate measures to justify a different way of understanding Jesus.

        1.   We have seen substantial evidence that Jesus' ministry was rooted in his apocalyptic views of the coming of a kingdom on earth.

        2.   Anyone who poses an alternative view must also work it out on the basis of evidence.

        3.   Some scholars have tried to do just that, to argue that Jesus was not an apocalypticist, even though our earliest sources independently indicate that he was.

    B.   One way to get around the problem of our early sources is by arguing that these sources—for example, Mark, Q, M, and L—are not the earliest ones. This is the view, for example, espoused by John Dominic Crossan, a member of the so-called "Jesus Seminar," whose books on the historical Jesus are among the most popular in the market.

        1.   Crossan thinks that Jesus was not a Jewish apocalypticist but obviously has to contend with the problem of the sources, which he does with wit and verve—and ingenuity.

2. Crossan claims that other lesser-known sources not found in the New Testament—including such documents as the Gospel of Peter and the Gospel of the Hebrews—preserve traditions that are much older than those found in the canonical sources. Because none of these other sources portrays Jesus as an apocalypticist, for Crossan, he evidently was not one.

3. The problem is that the documents Crossan refers to date from much later times. The Gospel of the Hebrews, for example, is not even mentioned or alluded to until the end of the second century. To say that it preserves traditions that are older than those found in a Gospel produced a full century or more earlier (Mark) is certainly possible, but it stretches one's credulity.

4. When the sources that virtually everyone agrees were produced first preserve traditions that portray Jesus apocalyptically and sources that virtually everyone agrees were produced later preserve traditions in which he is not portrayed apocalyptically, a trend is suggested.

C. Another way around the problem is to claim that these earliest sources do not portray Jesus as an apocalypticist.

1. This, too, is a bit problematic, because apocalyptic materials are found, for example, throughout Mark and Q.

2. Some scholars are convinced that Q is not only much earlier than Mark but also is not apocalyptic. Many members of the "Jesus Seminar" take this position.

3. That, too, is hard to maintain, because Q does contain apocalyptic traditions on the lips of Jesus (e.g., Luke 12:39 = Matt. 24:44; Luke 17:24, 26–27, 30 = Matt. 24:27, 37–39).

4. Proponents of a non-apocalyptic Jesus claim that even though our version of Q is apocalyptic, an earlier version of the document was non-apocalyptic—and that later an editor inserted apocalyptic traditions into the text. This later corrupted version of Q was then used by Matthew and Luke.

5. Remember that we don't even have Q. It's hard enough to claim that an ancient document in our possession went through multiple editions and to determine what it

looked like at every stage; to do so for a document that we *don't* have is really far more than is possible with such limited data.

D. In short, it is very difficult to get around the problem that our earliest sources independently show Jesus to be an apocalypticist. Moreover, both his words and deeds make sense in an apocalyptic context.

II. Jesus was baptized by John the Baptist, which demonstrates that he began his ministry by adopting an apocalyptic perspective.

A. We have already seen that this is one of the most securely rooted traditions in the early sources; it passes all three criteria with flying colors.

B. John proclaimed an apocalyptic message, as seen, for example, in Q (Luke 3:9). It is hard to imagine why Jesus would have chosen to associate himself with the Baptist if he didn't agree with John's message, because he could have easily associated with someone else (e.g., with a Pharisee or with the Essenes).

C. The baptism of Jesus shows that he essentially agreed with John in his apocalyptic message, although some scholars argue that Jesus later changed his mind. The evidence we have doesn't support this argument.

D. A similar conclusion can be drawn from Jesus' decision to call twelve disciples, one of the most well attested traditions in our sources.

    1. All the Synoptics agree that there were twelve insiders among Jesus' followers, but they don't agree on the names of who these twelve were (cf. Mark 3:14–19 and Luke 6:12–16). This evidence shows that it was known that there were twelve of them.

    2. Moreover, the tradition is supported by Paul, John, and Acts (1 Cor. 15:5; John 6:67; Acts 6:2).

    3. In addition, some of the sayings about the twelve appear to pass the criterion of dissimilarity. This is especially true of the Q saying of Jesus to his disciples that they would sit on twelve thrones to judge the twelve tribes of Israel in the coming kingdom (Matt. 19:28). No one would have made this saying up later, knowing full well that one of the twelve (Judas) betrayed Jesus.

E. This saying of Jesus (Matt 19:28; cf. Luke 22:30) may provide a key to the significance of the number twelve. It was a symbolic number in light of the ancient tradition that Israel had originally been formed by twelve tribes.

    1. The twelve disciples, therefore, represented true Israel and it was they—the ones who adhered to Jesus' teachings—who were the true people of God.

    2. Notice that in the Q saying, the focus is on their future role as rulers in the kingdom of God.

    3. This aspect of Jesus' teaching may have been responsible for another well-documented tradition in our sources—that the disciples had allowed their future prominence to go to their heads. Jesus constantly had to remind them that the first shall be last and that only those who humbled themselves like children and slaves would be allowed to enter into the kingdom (cf. Mark 9:33–37, 10:35–44 with Matt. 19–39).

III. Among Jesus' other activities, his associations with the wicked and the outcast are particularly prominent.

    A. His companionship with prostitutes, tax collectors (who were generally regarded as corrupt and collaborators with the Romans), and sinners (i.e., those who had no concern to keep the law) is attested throughout the early traditions of Mark, Q, M, and L (e.g., Mark 2:15–167; Matt. 11:19, 21, 31–32; Luke 15:1).

    B. Moreover, this is not the kind of tradition that Jesus' later followers, concerned about his reputation, would have likely invented.

    C. Jesus' choice to associate with sinners and outcasts make sense in light of his apocalyptic message. The kingdom would come to these people, not to the rich, eminent, powerful, and religious (cf. Mark 21:31 and Matt. 21:31 and its reversal of fortunes with the coming of the kingdom).

    D. Jesus also clearly associated with women in public.

        1. This is multiply attested in our traditions (e.g., Mark 15:40–451; Gospel of Thomas 114; Luke 8:1–3; John 4; and so on).

        2. These associations are significant, because women were widely regarded as inferior to men and, at least in

Palestine, were restricted in their abilities to engage in public activities.

   3. This also makes sense in an apocalyptic context. Remember the kingdom would have complete equality, and those who were oppressed would be exalted. Women were drawn to this message.

IV. Jesus' activities during his public ministry largely consisted of traveling through Galilee, proclaiming his gospel, and gathering followers.

   A. We do not know how long this ministry lasted.

   1. In Mark's Gospel it appears to last only a matter of months, from the early summer when grain had begun to ripen (Mark 2:23) until the Passover feast the following spring (14:12).

   2. John's later account, though, speaks of three Passover feasts (2:13, 6:4, 11:55), so the ministry must be assumed to have lasted at least a bit over two years.

   B. Jesus' ministry was probably restricted to rural areas.

   1. Jesus is never said to have visited the major city of Sepphoris, even though it was just a few miles from Nazareth, or any of the other major cities of Galilee.

   2. He is always in the small towns and villages and in the fields outside (e.g., Mark 1:45, 3:7, 4:1, and so on).

   3. He appears to have used Capernaum, on the Sea of Galilee, as his base of operation. This tradition is multiply attested (Mark 1:21, 2:1; Matt. 4:13; John 2:12, 6:59), and it's hard to see why Christians would have made it up.

   C. His ministry was almost exclusively to fellow Jews, whom he tried to convince, through his proclamations and interpretations of Scripture, that they needed to repent and turn to God in view of the coming destruction.

V. In light of the foregoing discussion, we can say that the most well attested deeds of Jesus all support the notion that Jesus was an apocalypticist, concerned to bring his message of the imminent arrival of the kingdom of God to the people of Israel before it was too late.

Essential Reading:

©2000 The Teaching Company Limited Partnership

Ehrman, *Jesus: Apocalyptic Prophet*, chap. 11.

Sanders, *The Historical Figure of Jesus*, chaps. 11–13.

Sanders, *Jesus and Judaism*, chap. 3.

Suggested Reading:

Allison, *Jesus of Nazareth.*

Chilton and Evans, *Authenticating the Deeds of Jesus.*

Questions to Consider:

1. In this lecture, we have considered a number of Jesus' most well documented activities and associations from an apocalyptic perspective, but by no means all of them. Just to pick one other—how might Jesus' well-documented fondness for children fit into his overall apocalyptic message?

2. Discuss Jesus' decision to associate with outcasts and sinners. Is it really plausible that he thought wicked people would come into God's kingdom before those who tried to be righteous? If so, what light might that cast on people today—even Christian people—who are bent on being highly moral instead of sinful?

Lecture Seventeen—Transcript
The Deeds of Jesus in their Apocalyptic Context

To this point, we've seen that when the historical criteria are applied to our earliest sources, what emerges is a Jesus who is thoroughly rooted in an apocalyptic view of the world. Jesus' proclamation focused on the imminent arrival of the Son of Man in judgment on Earth, and the appearance, then, of God's good kingdom. What's striking is that the ethical teachings of Jesus that most people see as especially characteristic of him fit well into that context. These were not ethics to help build a more just and equitable society for the long term. They were designed to show what the kingdom would be like when society was overthrown, and to prepare people to enter into that new social world that God would create. As we'll see in this lecture, the apocalyptic focus of Jesus also allows us to understand better the kinds of things that he's known to have done, as these also are established by considering the reports of his deeds in the Gospels in light of the various historical criteria we've established.

Before getting into this discussion of Jesus' deeds, though, I want to take a brief time-out, to stress that if anyone has a different way of understanding Jesus, for example non-apocalyptically, that it's not good enough simply to cite some verses and draw conclusions. We've seen substantial evidence that Jesus' ministry was rooted in his apocalyptic views of the coming of the actual kingdom on earth. Anyone who poses an alternative view has to work it out as well, on the basis of evidence. Some scholars have tried to do just that, argue that Jesus was not an apocalypticist, even though our earliest sources independently indicate that he was. I want to look at two ways that scholars have gotten around the problem that our earliest sources portray Jesus apocalyptically, when they think that he wasn't apocalyptic.

One way to get around this problem of our early sources is by arguing that these sources, for example Mark, Q, M, and L, do not preserve the earliest traditions about Jesus. This is the view, for example, espoused by a New Testament scholar named John Dominic Crossan, who's a leading member of the "Jesus Seminar," a group of scholars devoted to uncovering the historical words and deeds of Jesus, a group of scholars that meets together semi-annually to discuss each surviving tradition of all of our sources, and then to vote on its historical accuracy. Crossan, as I've said, is a leading member of the "Jesus Seminar," one whose books on the historical Jesus are among the most popular in the market.

Crossan thinks that Jesus was not a Jewish apocalypticist, but obviously, he has to contend with the problem of our sources. This he does with wit and verve, and with some ingenuity. Crossan claims that other, lesser-known sources not found in the New Testament, including such documents as the Gospel of Peter, that we've looked at, and the Gospel of the Hebrews preserve traditions that are much older than those found in the canonical sources. Since none of these other sources portrays Jesus as an apocalypticist, for Crossan, he evidently was not one. The problem is that the documents Crossan refers to themselves date from much later times. The Gospel of the Hebrews, for example, is not even mentioned or alluded to until the end of the second century A.D. To say that it preserves traditions that are older than those found in a Gospel produced a full century or more earlier, Mark, is certainly possible, but it stretches one's credulity.

When the sources that virtually everyone agrees were produced first preserve traditions that portray Jesus apocalyptically, and sources that virtually everyone agrees were produced later preserve traditions in which he's not portrayed apocalyptically, this should almost certainly suggest to us a trend, a trend away from seeing Jesus as an apocalypticist. To claim, as Crossan needs to do, that the later sources consistently portray the earlier traditions, and that the earlier sources consistently portray the later traditions, seems to be a peculiar case of special pleading.

Another way around the problem that our earliest sources seem to portray Jesus apocalyptically is the claim that in fact they do not—to take the same sources that we've been looking at and say that they do not portray Jesus apocalyptically. This is a bit of a problem, since apocalyptic materials are found, for example, throughout Mark and Q. Some scholars have been convinced that Q is not only much earlier than Mark, however—that Q was written maybe in the 50s, maybe 15 or 20 years before Mark—but also that Q was not apocalyptic. Many members of the "Jesus Seminar" take this very stand. It's a stand that is also hard to maintain, since Q does in fact contain apocalyptic traditions on the lips of Jesus, as we've seen. For example, Luke chapter 12, verse 39, also found in Matthew, of course; Luke chapter 17 verses 24 through 30. These are thoroughly apocalyptic types of tradition. How does one avoid this problem, then, if you want to say that the earliest sources don't portray Jesus apocalyptically?

Proponents of a non-apocalyptic Jesus claim that even though our version of Q is apocalyptical, an earlier version of the document was not apocalyptic, and that only at a later time did an editor come along and insert apocalyptic traditions in Q's non-apocalyptic text. According to this view, it was this later corrupted version of Q that was then used by Matthew and Luke, so that it appears to us to be apocalyptic but originally it wasn't apocalyptic. Again, it's an ingenious solution to a problem, but one has to wonder about the evidence.

It's important to recall that we don't even have Q. It's hard enough to claim that an ancient document in our possession went through multiple additions, to determine what it looked like at every stage. Sometimes we do that with ancient sources. We say, "It's edited this way, this way, and that way," but when we do that, we actually have the document. When we want to claim multiple editors for a text, it's possible when the text survives, but what about a text that doesn't survive? It's very hard to claim multiple editions of Q when we don't have Q. We simply don't have access to the document. The reason for people making this argument, I think, is precisely because they're not comfortable with the idea of Jesus being an apocalypticist, so if Q portrays him apocalyptically, you have to maintain that Q didn't originally do so until it went through multiple editions. Again, this strikes me as a case of special pleading.

In short, for me it's very difficult to get around the problem that our earliest sources independently show Jesus to be an apocalypticist. Moreover, as we'll see now, in this lecture, not only Jesus' words but also his deeds make sense within an apocalyptic context. I'm going to talk about several of Jesus' deeds and activities in this lecture, and several more in the next lecture.

It's quite clear, as we've seen, that Jesus was baptized by John the Baptist. That's one of his activities, the first one we know about, and it demonstrates pretty clearly that Jesus began his ministry by adopting an apocalyptic perspective. We've already seen that Jesus' baptism by John is one of the most securely rooted traditions in our sources. It passes all three of our criteria with flying colors. Moreover, we know that John proclaimed an apocalyptic message, as seen, for example, in his preaching in the Q document. It's hard to imagine why Jesus would have chosen to associate himself with the Baptist if in fact he didn't agree with his message, since he could have easily associated with someone else. Jesus could have joined up with a Pharisee, or with an Essene, or with somebody else, but instead, he joins up with John the Baptist.

The baptism of Jesus, then, above all shows that he essentially agreed with John in his apocalyptic message. People who think that Jesus is not an apocalypticist typically agree that he associated with John the Baptist. What is sometimes argued, then, is that Jesus started out apocalyptically, but then after the beginning of his ministry, he changed his mind, and so he shifted from John's harsh apocalyptic message of this coming end of the age to preaching a simple message of love, for example, or of sharing one's goods, or of giving up one's possessions for the sake of the spiritual life rather than a material life.

The difficulty with that way of arguing is precisely what I pointed out in an earlier lecture. You could say that fairly easily, if we didn't have evidence that the earliest communities of Jesus themselves were apocalyptic, because the continuity between the apocalyptic John and the apocalyptic Christian communities is Jesus himself. How do you explain that after he was gone, his followers still were apocalyptic? You almost would necessarily say, and this in fact is what John Dominic Crossan contends, that Jesus began apocalyptically, he changed his mind, stopped being apocalyptic for his ministry and preached something other than an apocalyptic message, and then after he died, his followers, instead of following his message, went back to John the Baptist's message, and became apocalyptic again. It's possible, of course; I mean, lots of things are possible in history, but one has to think about the probabilities. If Jesus begins by associating with John, and his followers afterward are also apocalyptic like John, it seems likely that Jesus himself provided the continuity. In any event, one deed that we're fairly certain about, one activity of Jesus that we're fairly certain about, is the baptism by John, apocalyptic.

A similar conclusion can be drawn from another datum from Jesus' life that we've established with relative certainty, namely, that Jesus decided to call twelve men to be his disciples. Jesus had twelve disciples. These aren't the only followers he had, but he chose kind of an inner group of twelve. How do we know that this is an authentic tradition? It's a tradition that's attested throughout our sources. All of the Synoptic Gospels, Matthew, Mark, and Luke, agree that there were twelve insiders among Jesus' followers. What's interesting to note is that the Synoptic Gospels don't agree on who the twelve were. Both Mark and Luke give lists of the names of the twelve, but the lists don't agree in every place. The way people have reconciled this over the years is to say, "Some of the people in the list actually had two names," and so, you know, Mark calls them one name, Luke calls them another.

Another way to look at it is that in fact everybody knew that there were twelve of these people, but not everybody knew who the twelve were. In the Book of Acts, as it turns out, the twelve apostles are mentioned again, but most of the twelve are never dealt with at all. We don't have very many traditions about most of these people. In any event, it appears that people knew there were twelve, whether they knew what the names of the twelve were or not. Moreover, in addition to the Synoptic Gospels, we have the tradition supported by the apostle Paul, who mentions the twelve in 1 Corinthians 15, by John, who's writing independently of the Synoptics in John chapter 6, and as I mentioned earlier, in the Book of Acts, chapter 6.

In addition to having this tradition be independently attested in our sources, there are some sayings about the twelve that appear to pass the criterion of dissimilarity, especially this passage that I mentioned in an earlier lecture, in which Jesus talks about the twelve being the future rulers of the kingdom. This is a Q saying, with the version in Matthew,

> Jesus said to them, "Truly I tell you, at the renewal of all things, when the Son of Man is seated on the throne of his glory, you who have followed me will also sit on twelve thrones, judging the twelve tribes of Israel."

The twelve disciples will be the twelve judges or twelve rulers of the people of Israel, in the kingdom of God. Why do I say this passes the criterion of dissimilarity? Because after Jesus' death, his followers knew that Judas, one of these twelve, had turned him in. The traditions were that Judas, then, committed suicide, or in some other way died. He commits suicide in the Book of Matthew. The Book of Acts says that he dies in some other way, and people try and reconcile the two, but people appear to have known that he died.

What Christian would make up the idea that Judas would be one of the twelve ruling the tribes of Israel? It's hard to imagine a Christian coming up with that. Where did the saying come from, then? It probably went back to Jesus. Jesus told his twelve that they were going to be the rulers of this future kingdom.

Among other things, in addition to supporting the idea that Jesus is giving them an apocalyptic message of the future kingdom, it shows pretty clearly that there were twelve disciples that Jesus chose. Moreover, this saying of Jesus may provide a key to the significance of the number twelve. Why did he choose twelve? Why not nine? Why not fourteen? What is it about twelve? This tradition suggests that in fact twelve is a symbolic number, that Jesus chose twelve precisely because of the ancient tradition that Israel was originally formed of twelve tribes; the twelve tribes of Israel then will be ruled by the twelve disciples. In other words, the choice of the twelve is a symbolic number because the twelve represent true Israel. It was they, the ones who adhered to Jesus' teachings, who were the true people of God.

Notice that in this Q saying, the focus is on their role in the future coming kingdom. Those who followed Jesus would be the ones who entered into the kingdom, and the twelve would be rulers over them. This aspect of Jesus' teaching may have been responsible for another well-documented tradition in our sources, namely that the disciples had allowed their future prominence to go to their heads. Jesus, throughout these early sources, constantly has to remind his followers, especially the twelve, that the first shall be last, and the last will be first, that only those who humble themselves like children, who become like slaves, would be allowed to enter into this future kingdom.

What we have, then, is a tradition that is firmly established, that Jesus had twelve close disciples that he himself had chosen. These twelve disciples, the fact that there are twelve fits in perfectly well with apocalyptic context. It explains other traditions in which Jesus affirms that this coming kingdom would come only to those who serve others, not those who lord it over others.

Among Jesus' other activities, his associations with the wicked and the outcast are particularly prominent. His companionship with prostitutes, tax collectors, and sinners is attested throughout the early traditions that we have of Mark, Q, M, and L. I mentioned in an earlier lecture something about what the tax collectors were all about. Probably the people that Jesus himself is referring to were not heads of the tax-collecting corporations that were established throughout Palestine. The way the tax collection worked in ancient Palestine was that there were corporations who bid to the Roman Empire, and the corporation that had the highest bid about the amount of taxes that they could bring in would be the one that would be allowed to collect the taxes on behalf of the local aristocracy, or on behalf of the Roman governor who was ruling at the time. The way these corporations made their money was by raising more taxes than the Romans themselves demanded. The people who went out and did the collection, then, of course, wanted to raise as much money as they could to help augment their own salaries. The tax collectors Jesus refers to in his own teachings, and that are referred to as associating with him, probably are not the leaders of these tax corporations, but are probably the people pounding on the doors actually raising the money.

In some Jewish sources from the later rabbis there were teachings that the tax collectors would never be able to have salvation because in Jewish tradition when one wrongs another, one not only has to pay back what one has defrauded, but has to provide some additional amount as a kind of a penalty beyond what the person was defrauded of. It was widely thought that since the tax collectors had defrauded so many people so many times, they couldn't possibly know what they would have to pay in restitution, and so no restitution ultimately would be possible. Tax collectors were widely seen, then, as people who were corrupt. Moreover, many people saw them as collaborators with Roman policies of domination, since they're the ones who are gathering the funds that are being paid to the Empire. Tax collectors, then, had a low reputation in this world.

In addition to the tax collectors, Jesus associates with a group called the "sinners." "Sinners," in this context, does not necessarily mean prostitutes, even though it's commonly interpreted that way, that "sinners" refers to prostitutes. Of course, prostitutes would have been understood as sinners, but there are traditions that specifically associate Jesus with prostitutes without calling them "sinners," and there are traditions that associate Jesus with sinners without calling them "prostitutes." In this context, the term "sinner" probably refers to people who had no intention ever, at all, of keeping God's law, for people who didn't try to observe the Torah, who were therefore seen by religious people like the Pharisees as beyond the pale. They were people seen as wicked, people who were sinful, people who were sinners.

It is well attested throughout our sources that these are the kinds of associates that Jesus had—prostitutes, tax collectors, and sinners. It's independently attested that he associated with such people; Mark chapter 2, Matthew chapter 11, Luke chapter 15, throughout our various early sources. Moreover, this is not the kind of tradition that you'd expect Jesus' later followers, who were concerned about his reputation, to have invented. In other words, they don't show that Jesus is associating with the great religious teachers, great leaders, people who are of high social standing. They show Jesus associating with the outcasts, with the lowly, with the people everybody thought were the sinful scum of the Earth. Who would make up a tradition like that? It appears that his followers would not, which means that probably these traditions actually go back to Jesus.

Why, though, did Jesus choose to associate with the sinners and the outcasts? It's firmly established that he did. The reason that he did would make sense in light of his own apocalyptic message. It was to people like these, according to Jesus, that the kingdom would come. The kingdom was not going to come to those who were rich, and eminent, and powerful, and religious, as Jesus tells the religious leaders of his own day, in the Gospel of Matthew chapter 21, verse 31: "The prostitutes and tax collectors will enter into the kingdom of God before you." This involved Jesus' apocalyptic message of the reversal of fortunes with the coming of the kingdom.

Jesus also clearly associated with women in public. This too, Jesus' association with women, is multiply attested in our traditions. For example, we have Jesus associating with women in Mark chapter 15, women actually go with Jesus from Galilee down to Jerusalem during the Passover; Gospel of Thomas, verse 114; Gospel of Luke chapter 8 indicates that Jesus had women who were his patronesses, who actually provided funding for him and his disciples; John chapter 4. These are four different independent sources that attest Jesus' involvement with women in public. It's a significant datum, because women were widely regarded as inferior to men, and at least in Palestine they were restricted in their abilities to engage in public activities outside of the home. Jesus, though, associated with them publicly. Why would he do so? Again, it makes sense in an apocalyptic context. Remember, in the kingdom there would be complete equality, and those who were oppressed would be exalted in the kingdom. It's no wonder that women were drawn to Jesus' message, and that he associated with them openly as an illustration of it. In the future kingdom, men and women would be equal.

Jesus' activities during his public ministry, then, largely consisted of traveling through Galilee, proclaiming his gospel, and gathering followers. We don't know how long this ministry lasted. In Mark's Gospel, our first account, the ministry of Jesus appears to last only a matter of months. The reason for thinking this is because in an early stage in the Gospel, Mark chapter 2, verse 23, there's an account of Jesus' disciples going through the grain fields and gathering some of the grain and eating it on the Sabbath. The Pharisees find this objectionable, and it leads to a controversy between Jesus and the Pharisees about the keeping of the Sabbath.

In terms of the chronology, though, the point is that this would have happened in the early summer when the grain was just beginning to ripen. At the end of Mark's Gospel in chapter 14, Jesus goes to Jerusalem during a Passover feast. That would be during the spring, so that the length of time between Mark chapter 2 and Mark chapter 14, the beginning and the end of the Gospel, appears to be a matter of months, the early summer to the following spring. John's account, on the other hand, our last account to be written, seems to take much longer. John speaks of there being three different Passover feasts during Jesus' public ministry. John mentions the Passover, one feast in chapter 2, a different feast in chapter 6, a different feast in chapter 11. In that case, the ministry of Jesus is assumed to have lasted at least a bit over two years, to accommodate the three different Passover feasts. There's some discrepancy, then, about the length of time the ministry lasted, anywhere from several months, as in Mark, to just over two years, as in John.

Jesus goes to villages and towns and the countryside, in the Galilee. It's striking that Jesus is never said to have visited the major cities of the area—Sepphoris, which was just a few miles' walking distance from Nazareth, or any of the other major cities of Galilee. I want to stress the point because a lot of modern scholars have been excited about the excavations, the archaeological digs at Sepphoris, which indeed have been exciting because they've shown us something about urban life in Galilee. Sepphoris is a major city, a big place, and within walking distance of Nazareth, and so people have concluded that Jesus must therefore have been a fairly urbane, sophisticated, cultured person, because he lived so close to a major urban center.

The problem is, the New Testament never said that Jesus even visited there. The word "Sepphoris" never even occurs in the New Testament. Therefore, to think that the urban environment of Sepphoris is the principal context for understanding Jesus doesn't work, because Jesus is never associated with Sepphoris; nor is he associated with Tiberias, the other major city near the area. Jesus doesn't go to the major cities. He spends all of his time in the small towns and villages, and in the fields outside of them. Jesus appears to have been most comfortable in the rural areas. He doesn't associate with people in the urban areas. The only time he goes to a city is at the end of his life, Jerusalem. In Mark's Gospel, there's no indication that he had gone back and forth from there to Galilee. It's when he makes his major pilgrimage, to Jerusalem at the end of his life. Jesus appears to have used as his sort of base of operation the town of Capernaum, on the Sea of Galilee. I think that that's probably historically accurate that that's where Jesus used as his base, because the tradition is multiply attested in Mark and M, and in John. It's also hard to say why a Christian would have made up that tradition; they don't gain anything by it.

Jesus' ministry appears to have been conducted exclusively to fellow Jews, whom he tried to convince through his own proclamation and his interpretation of the scripture, that they needed to repent, and turn to God, in view of the coming destruction.

In sum, we can say that the best attested deeds of Jesus, his baptism by John, his selection of twelve disciples, his associations with outcasts, sinners, and women, and his itinerate preaching ministry in Galilee, all support the notion that Jesus was an apocalypticist concerned to bring his message of the imminent arrival of God to the people of Israel before it was too late. In another lecture, we'll see how this apocalyptic orientation can also explain the activities of Jesus that we're best informed about, those that occurred during the last week of his life, after he took his final and fatal trip to Jerusalem during the Passover feast sometime around the year 30.

Before moving to that point, though, we need to consider some of the other words and deeds of Jesus that are found throughout our tradition, in particular his well-known claims that in some sense, the kingdom of God had already arrived, and his most famous deeds, the miracles that he's alleged to have done. This aspect of his teaching, that the kingdom's already arrived, and this aspect of his activities, his alleged miracles, are two special cases that I think we need to spend some time thinking about carefully, so these two areas will be the topics of our next lecture.

Lecture Eighteen
Still Other Words and Deeds of Jesus

Scope:

The most commonly reported activities of Jesus are his miracles, especially his abilities to cast out demons and heal the sick. The reports of Jesus' miracles create special problems for historians, not because they must take the philosophical view of the Enlightenment that miracles cannot happen, but because even if one concedes that miracles can happen, historians cannot demonstrate them. Historians are restricted to marshaling evidence from the public record, available to all people of every religious conviction, concerning what probably happened in the past. Because historians work with probabilities (never absolute certainties) and because miracles by their very nature are the most improbable of events, historians can never show that they probably happened. The historian can, though, discuss the reports of miracles and that is what we will do in this lecture. We will also address the issue of the relationship of the present to the future in Jesus' proclamation of the Kingdom. Was it, as some scholars assert, present and perhaps complete in Jesus' earthly ministry, or was it a Kingdom yet to come, brought by the Son of Man in judgment.

Outline

I. The ubiquitous Gospel reports of Jesus' miracles create special problems for historians, who are committed to establishing what probably happened in the past.

   A. These miracle traditions create a special problem for historians. Some people since the Enlightenment have insisted that miracles cannot happen. For such people, because miracles don't happen, Jesus did not do miracles. This view can be called the "philosophical" problem of miracle. I want to state emphatically that this is not the issue I want to address in this lecture.

   B. For the sake of the argument, I'm willing to concede that miracles can and do happen. Even if miracles are possible, however, the historian still has no way to show that they have ever happened. I'll call this the "historical" problem of miracle.

II. We must begin by comparing the ways in which historians engage in their craft to the ways in which natural scientists engage in theirs.

A. The natural sciences operate through repeated experimentation, seeking to establish predictive probabilities based on past occurrences.
might call "presumptive probability." A "miracle" would involve a violation of this known working of nature.

B. The historical disciplines are not like the natural sciences, in part because they are concerned with establishing what *has happened* in the past, as opposed to predicting what *will happen* in the future, and in part because they cannot operate through repeated experimentation.

  1. An occurrence is a one-time proposition; once it has happened, it is over and done with.

  2. Because historians cannot repeat the past to establish what has probably happened, there will always be less certainty about past events. The farther back you go in history, the harder it is to mount a convincing case for a miracle.

C. This is what makes alleged miracles so problematic.

  1. Most things that happen are not so unlikely as to defy the imagination, because they happen more or less all the time.

  2. What about events that do not happen all the time? As events that defy all probabilities, miracles create an inescapable dilemma for the historian.

D. For historians, a miracle can never be the most probable occurrence. That means that historians can never show—by the very nature of the case, given the constraints imposed on them by historical methods—that miracles probably happened.

  1. This is a problem for all historians of every religious or even non-religious stripe.

  2. Even if otherwise good sources exist for a miraculous event, the very nature of the historical discipline prevents the historian from arguing for its probability. By their very nature, miracles are the least probable occurrence in any given instance.

E. A related issue is that the only kind of evidence that historians can look at is what is available in the public record.

  1. The historian has no access to "supernatural forces," only to events that can be observed and interpreted by any reasonable person, of whatever religious persuasion.

  2. If a miracle requires belief in the supernatural realm, but historians—when they are acting as historians—have access only to the natural realm, then they can never even discuss the probabilities of a miracle.

F. I should emphasize that historians do not have to deny the possibility of miracles or deny that miracles have actually happened in the past.

  1. Many historians, including Christians, Jews, and Muslims, believe that miracles have happened.

  3. When they think or say this, however, they do so not as historians but as believers

  4. In this discussion, I am not taking the position of the believer; I am taking the position of the historian.

  4. When reconstructing Jesus' activities, I will not affirm or deny the miracles that he is reported to have done. These events—even if they did happen—are beyond the purview of the historian. As a historian, however, I can talk about the reports of his miracles, because these are a matter of public record.

III. Jesus clearly had the reputation of being an exorcist.

  A. The accounts of his exorcisms are multiply attested; they are found throughout Mark, M, and L. But how about the other criteria?

  1. The accounts cannot pass the criterion of dissimilarity, because followers who believed that Jesus was could overcome the forces of evil may well have made up stories to show that he did.

  2. The accounts pass contextual credibility only to the extent that other miracles workers, such as the pagan Apollonius of Tyana and some other Jewish holy men, were also thought to have power over.

  3. The historian cannot say that demons—real live supernatural spirits that invade human bodies—were actually cast out of people. To do so would be to transcend the boundaries of the historical method

4. We certainly can say that Jesus was widely recognized by people of his own time—who did believe that demons existed and could be exorcised—to have the powers to cast them out.

B. What is especially interesting for the historian is how these alleged miracles were interpreted by Jesus' earliest followers.

1. When Jesus is charged with casting out demons by the power of Satan, he responds by saying, "If I cast demons out by Beelzeboul, by whom do your sons cast them out? But if I cast demons out by the spirit of God, behold the Kingdom of God is come upon you" (Matt. 12:27–30; cf. Luke 11:19–23).

2. Notice that everyone—Jesus and his opponents—admits that both Jesus and other Jewish exorcists can cast out demons. Even more important, Jesus' exorcisms are interpreted apocalyptically. They show that the kingdom of God was at hand.

3. It is striking that this apocalyptic view is the earliest understanding of the widespread tradition that Jesus could cast out demons.

IV. Similar results accrue to a historical understanding of Jesus' miracles of healing.

A. The reports of his abilities to heal the sick and raise the dead are multiply attested, but they cannot pass the criterion of dissimilarity.

B. Even more significant is the interpretation commonly given to his ability to heal.

1. His healing miracles were not taken to be signs that Jesus was God. They were the sorts of things that Jewish prophets did. Jesus simply did them better than anyone else. The earliest traditions assign apocalyptic meaning to these acts.

2. Recall that in the kingdom, disease and death would no longer exist. Jesus healed the sick and raised the dead. In a small way, then, the kingdom was already becoming manifest.

3. According to an account in Q, when John the Baptist wanted to know whether Jesus was the final prophet before the end or whether another one could be expected, Jesus reportedly replied:

   Tell John the things you have seen and heard: the blind are regaining their sight, the lame are starting to walk, the lepers are being cleansed, the deaf are starting to hear, the dead are being raised, and the poor are hearing the good news! (Luke 7:22; Q; 4

4. Again, Jesus' miracles are interpreted apocalyptically to show that the end had arrived and a final climax was soon to come.

V. This leads us to a final point: To what extent did Jesus proclaim that the end had already begun to make itself manifest? Scholars have long debated the extent to which Jesus thought that the kingdom had already arrived.

A. Some have gone to the extreme of claiming that, for Jesus, the kingdom was already completely present and nothing more was going to occur—no cataclysmic break in history brought by God, other than the appearance of Jesus himself (this view is termed "realized eschatology").

   1. This view is largely based on such verses as Luke 17:20–21: "the Kingdom of God is in your midst."
   2. Unfortunately, the verse is not multiply attested, and we have seen many examples of clear apocalyptic proclamations scattered throughout the earliest sources.
   3. In some sense, though, it seems as if Jesus thought that the end had already become manifest in the present.

B. Most scholars would say that Jesus understood that the kingdom had already begun to appear, but a cataclysmic ending was still to come with the arrival of the Son of Man.

C. We have already seen a sense of the coming of the kingdom in both Jesus' teachings of ethics and the reports of his miracles.

   1. People who follow Jesus are to implement the ideals of the kingdom in the present. Because war will not exist, people should not commit any acts of violence now; because hatred will not exist, people should engage only

in love now; because oppression will not exist, people should work for justice now.

   2.   The reports of Jesus' miracles also show the beginning of the kingdom in the present. Because the forces of evil will not exist, Jesus casts out demons now; because illness will not exist, Jesus heals the sick now; because death will not exist, Jesus raises the dead now.

D. Many of Jesus' parables present this view: that the kingdom has started to appear in the ministry of Jesus and the lives of his disciples, but that what they were experiencing was merely a foretaste of the glories that were to come when the kingdom of God arrived in power.

E. The parable of the mustard seed (in both Mark and Thomas) stresses that the small and inauspicious beginnings in the present would erupt into enormous consequences in the end.

F. The parable of the leavened dough (Q) emphasizes that what is small and hidden now will affect the whole world later.

VI. For Jesus and his earliest followers, the apocalyptic message of the coming destruction had serious implications for the present.

A. Those who implemented the ideals would be qualified to enter the kingdom when it arrived with the powerful appearance of the Son of Man. They had also begun to realize what life would be like in that kingdom, which would be ruled by peace, harmony, justice, and love.

B. Those who saw in Jesus a great worker of miracles saw still further manifestations of the kingdom.

   1.   Historians cannot affirm that Jesus did (or did not) perform supernatural feats that violated what we might call natural laws—that kind of judgment lies beyond the purview of what we can know historically.

   2.   Historians can say that Jesus was commonly *believed* to have done such things, and that this belief was typically understood apocalyptically. By casting out demons, healing the sick, and raising the dead, Jesus was embodying what life would be like when the kingdom of God arrived.

Essential Reading:

Ehrman, *Jesus: Apocalyptic Prophet*, chap. 11.

Meier, *A Marginal Jew*, vol. 2.

Sanders, *The Historical Figure of Jesus*, chap. 10.

Suggested Reading:

Fuller, *Interpreting the Miracles.*

Kee, *Miracle in the Early Christian World.*

Questions to Consider:

1. Explain why a miracle that was reportedly done by a modern faith-healer—even if attested to by eyewitnesses and discussed in the newspapers—cannot be established as historically probable. (If it seems to you that it *would* be probable if reported by eyewitnesses, listen or read through this lecture again and think about the logic behind the claim that historians cannot establish that a miracle, by its very nature, probably happened in the past.) Does the fact that it can't be established as probable mean that it cannot be accepted as true?

2. For the sake of argument, I presupposed in this lecture that miracles can and do happen (even though they cannot be established as probably happening). Now for the sake of a different argument, presuppose something quite different—that Jesus did *not* do any miracles at all. Assuming such a view, how might you account for the abundance of miracles attributed to him throughout the tradition?

Lecture Eighteen—Transcript
Still Other Words and Deeds of Jesus

I've spent the last three lectures trying to unpack the apocalyptic substance of Jesus' words and deeds. We've seen that he anticipated the imminent arrival of the Son of Man from heaven, a cosmic judge who would wreak vengeance on the enemies of God, and bring an eternal rule of peace and harmony on Earth for those who did what God demanded, in the kingdom of God that was soon to arrive.

Jesus' ethical teachings fit in with this apocalyptic message. Jesus' followers were to repent of their past sins, and turn to God, loving Him with their whole heart, and loving their neighbors as themselves, forgiving one another, following the Golden Rule, adhering to the demands that God made upon His people in the Jewish scriptures. Moreover, Jesus' activities reflected this message as well: His being baptized by John, an apocalyptic prophet in the wilderness; his selection of twelve disciples, who were to rule over the remnant of the nation of Israel that entered into the kingdom; his active and public associations with outcasts, sinners, the poor, women. There are, of course, numerous other traditions recorded about Jesus in our surviving Gospels. I therefore need to stress once again that we're looking only at materials that can be plausibly accepted as historically accurate, based on the historical criteria we've discussed.

In this lecture, I want to turn my attention to two other prominent aspects of the early accounts of Jesus, to see what we can say about their historical value; first, the reports of his miracles, and second, his sayings that the kingdom of God was already, in some sense, present on Earth.

The reports of Jesus' miracles create a special problem for historians, who are committed to establishing to the best of their ability what probably happened in the past. On the one hand, the miracles of Jesus are virtually ubiquitous in our Gospel traditions. Nearly everywhere you turn, Jesus is healing the sick, casting out the demons, raising the dead, multiplying the loaves, walking on the water, and so on. These traditions infiltrate our Gospel traditions. Some people, since the Enlightenment in Europe, have insisted that such miracles cannot happen. For people like this, since miracles don't happen, Jesus necessarily did not do miracles. This view can be called the "philosophical" problem of miracle. I want to state emphatically that this is not the issue that I want to address in this lecture.

I'm not dealing with the philosophical problem of whether or not miracles are possible. That's not what I want to deal with. For the sake of the argument, I'm willing to concede that miracles can and do happen. For the sake of the argument, I concede that they happen. There still remains a huge, and I'd say, insurmountable problem when discussing Jesus' miracles. Even if miracles are possible, there is no way for the historian to show that they've ever happened. I'm going to call this the "historical" problem of miracle, as opposed to the philosophical problem. Let me explain the historical problem of miracle at some length.

One way to approach the question is by reflecting for a moment on the ways in which historians engage in their craft in contrast, say, to the ways in which scientists engage in theirs. The natural sciences operate through repeated experimentation, as they seek to establish predictive probabilities based on past occurrences. To illustrate on just the most simple level, suppose that I wanted to demonstrate that a bar of iron will sink in a tub of lukewarm water, but a bar of Ivory soap will float. I could prove my thesis, simply by repeated experimentation with tubs of water, and with bars of both iron and soap. Simply line up the tubs, and start throwing in. The bars of iron are going to sink every time, the bars of Ivory soap are going to float every time, and this would provide an extremely high level of what we might call "presumptive probability;" namely, that if I keep repeating this experiment, I'm going to keep getting the same results, so that we can predict that in the future, that's probably what's going to happen.

This is what natural science does, is it makes predictions about what's going to happen, based on repeated experimentation of what already has happened. In common parlance, a miracle within this schema would involve a violation of this known working of nature. It would be a miracle, for example, if a preacher prayed over a bar of iron, and chucked it into a vat of lukewarm water, and it floated. We would call that a miracle.

The historical disciplines are not like the natural sciences, because they're concerned with establishing what has happened in the past, as opposed to predicting what will happen in the future, and in part because the historical disciplines do not operate through repeated experimentation. An occurrence is a one-time proposition. Once it's happened, it's over and done with. Since historians cannot repeat the past, in order to establish what has probably happened, there will always be less certainty than there would be in the natural sciences, where you can demonstrate things through repeated experimentation.

It's much harder to convince people that John F. Kennedy was the victim of a lone assassin than it is to convince them that a bar of Ivory soap will float, because you can repeat one, and you can't repeat the other. In addition, the farther back you go in history, the harder it is to mount a convincing case. It's one thing to mount a convincing case of an event that happened in 1963, where you actually have videotape, but to try and convince somebody of what happened in the year 63 is extremely difficult. You cannot only not repeat it, but the sources available to you are highly problematic.

This, though, is what makes alleged miracles so hard for historians, so difficult, and in fact why they pose an insurmountable difficulty for historians. Of course, everything that happened at all is improbable. Everything that happens is improbable, but most things that happen are not so unlikely as to defy the imagination, because they happen, more or less, all the time. If you, five years ago, had tried to calculate the probability of your sitting right now where you're sitting, it'd be a remote possibility, five years ago, but there's nothing improbable about the fact itself. You have to be sitting somewhere. If, though, five years ago, you tried to predict the probability of your right now, say, levitating 20 feet in the air, how would you even calculate the probability of that, since you don't levitate? You see, both are improbable, but the improbability of you levitating at this point is so infinitesimally remote that you can't even calculate it.

Events that don't happen all the time defy probabilities. That's why miracles create an inescapable dilemma for the historian. Let me put it like this: Since historians can only establish what probably did happen in the past, and the chances of a miracle happening by definition are infinitesimally remote, a miracle can never be the most probable occurrence. That means that historians can never show, by the very nature of the case, given the constraints imposed on them by the historical methods, that miracles probably happened.

This is not a problem for only one kind of historian, for example atheists, or agnostics, or Buddhists, or Roman Catholics, or Baptists, or Jews, or Muslims. It's a problem for all historians of every stripe, even if there are otherwise good sources for a miraculous event. The very nature of the historical discipline prevents the historian from arguing for its probability. By their very nature, miracles are the least probable occurrence in any given instance.

Another way to look at this problem is to point out ways that the historical disciplines are like the natural sciences. Both historical and natural disciplines deal with phenomena that can be observed by all interested parties apart from their ideological or religious beliefs. The historian can only look at evidence, in other words, that's available in the public record. As a historian, the person has no access to supernatural forces; only to events that can be observed and interpreted by any reasonable person of whatever religious persuasion. If a miracle requires belief in the supernatural realm, but historians, as historians, only have access to the natural realm, then they can never even discuss the probabilities of a miracle, because it requires belief in the supernatural.

Let me emphasize that historians don't have to deny the possibility of miracles, or deny that miracles happen. I'm not saying that. Many historians—committed Christians, observant Jews, practicing Muslims—believe in fact that miracles have happened. When they think this, though, they're thinking it not as historians, but as believers. In the present discussion, I'm not going to be taking the position of the believer, nor saying that you should or shouldn't take that position. I'm taking the position of the historian who, on the basis of a limited number of problematic sources, has to determine, to the best of his or her ability, what the historical Jesus actually said and did.

As a result, when reconstructing Jesus' activities, I won't be able to affirm or deny the miracles that he's reported to have done. These events, even if they did happen, are beyond the purview of the historian. However, as a historian, I can at least talk about the reports of Jesus' miracles. Since the accounts that people thought he did miracles are part of the public record, there's nothing problematic with the belief that people thought Jesus did miracles, and so we can talk at least about the reports of Jesus' miracles even if we can't affirm as historians that he did them.

And so, the reports of Jesus' miracles. Jesus clearly had the reputation in his own day of being an exorcist, somebody who could cast out demons. It's interesting to consider the accounts of Jesus as an exorcist, in light of the criteria that we have for establishing historically accurate material. The accounts of Jesus' exorcisms are multiply attested, found throughout Mark, M, and L. Of course, these traditions that Jesus could cast out demons do not pass the criterion of dissimilarity, since his followers, who believed that Jesus was all-powerful and could overcome the forces of evil, may well have made up a lot of stories to show that he did precisely that. Therefore, they're multiply attested, but they don't pass dissimilarity. They pass contextual credibility only to the extent that other miracle-workers like the pagan Apollonius of Tyana that we've talked about, and some other Jewish holy men from the day, were also thought to have power over demons, which means among other things that anyone who wants to think that Jesus did miracles of this sort has to allow for the possibility that Apollonius did as well.

In terms of the historicity of the traditions of Jesus being an exorcist, as I've pointed out, the historian cannot say that demons, that is, real live supernatural spirits that invade human bodies, were actually cast out of people. To make that claim would be to transcend the boundaries imposed on the historian by the historical method, so that it would require, in other words, a religious belief system that involves a supernatural realm that's outside of the historian's province. We can certainly say, though, that Jesus was widely recognized by people of his own time, who did believe that demons existed and could be exorcised—Jesus was believed to have powers to do just that.

What's especially interesting for the historian is how these alleged miracles were interpreted by Jesus' earliest followers. When Jesus is charged with casting out demons by the power of Satan by his enemies, he responds in our early traditions by saying, this is a quotation from Q, the form of Matthew: "If I cast demons out by Beelzeboul," the devil, "by whom do your sons cast them out? But if I cast them out by the spirit of God, behold, the kingdom of God is upon you." Matthew chapter 12, verse 27. It's worth noticing that everyone, Jesus and his opponents together, everyone admits not only that Jesus can cast out demons, but other Jewish exorcists can do so as well. Even more important, though, for our present discussion, Jesus' exorcisms are interpreted apocalyptically. They show, according to this early tradition, that the kingdom of God was at the doorstep. It's striking that this apocalyptic view is the earliest understanding of the widespread tradition that Jesus could cast out demons.

Very similar results accrue to a historical understanding of Jesus' miracles of healing. Once again, the reports of Jesus' abilities to heal the sick, to raise the dead, are multiply attested. We find them throughout our sources. Jesus is always healing people of various kinds—those who are blind, those who are mute, those who have various kinds of paralysis, those who have leprosy. Jesus is able to heal people of this sort. Thus, the traditions of Jesus' healing are multiply attested; of course, also, though, they do not pass the criterion of dissimilarity. People telling the stories about Jesus want to portray him as a powerful miracle-worker, and so in the cases of the stories of healing, we have to assume that these are similar to what Christians wanted to say about him, so they don't pass our criterion.

Historians, moreover, who cannot subscribe to one theological set of beliefs over another, when trying to decide what probably happened in the past, can't affirm that these miracles must have happened because it would involve them in accepting perspectives that are beyond the historical realm. In any event, it's quite clear that Jesus had a reputation for being able to heal others with a word or a touch.

Even more significant is the interpretation, once again, given Jesus' ability to heal. People today have often thought that Jesus' being able to heal others shows that in some sense he was divine. This is a common argument used by Christians today trying to show the divine character of Jesus, that of course only God could heal somebody who was blind, or who could cure paralysis, or could cure leprosy by a word alone—that this shows that Jesus is divine. It's a strange argument when you think about it, because also within these circles where this kind of argument is used, you have people who are faith healers, who themselves are not thought to be divine. They're thought to be representatives of God; the power of God works through them. Thus, the ability to work miracles doesn't show anything about a person's divinity.

Moreover, there are lots of instances in antiquity where people are thought to heal, and nobody ever claimed that the result of this was that therefore the person was himself divine. Even in the Hebrew

Bible, we have cases of miraculous events by people who are prophets, but who are completely human beings, even to the extent of raising people from the dead. In the Hebrew Bible, we have an account of the prophet Elijah, who raises a dead boy up after the boy was completely dead, but nobody thought that this made him divine. The earliest sources we have about Jesus don't indicate that his miracle-working abilities said anything about his divinity; and these were the sorts of things that everybody knew that Jewish prophets did.

There was an idea that Jesus did these miracles better than anyone else. He does miracles almost effortlessly. The interesting thing is how these miracle traditions are again interpreted by his earliest followers, though. Recall in Jesus' own teaching, in the future kingdom of God, there's going to be no more evil, but that also means that there's going to be no more illness, and there'll be no more death. Jesus embodies the kingdom in his ministry of these healing stories, because he embodies what the kingdom is going to be like. In the kingdom, there'll be no disease, and so Jesus heals disease. In the kingdom, there'll be no more death, and so Jesus raises people from the dead.

We have this very interesting account in the Q source, in which John the Baptist, who's in prison, wants to know whether to expect someone else to come, or whether Jesus himself was the final prophet before the end. He sends word to Jesus asking him: "Are you the one, or should we expect somebody else?" Jesus replies; this is the Q source, this is the account found in Luke chapter 7. "Tell John," says Jesus, "the things you've seen and heard. The blind are regaining their sight. The lame are starting to walk. The lepers are being cleansed. The deaf are starting to hear. The dead are being raised, and the poor are hearing the good news." What's striking here is that Jesus' miracles in this Q source are being interpreted apocalyptically, to show that the end had arrived and was soon to come to a final climax.

Thus, for both of these areas of the traditions of Jesus, the exorcisms, that's casting out demons, and the healings, we have the same results. Historians can't say that these things happened, because to do so would be to accept belief in the supernatural, and that's beyond the purview of the historian as a historian. Moreover, to say that he probably did these things would be to say that the least probable occurrence, a miracle, is the most probable event. Just logically, you can't say that as a historian. The accounts are independently attested though, that Jesus had the reputation for doing these miracles, and what is most striking of all in both instances—the exorcisms and the healings—in both instances, these kinds of miracles are interpreted apocalyptically to indicate that the end of the age was imminent.

This leads us now to a final point of consideration. To what extent did Jesus proclaim that the end that was going to be imminent, had already begun to make itself manifest? To what extent did Jesus think that the kingdom of God, that was going to be brought by the coming Son of Man, and that act of judgment against the world, had already in some way begun to be realized in the present age? This has been a matter of long and protracted scholarly debate. The question being, to what extent did Jesus think the kingdom had already arrived?

Some scholars have gone to the extreme of claiming that, for Jesus, the kingdom was already completely present, and there was nothing more that was going to occur; no cataclysmic break in history to be brought by God, other than the appearance of Jesus himself. This is a point of view that is sometimes called by scholars "realized eschatology." Eschatology is a person's teaching about the end times, beliefs about the end times; "realized eschatology" is the notion that the end times have been realized already in the present, so that in Jesus' ministry itself, the kingdom of God has already appeared.

Scholars who have subscribed to this view of realized eschatology have based their views largely on a verse like Luke chapter 17, verses 20 and 21, that I pointed out before. Jesus says in these verses in Luke that the kingdom is not going to come by signs that you can see, it's in your midst, or is among you. Unfortunately, this verse is not multiply attested, and we've seen example after example of clear apocalyptic proclamations scattered throughout our earliest sources otherwise. Moreover, as we've begun to see, Jesus' apocalyptic teachings can well accommodate this idea that the kingdom is already present in some sense. In other words, you don't have to sacrifice the future aspect of the kingdom to affirm that in some sense for Jesus the kingdom had already arrived.

We've already seen both in Jesus' teaching of ethics, and in the reports of his miracles, that there's something going on with the present in-breaking of the kingdom in Jesus' teachings and his activities. Think about the ethics; people who follow Jesus are to implement the ideals of the kingdom in the present. In the future kingdom, there'll be no war, and so Jesus' followers should not commit any acts of violence now. In the kingdom, there'll be no hatred, and so people should engage in acts of love now. In the kingdom, there'll be no oppression, and so people should work for justice now. In other words, the ideals of the kingdom are already being manifested by people who follow Jesus' teachings. Moreover, the reports of Jesus' miracles show in-breaking of the kingdom in the present. There will not be any forces of evil in the kingdom, and so Jesus can reputedly cast out demons. There'll be no illness in the kingdom, and so Jesus heals the sick. There'll be no death in the kingdom, and so Jesus raises the dead.

In Jesus' apocalyptic ministry, then, there's a sense that the kingdom has already begun to arrive. Many of Jesus' parables actually present this view, that the kingdom has started to appear in Jesus' ministry and in the lives of his disciples. The emphasis of these parables is that even though this is started, what they are experiencing now is merely a foretaste of the glories that are to come when the kingdom of God arrives in power.

Take for example the parable of the mustard seed. It's a parable found independently attested. It's in Mark, and it's also in Thomas. The parable is that you take a little mustard seed, which Mark says is the smallest seed on the earth, it gets planted in the ground, and lo and behold, what emerges is a huge bush, or a tree, so large that the birds of the sky can make their nests in its branches. What's the point of this parable? Some interpreters have said various things about this parable. The most recent interpretation, popular interpretation, is that the point of the parable is that the kingdom of God is like this weed that nobody wants, so it's kind of surprising, because who wants a mustard weed in their garden? No, people try and get rid of mustard. This was to shock people into realizing that the kingdom isn't what they expected.

It's an interesting interpretation, but it doesn't stress what the parable itself stresses. What the parable stresses is that this tiny seed turns into a huge bush. What is that about? The kingdom of God is like that, in that the kingdom of God has a partial beginning now, an inauspicious start in the ministry of Jesus and in the lives of his disciples; it has a small beginning, but when the Son of Man arrives, it's going to be huge. It's going to take over the Earth. A similar lesson is conveyed by the parable of the leaven, in which a woman takes a little bit of leaven, puts it into a batch of dough, and it leavens the entire batch; again, emphasizing that what's small and hidden now will affect the whole world later.

In conclusion, we can say that for Jesus and his earliest followers, the apocalyptic message of the coming destruction had serious implications for the present. Those who implemented the ideals of the kingdom would not only qualify to enter the kingdom when it arrived with the powerful appearance of the Son of Man, they had also begun to realize what life would be like in that kingdom. It would be ruled by peace, harmony, justice, and love. Those who saw in Jesus a great worker of miracles saw still further manifestations of the kingdom.

Historians cannot affirm that Jesus did or did not perform supernatural feats that violated what we might today call natural laws. That kind of judgment, that Jesus could actually do that sort of thing, lies beyond the purview of what we can know historically. Historians can say, however, that Jesus was commonly believed to have done such things during his lifetime. Even more importantly, this belief was typically understood apocalyptically. By casting out demons, healing the sick, and raising the dead, Jesus was already embodying what life would be like when the kingdom of God arrived in power.

Lecture Nineteen
The Controversies of Jesus

Scope:

In this lecture, we will explore the traditions of Jesus' widespread rejection and some of his controversies with the Pharisees, especially over the meaning of the commandment of Scripture to keep the Sabbath day holy and the Pharisaic rules concerning tithing. We will then consider whether Jesus' radical emphasis on the command to love led him to violate the Scriptural demands for ritual purity, especially with regard to kosher food laws.

Outline

I. The past lectures clarify why Jesus would acquire a following.

    A. To people who were suffering, he brought a message of hope, that God would soon intervene in the world to relieve their suffering and reward their faithfulness.

        1. The Romans and other evil forces would be removed from power.

        2. The poor, oppressed, and outcast would be brought into God's kingdom and pain, injustice, poverty, disease, and death would no longer exist.

    B. His followers had already begun to form a tightly knit community organized around the principles of love, as taught by God in the Jewish Scriptures.

    C. Jesus was thought to have done great miracles that showed that the kingdom had already begun to appear.

    D. Many, perhaps most, people today assume Jesus had thousands of avid followers and only a few powerful enemies. This was not the case.

II. Traditions of Jesus' rejection cover most of those with whom he came in contact: his own family, his townspeople, people living in surrounding towns and villages, the Jewish religious leaders, the aristocracy in Jerusalem, and of course, the Roman overlords.

    A. The tradition that Jesus' own family rejected him is firmly rooted. This may seem hard to accept for those who know about the annunciation story in the Gospel of Luke (where the angel Gabriel informs Mary who her son will be). This story, of course, cannot pass the criteria of independent attestation or dissimilarity.

1. The theme of Jesus' rejection by his family is attested in multiple and independent traditions and is not the sort of thing later Christians would be likely to make up. It passes our criteria.
2. Early in his ministry, according to our first account, Jesus' family tried to seize him from the public eye because they thought he had gone mad (Mark 3:21); he in turn spurned them when they came to see him (Mark 3:31–35).
3. His brothers are said in a later source not to have believed in him (John 7:5), and he had no relatives among his closest followers. Paul implies that Jesus' brother James became a believer only after Jesus' resurrection (1 Cor. 15:7).
4. Only the latest Gospel, John, tells us what Mary thought of him. It says that she was with him till the end, although the Book of Acts indicates that she was one of the early believers immediately after the resurrection (John 19:25–27; Acts 1:14).

B. Jesus was clearly rejected in his own hometown in Nazareth.
1. This is shown by the rejection scene recorded in our earliest narrative, Mark 6:1–6 (cf. Matt. 13:53–58), and amplified by independent traditions in Luke 4:16–30.
2. This rejection is supported even more firmly by Jesus' widely attested saying "a prophet is not without honor except in his own country" (Mark 6:4; John 4:44; "in his own village," G. Thom. 31). In the earliest form of the saying, Jesus indicates that the prophet is also dishonored "among his own relatives and in his own house," suggesting that Jesus was not well received at home.

C. Other towns and villages of Galilee also seem to have rejected Jesus.
1. This is best seen in Q materials, which are early and appear to pass the criterion of dissimilarity:

Woe to you Chorazin, woe to you Bethsaida. For if the great deeds that have been done among you had been done in Tyre and Sidon, they would have repented long ago and sat in sackcloth and ashes. But it will be more tolerable for Tyre and Sidon in the day of judgment than for you. And you Capernaum, you will not be exalted up to heaven will you? No, you will descend into hell. (Luke 10:13–15; Matt. 11:20–24)

    2. Note that Jesus' response to his own rejection is couched here in apocalyptic terms of judgment, condemnation, and destruction.

D. The widespread rejection of Jesus and his message would make sense of several other early traditions associated with Jesus.

    1. In Q, he laments that even though foxes and birds have places to stay, he has nowhere (Matt. 8:20; Luke 9:58).

    2. In Mark and Thomas, he intimates that the reason the kingdom has such a small and inauspicious beginning is that most of his proclamation is falling on deaf ears (for example, the parable of the sower: Mark 4:1–9; G. Thom. 9).

    3. He claims, in a completely independent source, that he is "hated by the world" (John 15:18).

E. Above all, Jesus was rejected by the religious leaders of his people.

    1. At the end of his life, as we'll see, his rejection by the aristocracy that ran the Temple—the Sadducees and the chief priests—ultimately led to his execution by the Romans.

    2. During his preaching ministry in Galilee, though, Jesus had no confrontations with the powerful Jews of Jerusalem's Temple, but only with local teachers who belonged to the Pharisees.

III. During his public preaching ministry, Jesus was harshly opposed by Pharisees and experts in the Jewish law (known as scribes), who thought that his teachings were wrong, that he misunderstood what God wanted, that he and his followers profaned the law, and that as a result, his powerful deeds could not come from God but were from the devil.

A. The controversies Jesus had with these other Jewish teachers were not over whether the law of God should be followed, but rather over the proper interpretation of the law. These were internal Jewish debates, no more harsh or vitriolic than those going on between other Jewish groups, for example, between the Essenes and the Pharisees.

B. Some of Jesus' disagreements with Pharisees involved moral decisions that were made difficult by the fact that the Law of Moses was incomplete and ambiguous.

    1. An example is the law concerning divorce. Moses allowed a man to divorce his wife (cf. Deut. 24:1–4), but what should be the permissible legal grounds?

    2. Like some Pharisees, but unlike others, Jesus himself took a fairly radical stand, that the legal grounds provided by Moses were simply a makeshift measure and that God preferred people never to divorce (Mark 10:2–9).

C. Other disputes involved ethical and religious matters not directly dealt with by the law.

    1. As an example: Should one support a corrupt civil government (i.e., Rome) by paying taxes? The Law of Moses doesn't say, and different Jewish scholars had different opinions.

    2. For Jesus, given that the end of the present order was imminent, taxes were a matter of indifference: "Render unto Caesar the things that belong to Caesar" (that is, the money Caesar minted that bore his own impression; Mark 12:13–17; G. Thom. 100).

IV. Far more vitriolic were the disputes Jesus had with Pharisees over the proper interpretation of laws that both sides agreed were given by God and were to be followed. An illustrative example involves the law to keep the Sabbath day holy—one of the Ten Commandments.

A. It would be a mistake to accept what Jesus' opponents said and think that he both broke the Sabbath and encouraged others to do likewise.

    1. In fact, it's difficult to find any place in the Gospel traditions where Jesus actually does anything in violation of the Sabbath laws found in the Hebrew Scriptures.

    2. Instead, in nearly every instance, Jesus has broken the Pharisees' interpretation of the Sabbath laws—for example, by healing on the Sabbath or allowing his disciples to pluck some grain to eat on the Sabbath.

3. Healing on the Sabbath is nowhere forbidden in the Law of Moses, and Jesus is not said to have plucked grain on the Sabbath.

B. For Jesus, an overarching principle determines what is appropriate to do on the Sabbath: "Sabbath was made for humans, not humans for the Sabbath" (Mark 2:27).

1. This shows that Jesus affirmed the goodness of the Sabbath, but maintained that part of its goodness involved not imposing it as an inordinate burden on anyone. God meant the Sabbath as a way to help people, not hurt them. As a result, it is always right to do what helps others, not what hurts, on the Sabbath (Mark 3:4).

2. To some extent, the Pharisees agreed with this judgment. We know, for example, that the Pharisees judged that if a farmer had an animal that fell into a pit on the Sabbath, it was all right to pull it out. (In contrast, the Essenes claimed that this ruling was far too lax, as we now know from the Dead Sea Scrolls.)

3. Jesus alludes to the Pharisaic view in both Q (Luke 14:5; Matt. 12:11) and L (Luke 13:15), but takes it a step further: Humans are worth more to God than animals, so it's perfectly acceptable to do something that might benefit someone on the Sabbath.

4. Moreover, it is multiply attested that Jesus cited biblical precedent for such views, pointing out that even in the Hebrew Bible, God extends his approbation of certain activities on the Sabbath (Mark 2:25–26; John 7:22–23).

5. Any interpretation of the law that did not have as its principal aim the love of others above all else was, for Jesus, completely misguided.

6. Thus, what put the Pharisees at odd with Jesus was how the law—in this case, the law to keep the Sabbath day holy—was to be interpreted, not whether it should be kept.

C. Jesus occasionally found the Pharisaic oral laws to be far too restrictive and counterproductive. An example is the Pharisaic law of tithing.

    1. Moses commanded that ten percent of all crops grown should be given to the priests in the temple (called a "tithe").

    2. Pharisees were concerned, though, over what to do when they purchased vegetables in the market, when they didn't know whether or not the tithe had been paid. To guarantee that the law had been followed, Pharisees opted to tithe what they purchased, as well as what they produced.

    3. Jesus didn't consider such interpretations, distinctive to the Pharisees, to be ultimately of any significance, in comparison to the need to love one's neighbor above all else.

    4. For Jesus, anyone who insisted that what really mattered to God was the amount of mint and cumin his priests had received was completely missing the point. What God wanted was a people committed to loving him above all else and loving their neighbors as themselves (Q: Matt. 23:23; Luke 11:42).

V. At times, Jesus pushed his emphasis on love to such an extreme that it seemed to others that he discounted the law, e.g., with respect to the laws of purity that are so central to the Hebrew Bible.

    A. At one point, for example, he denies the necessity of the Pharisaic practice of washing one's hands before a meal, washing done not to get rid of germs—these people didn't know about germs—but to become "ritually clean" before God.

    B. In our earliest tradition about the matter, Jesus says, "There is nothing outside a person that can bring defilement by entering into him; but it is the things that are outside of a person that bring defilement" (Mark 7:16). In context, Jesus is not abrogating the Mosaic food laws, but denying the Pharisaic ruling that a person should wash before eating.

C. Jesus taught that what matters to God is not the oral laws of the Pharisees about how to keep Sabbath, what to tithe, and how to eat.

1. Anyone who keeps the Sabbath, tithes, and washes his or her hands, but then commits murder or adultery, or deceives or slanders another, or exalts oneself over or oppresses others, has completely missed out on what God wants.

2. The Pharisees, in other words, emphasized the wrong things. In Jesus' words from Matthew, they "strain out the gnat but swallow the camel" (Matt. 23:24).

VI. It is clear that Jesus face widespread rejection among the Jewish people to whom he preached and had numerous controversies with other Jewish teachers of his day.

A. It was not these legal disputes with the Pharisees that ultimately led to Jesus' execution. The Pharisees were not the power players in Jesus' day; they had no political clout, civil authority, or legislative jurisdiction. They were a group of highly respected and seriously religious Jews, but they were not influential, at that time, in political affairs. Their disputes with Jesus could not have led to his crucifixion.

B. The religious authorities responsible for Jesus' arrest and trial were the Sadducees and high priests in the Temple of Jerusalem.

1. When Jesus left the familiar rural environs of his childhood and took his apocalyptic message of the coming judgment of God to the capital city of Jerusalem, he aroused the opposition of those who were powerful enough to silence him.

2. Once he offended them by proclaiming that they too would face God's coming wrath, his own days became numbered.

Essential Reading:

Ehrman, *Jesus: Apocalyptic Prophet*, chap. 11.

Meier, *A Marginal Jew*, vol. II.

Sanders, *The Historical Figure of Jesus*, chap. 14.

Suggested Reading:

Sanders, *Jesus and Judaism*, chaps. 9–10.

Questions to Consider:

1. How do you think we can explain the persistent report that Jesus was widely rejected by those who knew him, including his own family? How could they not realize who he was?

2. Think of the most heated arguments that you've gotten into. Are they with people who are close with you or with people you scarcely know? In light of your experience, what do you make of Jesus' heated disagreements with the Pharisees? Is it possible that they were at such odds precisely because they knew each other well and agreed on some of the most basic issues?

Lecture Nineteen—Transcript
The Controversies of Jesus

From the past several lectures, it should be clear why Jesus would acquire a following. To people who were suffering, he brought a message of hope that God would soon intervene in the affairs of the world, to relieve their suffering and to reward their faithfulness. The Romans and all other evil forces would be removed from power. The poor and oppressed and outcast would be brought into God's kingdom. There would be no more pain, injustice, poverty, disease, or death. Moreover, his followers had already begun to form a tightly knit community, organized around the principles of love as taught by God Himself in the Jewish scriptures. Jesus himself was thought to have done great miracles, miracles that showed that in fact the kingdom of God had already begun to appear.

All this makes it all the more striking that the early traditions of Jesus suggest that he was by and large rejected by nearly everyone he came in contact with. This may seem odd to anyone today who simply assumes that Jesus had thousands of avid followers, and only a few, though powerful, enemies. The traditions of Jesus' rejection involve most of those with whom he came into contact; his own family, his townspeople, people living in surrounding towns and villages, the Jewish religious leaders, the aristocracy in Jerusalem, and of course, the Roman overlords.

It's a firmly rooted tradition that Jesus' own family rejected him. This may seem hard to accept for those who know about the annunciation story in the Gospel of Luke. That's the account in Luke chapter 1 where the angel Gabriel comes to Mary and tells her that she's going to bear a special child; the Holy Spirit will impregnate her so that the one born of her will be the Son of God. Naturally, you would assume, then, on the basis of this story, that Mary knew full well about Jesus, and of course accepted him as the Son of God, as would her husband, then, Joseph, and anyone else who was in the family. This annunciation story, though, cannot pass the criteria we've discussed for establishing authentic tradition. It's only found in Luke, so it doesn't pass independent attestation, and it certainly does not pass the criterion of dissimilarity.

On the contrary, the theme of Jesus' rejection by his family is attested in multiple and independent traditions. It's also not the sort of thing, of course, that later Christians would be likely to make up. That is, the idea of his being rejected by his family does pass our criteria. Early on in his ministry, according to our first account, the Gospel of Mark, his family tried to seize him from the public eye because they thought he'd gone out of his mind. Mark chapter 3, verse 21. This included, apparently, his mother and his brothers, who then come to see him ten verses later; Mark chapter 3, verse 31. They come to see him, and he's teaching a crowd of people; they can't get in through the door, and someone announces, "Your mother and brothers and sisters are here to see you." Jesus says, "Who are my mother, brothers, and sisters? Those who hear the word of God; you all are my mother, brothers, and sisters."

It appears that relationships were somewhat strained during Jesus' ministry, at least during the early part. We're told in some sources that his brothers did not believe in him; John chapter 7, verse 5. It's also striking that even though Jesus had a number of close followers, none of his relatives were among them. The apostle Paul seems to imply that it was only after the tradition of Jesus' being raised from the dead that his brother James became a believer (1 Corinthians chapter 15). It's difficult to know what Jesus' mother actually thought about him. It's only in our latest Gospel, John, that she's said to have been with him to the very end. She's there for the crucifixion, although the Book of Acts does indicate that she was one of the early believers immediately after the resurrection (Book of Acts, chapter 1). In any event, the tradition is fairly clear that Jesus was rejected by his own family during his ministry, even though afterward some of them apparently became believers in him.

Not only was Jesus rejected by his family; secondly, he was rejected in his own town, the village of Nazareth. This is shown by the rejection scene recorded in our earliest narrative, Mark chapter 6, verses 1-6, where Jesus comes to his town and speaks in the synagogue, and the people are amazed at his teaching and can't understand how he could be saying such things. Because he had no repute among them previous to this, he then is rejected by them. This scene is amplified in the Gospel of Luke chapter 4, where Luke supplements Mark's accounts by independent traditions available to him, apparently through the L source, in which there's a clear rejection of Jesus. The people in his hometown actually try to kill him because they take offense at what he said.

The idea that Jesus was rejected in his hometown by people who had known him earlier is especially supported by a widely attested saying found in Mark, John, and the Gospel of Thomas. Three completely independent sources have the saying of Jesus: "A prophet is not without honor except in his own country." In other words, it's only where you grow up that you lack honor. In the Gospel of Thomas, the wording is a little bit different: "A prophet is not without honor except in his own village." In the earliest form of this saying, Jesus seems to indicate that "a prophet is also dishonored among his own relatives and in his own house;" Gospel of Mark. This again may suggest that Jesus was not well received at home.

Again, I should point out that this tradition is not only multiply attested in independent sources, it's also not the kind of tradition that a Christian would have been likely to have made up. My conclusion is that Jesus did not make a huge impact among the people that he grew up with when he was a kid. As a child, he evidently wasn't thought of as somebody special with any kind of religious or spiritual authority, because he appears to have been rejected by the people he grew up with when he was an adult.

Third, Jesus is rejected not only by his family and by his own townspeople. It appears that during his public ministry, Jesus was rejected by the towns and villages of Galilee that he visited as an itinerant preacher. This is probably best seen in the materials preserved in our document Q. These materials are obviously early, and they appear to pass the criterion of dissimilarity. Again, this is not a tradition that later Christians would want to say, that Jesus was by and large rejected by the very people he was trying to minister to.

The Q saying that probably best attests this tradition is found in Luke chapter 10 and Matthew chapter 11, where Jesus declaims against two of the villages that he had been ministering to. He says, "Woe to you Chorazin," that's one of the towns, "woe to you Bethsaida," another one of the towns, "for if the great deeds that had been done among you had been done in Tyre and Sidon, they would have repented long ago and sat in sackcloth and ashes." Tyre and Sidon were two places in the Hebrew Bible that were destroyed because they rejected God. Jesus is saying, "If they had seen the miracles you all had seen, then they would have repented long ago." He goes on, "But it will be more tolerable for Tyre and Sidon in the day of judgment than for you. And you, Capernaum, you will not be exalted up to heaven, will you? No, you will descend to hell." Luke 10, Matthew 11. As we saw in an earlier lecture, Capernaum was the town that Jesus used as his base of operation. It appears that the people there also didn't accept his message. It's worth noting in passing that Jesus' response to his own rejection in this Q material is couched in clear apocalyptic terms, that on the day of judgment these places are going to be destroyed. The images are of judgment, condemnation, and destruction.

The widespread rejection of Jesus and his message in these various places makes sense of several other early traditions associated with Jesus. For example, we have this saying in Q, in which Jesus laments that "foxes have lairs, birds have nests, but the Son of Man has nowhere to lay his head." No place welcomes him, accepts him into their home; Matthew 8, Luke 9. That's a saying that supports this idea that he's being widely rejected. Or a parable that's found both in the Gospel of Mark and in the Gospel of Thomas, a parable that indicates that the reason the kingdom of God has such a small, inauspicious beginning, is because Jesus' proclamation is falling on deaf ears. This is the parable of the sower, best known from its occurrence in Mark chapter 4. Jesus says that there's a sower, a farmer, who goes out to sow his seed. He throws his seed. Some of the seed falls on the pathway; birds come and eat it. Some of the seed falls on soil that is rocky; there is rock underneath the soil, so there's just a thin layer of soil, and the seed grows up quickly, but there's no root, so it quickly withers when the sun comes. Other seed falls on thorny soil, so that thorns grow up and strangle it, and finally, some of the seed falls on the good soil. The seed that falls on the good soil, then, produces fruit, thirty-fold, sixty-fold, one hundred-fold. In the Gospel of Thomas, you have the same parable. Interestingly, I'm not quite sure what to make of this, but the seed that falls on the good soil produces "60 per measure and 120 per measure." He had a different enumeration system; I'm not sure what.

In any event, the parable appears to be indicating that Jesus, the one who sows the word, is not well received by most of his hearers. Most of the seed falls somewhere other than on good soil. This again is an indication, perhaps, that Jesus is being rejected by most people who hear him. The same idea is found independently attested in a completely different source, the Gospel of John, in which Jesus says on several occasions that he is "hated by the world." John chapter 15, verse 18, for example. In short, it looks like most of the people Jesus is preaching to aren't accepting his message. It stands counter to what we might imagine when we think about Jesus going through the Galilean countryside with thousands and thousands of people following him, and only a few people, kind of the outskirts of the crowd, kind of grumbling about things. It looks like it wasn't that way at all. It looks like that, on the contrary, most of the people hearing Jesus are rejecting him, and he's responding to this rejection by proclaiming coming judgment against those who don't accept his message.

The fourth, and probably most significant, group of people that rejected Jesus are the religious leaders of his own people. It is quite clear that Jesus was not widely accepted by those who were construed to be the religious leaders of the Jews in Palestine. As we'll see in a later lecture, at the end of his life, it was the rejection by the aristocracy among the Jews that ran the Temple in Jerusalem, namely the Sadducees and the chief priests, that ultimately led to Jesus' execution by the Romans. It's his conflicts with Sadducees, the chief priests, that lead to his execution. This is a conflict that happens at the very end of his life.

During his preaching ministry in Galilee, though, where he spent almost all of his time up in the Galilee in these rural areas preaching to towns and villages and out in the countryside, during this preaching ministry, Jesus did not have confrontations with the powerful Jews of Jerusalem's Temple, the Sadducees and chief priests, but only with the local teachers who happened to belong to the sect of the Pharisees, along with experts in the Jewish law who were called "scribes." They're called "scribes." This is our English word, scribe, comes from the Latin word *scribo*. These are people who were able to write, and people who could write in Palestine were people who were scribes, who could actually transcribe the sacred texts, the Hebrew Scriptures; so these were people who were experts in the Jewish law, because they're the transcribers and interpreters of these texts. The Pharisees, including the scribes who were among the Pharisees, thought that Jesus' teachings were wrong, that he misunderstood what God wanted, that both he and his followers had profaned the law, and that as a result, his powerful deeds did not come from God, but were from the devil.

As we've seen already, the controversies Jesus had with these and other Jewish teachers were not over whether or not the law of God should be followed. Remember, Jesus and his disciples kept Jewish customs, they observed Jewish festivals and they followed the Jewish law. The disputes, instead, were over the proper interpretation of the law. Let me stress that these were internal Jewish debates. They were no more harsh or vitriolic than those going on between other Jewish groups, for example, between the Essenes and the Pharisees, who were completely at each others' throats, or the Essenes and the Sadducees, or even disputes among different Pharisees. Disputes could be harsh. You often have harsher disagreements with your own family members than you have with people on the outside. Jesus was engaged in internal kinds of disputes, especially because of where he was living and where he was teaching, among Pharisees. I want to talk about some of the kinds of disputes that Jesus had with the Pharisees during his public ministry.

First, some of the disputes that Jesus had were involving moral decisions that were made difficult by the fact that the Law of Moses was incomplete and ambiguous; disputes over what to do in cases where the Law of Moses was incomplete or ambiguous. These were matters of debate among a number of Jewish teachers, even among different groups of Pharisees. I'll give you one example; law concerning divorce. In the Torah, the law, Moses had allowed a man to divorce his wife; Deuteronomy chapter 24. What should be the permissible legal grounds for divorce? It was a disputed matter.

Like some Pharisees, but unlike other Pharisees, Jesus himself took a fairly radical stand, that the legal grounds provided by Moses for divorce were simply a makeshift measure, and that God preferred people never to get a divorce; Mark chapter 10. This was an issue that was debated among Jewish teachers, and Jesus took a stand like other teachers. Divorce—even though Moses allowed for it, people should not get divorced. Some people have seen this, by the way, as a positive step towards liberation for women, because in that day, a man could divorce a woman, but then the woman was left without any protection, since she had to be under the authority of a man, either a husband or a father. If the father's dead and the husband's left her, then she's by herself, and it made it extremely difficult. This, by disallowing divorce, it was in fact supporting the cause of women.

A second area of dispute involves not where the law of Moses was incomplete or ambiguous, but involved ethical and religious matters that were not directly dealt with by the law. What about issues not dealt with by the Law of Moses? Jewish teachers, of course, had different views of what to do in such cases. I'll give you an example. Should a Jew support a corrupt civil government by paying taxes? Should Jews pay taxes to Rome or not? The Law of Moses doesn't say. Different Jewish scholars had different opinions. Jesus' opinion is best expressed in the saying found both in Mark and in Thomas. This is a multiply attested saying, that "You should render under Caesar the things that belong to Caesar, and the things that belong to God, to God." In other words, this takes place within this situation where Jesus is given a coin. They say, "Should you pay taxes?" Jesus says, "Let me see the coin." They show him a Roman coin. It has the image of Caesar on it, and he says, "It has Caesar's image on it, so give to Caesar what belongs to Caesar, and to God what belongs to God." In the Gospel of Thomas, he adds a third line to this, where he says, "And give to me what's mine." Interesting little twist. In any event, it appears clear that Jesus thought that "Yes, go ahead and pay the taxes." It makes sense within Jesus' own apocalyptic context; it's exactly what he would say. For Jesus, the end of the present order was imminent anyway. Paying taxes, then, was a matter of indifference.

A third kind of dispute that Jesus has with the Pharisees is a more vitriolic dispute. It involves the proper interpretation of laws that both sides agreed were given by God and needed to be followed. Interestingly, this is where you get a lot of animosity between the two sides, over the proper interpretation of laws that both Jesus and the Pharisees knew that God had given and believed should be followed. Key illustration involves the law to keep the Sabbath day holy, one of the Ten Commandments. You should keep the Sabbath day holy.

It would be a mistake to accept what Jesus' opponents said about him and to think that he both broke the Sabbath and encouraged others to do likewise. That's what his enemies said, and interestingly, Jesus' friends ever since have agreed, that in fact it was true, that Jesus broke the Sabbath. In fact, it's very hard to find any place in the Gospel traditions where Jesus does anything in violation of the Sabbath that's found in the Hebrew Scriptures. Instead, in nearly every instance, Jesus has broken the Pharisees' interpretation of the

Sabbath laws, not the Sabbath laws of the Hebrew Bible themselves. How does he break the Pharisees' interpretation of the Sabbath laws? For example, by healing on the Sabbath or by allowing his disciples to pluck grain and to eat it on the Sabbath. Nowhere, however, does the Law of Moses forbid somebody to heal on the Sabbath. In addition, Jesus himself is not said to have plucked grain on the Sabbath; this is something that his disciples did. You're hard-pressed to find a single instance in the Gospels where Jesus actually violates the dictates of scripture concerning the Sabbath.

Jesus' view about the Sabbath is best embodied in an overarching principle that determines what's appropriate to do on the Sabbath day. It's a principle that is expressed in our earliest source, Mark chapter 2, verse 27, where Jesus says: "The Sabbath is made for humans, not humans for the Sabbath." It's an interesting saying, because the way Mark actually gives it is, let me use the non-generic, non-inclusive phrasing that's often found in English Bible translations that give the verse as Mark gives it: "Sabbath was made for man, not man for the Sabbath. Therefore, the Son of Man is lord of the Sabbath." This is how it's given in most translations of Mark 2:27. It's an odd way of putting it: "The Sabbath is made for man, not man for the Sabbath. Therefore the Son of Man is lord of the Sabbath." Why's the "therefore"? Why is Jesus, then the lord of the Sabbath, if the first part's true?

This is one of those sayings that make better sense if you translate it back into Aramaic, Jesus' own language. In Aramaic, the term "man" and the term "Son of Man" are the same. It's the term *barnasha*. If you say this with "man" and "Son of Man" in Aramaic, it's "The Sabbath was made for *barnasha*, not *barnasha* for the Sabbath. Therefore, *barnasha* is lord of the Sabbath." Mark translated the third *barnasha* as "Son of Man" rather than "man"—it could mean both things—to mean it's a title for Jesus. It makes better sense in the Aramaic. It means that humans are to lord it over the Sabbath, the Sabbath isn't to lord it over humans. In other words, Jesus is affirming the goodness of the Sabbath, but maintaining that part of its goodness involves not imposing it as an inordinate burden on anyone. God meant the Sabbath as a way to help, not to hurt, people. As a result, it's always right to do what helps, not what hurts, other people on the Sabbath.

I should point out to some extent that the Pharisees agreed with this judgment. We know, for example, that the Pharisees thought that if a farmer had an animal that fell into a pit on the Sabbath, the Pharisees said it was okay to pull the animal up out of the pit rather than to incur the financial loss. We know that this was a point the Pharisees made, because the Essenes in the Dead Sea Scroll community disagreed with this view and thought the Pharisees were completely lax in taking this stand, that they were kind of lightweights when it came to following the law. Jesus agrees with this judgment of the Pharisees, however; Luke chapter 4, verse 5. He takes it a step further, though. Humans are worth more than animals, and so, it's perfectly acceptable to do something that might benefit them on the Sabbath. What put the Pharisees at odds with Jesus was, in this case, how the law of the Sabbath was to be interpreted, not whether or not the Sabbath was to be kept. For Jesus, any interpretation of the law that didn't have as its principle aim the love of others above all else was completely misguided.

A fourth area of conflict with the Pharisees involves laws that the Pharisees had developed, the oral laws of the Pharisees that Jesus found to be too restrictive or counterproductive. Just one very quick example; the Pharisees knew that the scriptures taught that a person needed to give ten percent of everything that they grew (since they were farmers) to God. What, though, about materials you buy, produce you buy in the market, that hasn't been tithed previously? Then you should give a tithe of that to cover the law. What about buying things that you don't know whether the farmer who raised these crops tithed? The Pharisees said, "You should tithe that too, just in case. If it was tithed already, and it gets tithed a second time, so much the better for the priests who get the tithe, but this way you make sure you follow the law." Jesus thought that this kind of restriction on tithing what you purchase as well as what you grow was really going overboard, because people who were doing this were so concerned about this minutia that they were avoiding bigger issues, like showing mercy and justice and love. Thus, Jesus maligns those who engage in this kind of activity, saying that in fact it's more important to be concerned with major parts of the law, not to be worried about the little things, such as tithing everything to make sure that you have covered your bases.

Let me stress that throughout these conflicts that Jesus had with the Pharisees, most of the conflicts have to do with how one keeps the law, whether one needs to follow the oral law developed by the Pharisees in order to be right with God. Jesus insisted that one did not. In Jesus' words, from the Gospel of Matthew—the Pharisees are so concerned, he thinks, with following the little things; they tithe cumin and mint, but they are not worried about big things like love and justice; in Jesus' words, "They strain at the gnat, but they swallow the camel." They're not concerned about the major things. Matthew 23, verse 24.

In conclusion, it's clear that Jesus faced widespread rejection from the Jewish people to whom he preached, and that he entered into numerous controversies with other Jewish teachers of his day. We have independently attested traditions that are scattered throughout our sources, that Jesus was not well-received by people from the towns and villages of Galilee, where he spent most of his preaching ministry; that he was spurned by the people of his own village Nazareth, and most striking of all, that he was rejected even by his own family. He was also not well-liked by the other Jewish teachers of his day, especially the Pharisees, with whom he had regular and heated differences of opinion, not over whether one should keep the law of Moses, but over how one could best keep it.

I should emphasize that these heated disagreements with the Pharisees were not particularly out of place in Jesus' world of first-century Palestinian Judaism. There were lots of internal disputes among Jewish teachers, sometimes teachers within the same party. It was not a case, in other words, of Jesus against everyone else. There were lots of views that all contended with one another, each group insisting that it was right, and that the others were tragically wrong. Moreover, it was not these legal disputes with the Pharisees that ultimately led to Jesus' execution, a point that many people don't realize. These disputes are simply legal disputes; they're inner debates that are going on all the time. There aren't Pharisees going off and being crucified because they disagreed with other Pharisees. These are simply disputes going on among other Jewish teachers.

Moreover, the Pharisees were not the power players in Jesus' day. They weren't the ones who had political clout, civil authority, or legislative jurisdiction. The Pharisees were a group of highly respected and seriously religious Jews, but they were not influential at that time in political affairs. Their disputes, then, with Jesus would not have led to his crucifixion. As we'll see in the next lecture, the religious authorities responsible for his arrest and trial were the Sadducees, and the high priests in the Temple of Jerusalem. It was only when Jesus left the familiar rural environs of his childhood and took his apocalyptic message of the coming judgment of God to the capital city of Jerusalem that he aroused the opposition of those who were powerful enough to silence him. Once he offended them by proclaiming that they, too, would face God's coming wrath, his own days became numbered.

Lecture Twenty
The Last Days of Jesus

Scope:

We have better documentation for Jesus' final week than for any other period of his life. He left Galilee for the capital of Jerusalem, Judea, to celebrate the Passover feast. It appears that he did not go to the festival as a pilgrim, but as an apocalyptic prophet to deliver his message of imminent destruction and salvation to the heart of Israel, the Temple of Jerusalem, to urge people to repent before it was too late. This lecture will discuss what happened when Jesus entered the Temple and caused a disturbance, an action probably meant as a parable, demonstrating in a small way the kind of destruction that would occur when the Son of Man arrived—the Temple itself would be destroyed. We will observe Jesus preaching his message and acquiring greater numbers of listeners frightening the local authorities, who feared riots among the crowds. They arranged to have Jesus removed quietly from the public eye. Before he was arrested, Jesus realized that his time was up and had a last meal with his disciples in which he may have informed them that his enemies were about to make their move against him.

Outline

I. We must draw a connection between the content of Jesus' apocalyptic message and the reason for his death.

A. Some hypotheses of what Jesus ultimately stood for run aground on this connection. They sound completely plausible in reconstructing what Jesus said and did, but they can't make sense of his execution by the Romans.

1. If Jesus is to be understood as a Jewish rabbi who taught that everyone should love God and be good to one another, then why did the Romans crucify him?

2. If Jesus was mainly interested in opposing the materialistic world that he found himself in, urging his followers to give up their possessions and live simple, natural lives, apart from the trappings of society, why would he have been sentenced to death?

B. Let me explain how I understand the connection between Jesus' life and death. In this lecture and the next, I'll go into some of the details.

1. At the end of his life, Jesus brought his apocalyptic message of the coming judgment to Jerusalem. This judgment would be inflicted by the Son of Man, who would destroy all those opposed to God before establishing his kingdom.
2. Those who refused to accept this message would be condemned—even if they, like the Pharisees, followed the Torah of God exactly, or maintained the purity regulations of the Essenes, or remained faithful to the sacrificial cult of the Temple as the Sadducees did.
3. Religious leaders among these various groups, and the institutions they represented, would be destroyed by the Son of Man. So, too, would the Temple be destroyed.

C. Jesus acted out this message when he arrived in Jerusalem. He entered the Temple and engaged in symbolic destruction as a warning of what was to come, overturning tables and causing a mild ruckus.
1. This public display and its accompanying message angered some of the chief priests, who recognized how explosive the situation could be during the Passover.
2. Fearing an uprising, the priests conferred, had Jesus arrested, and questioned him about his words against the Temple.
3. Realizing that it would be dangerous to let Jesus run loose, the priests decided to have him taken out of the way. They could not handle the matter themselves, however, because the Romans did not allow Jewish authorities to execute criminals.
4. They delivered Jesus to the governor, Pontius Pilate, who had no qualms at all about disposing of yet one more troublemaker who might cause a major disturbance. Jesus was then executed by the Romans on political charges.

II. We are better informed about Jesus' last days than about any other period of his life. For the Gospel writers, his life was mostly preparation for his death.
A. Thus, the focus of the earliest surviving accounts is on Jesus' last days. Mark devotes five of his sixteen chapters to the final week of Jesus' life, and John devotes ten out of twenty-one.

2. It is no stretch to say that the Gospels are principally concerned about Jesus' passion, that is, the accounts of his suffering and death. Some scholars have said that the Gospels are passion narratives with long introductions.

B. There can be no doubt, historically, that for the last week of his life, Jesus left the place of his public ministry, rural Galilee, and went with his disciples to the capital city of Judea, Jerusalem. Why he did so may not seem quite as obvious.

    1. A theologian, of course, might say that Jesus traveled to Judea to die for the sins of the world. This view is based on Gospel sayings (such as Jesus' predictions of his own passion in Mark 8:31, 9:31, and 10:33–34) that cannot pass the criterion of dissimilarity, in that they portray Jesus as knowing the details of his own fate.

    2. From a strictly historical perspective, that is, restricting ourselves to what we can show on historical grounds, we should recall that Passover was an enormously popular festival. Maybe, then, Jesus went to Jerusalem simply to celebrate the Passover.

    3. On the other hand, Jesus' actions in Jerusalem appear to have been well thought out. When he arrived, he entered the Temple and caused a disturbance. He then spent several days, in the Temple, teaching his message of the coming kingdom.

C. Given Jesus' understanding that this kingdom was imminent, perhaps it is best to conclude that he went to Jerusalem as part of his mission, precisely to proclaim his apocalyptic message in the heart of Israel itself—the Temple on Passover.

III. The account of Jesus' "triumphal entry" is hard to accept historically.

A. Even though the account is multiply attested (see Mark 11:1–10; John 12:12–19), it cannot pass the criterion of dissimilarity, because it is explicitly said to have fulfilled a prophecy of Hebrew Scripture about the coming messiah (see Isa. 62:11; Zech. 9:9, cited in Matt. 21:5).

B. What we know of the political situation makes it even more difficult to accept the account as historical.

1. The week before Passover was a tense and potentially dangerous time in the view of the Roman authorities.
2. This was the one time of year that the Roman governor, who usually stayed in Caesarea on the coast, would come to the capital with troops in tow to quell any possible uprisings.
3. If Jesus actually entered the city with such fanfare, with crowds shouting their support for him as their new ruler, the king who fulfills the prophecies (who would, therefore, overthrow the current ruler and his armies), it is nearly impossible to understand why he wasn't arrested and taken out of the way immediately.
4. Probably the most we can say is that Jesus did enter Jerusalem, that he was one of the pilgrims coming for the feast, and that he (like others) may well have come on a donkey.
5. It is also possible that some of the crowds in Jerusalem had already heard about Jesus' teachings and remarkable deeds and, when he came to the city, wondered if this could be the messiah.
6. Such speculation would not have been extraordinary. We know of other Jews both before Jesus' day and afterwards who were thought by some to be the future ruler of Israel. Typically, such potential threats to the Roman authorities were executed.

IV. One of the most solidly established traditions about Jesus is that when he arrived in Jerusalem, he caused a disturbance in the Temple, driving out those who sold animals and overturning tables of the moneychangers.

   A. The account is multiply attested in both Mark (chap. 11) and John (chap. 2).

   B. To understand the event, we must have some background information.
   1. The Temple compound was an enormous place. The walls around it were ten stories high, and they enclosed enough space to hold twenty-five American football fields.

2. The Temple was the one place where Jews from around the world could sacrifice animals to God, as prescribed by the Torah.
3. Jews obviously couldn't bring animals with them from afar; the animals had to be purchased on the spot. It wouldn't make sense to use imperial money, with an image of Caesar on it, to purchase animals in the Temple of the one God who forbade the use of images. A currency exchange was set up to allow the purchase of animals with Temple money.
4. It's hard to see how the Temple could function without some system like this. Our early accounts, though, indicate that Jesus entered the Temple, drove out those who were selling sacrificial animals, and overturned the tables of the moneychangers.

C. It is difficult to know, historically, what Jesus actually did when he entered the Temple and what he meant by it. Most scholars recognize that some aspects of the accounts appear to be exaggerated. This is particularly true of Mark's claim that Jesus completely shut down the operation of the Temple.
1. Again, the Temple complex was immense, and armed guards would have been present to prevent any major disturbances.
2. Moreover, if Jesus had created a problem in the Temple, it's nearly impossible to explain why he wasn't arrested on the spot and taken out of the way before he could stir up the crowds.
3. For these reasons, it looks as if Mark's account represents an exaggeration of Jesus' actions. Exaggerations aside, we're almost certain that Jesus did something that caused a disturbance in the Temple. The event is multiply attested in independent sources and the event coincides with Jesus' predictions that the Temple would soon be destroyed.

D. For this reason, a good number of scholars—beginning in the 1970s with E. P. Sanders—have begun to recognize that Jesus' actions in the Temple were meant as a symbolic expression of his proclamation.

1. Jesus sometimes engaged in symbolic acts that illustrated his apocalyptic message (for example, by associating with tax collectors and sinners to illustrate his message that the kingdom was for the outcast and lowly).

2. In view of Jesus' message of the coming destruction of the Son of Man, perhaps it is best to see his action in the Temple as a kind of prophetic gesture, an enacted parable, in which he demonstrated on a small scale what was soon to happen in a big way on the Day of Judgment. The Temple was going to be destroyed.

E. It is hard to know, though, what exactly Jesus found to be offensive about the Temple, i.e., whether he found the priests operating it to be corrupt or had some other problem with it.

1. The words quoted in the accounts may not go back to Jesus himself, because the charges of corruption in the Temple may represent later Christianization of the tradition.

2. On the other hand, we do have accounts of other Jews both before Jesus (e.g., Jeremiah 7) and in his own day (e.g., the Essenes) who believed that the Temple system had become corrupt.

3. As a country fellow from rural Galilee, who preached against wealth and power, the sheer opulence of the place may have made Jesus' blood boil on principle.

F. There are two ways we can understand the significance of Jesus' prediction that the Temple would be destroyed in the context of his broader apocalyptic message.

1. Jesus may have believed that the coming kingdom would have a new Temple, one totally sanctified for the worship of God. This was the view of the apocalyptically minded Essenes of the Dead Sea Scroll community, who were his contemporaries.

2. Alternatively, Jesus may have believed that the Temple would not be needed in the coming kingdom, because evil and sin would no longer exist; therefore, the cultic sacrifice of animals to bring atonement would not be needed either. This view was later embraced by some of Jesus' apocalyptic followers, such as the author of the Book of Revelation (see Rev. 21:22).

3. In either case, the implication of Jesus' actions was clear: For Jesus, the Temple cult and the officials in charge of it were a temporary measure at best and a corruption of God's plan at worst. They would be eliminated when the kingdom arrived.

V. Jesus' dire predictions against the Temple did not escape the notice of those in charge, the chief priests who also happened to have jurisdiction over the local affairs of the people in Jerusalem.

A. These priests were mostly Sadducees, who acted as chief liaisons with Roman officials, in particular with the Roman prefect, Pontius Pilate.

B. At this point in our earliest account, Mark, Jesus begins to have serious arguments with the Jewish authorities in Jerusalem, sometimes engaging in public debates with them and sometimes speaking ill of them to anyone who would gather around to listen (see, for example, Mark 11:27–33, 12:1–12, 18–27, 14:1).

C. Jesus spent the week teaching and engaging his foes in the Temple.

1. His most explicitly apocalyptic message, in fact, is said to have been delivered there, according to all three of the Synoptic Gospels (Matthew 24–25; Mark 13; Luke 21).

2. As the crowds began to swell, Jesus evidently started to attract more attention. The Jewish authorities in the Temple became concerned about an uprising. It had happened before and was to become a constant threat in the years to follow.

D. For their part, the Roman authorities were armed and ready to act. It was decided to have Jesus taken out of the public eye by stealth to avoid any problems.

E. Before his arrest, Jesus had a last meal (possibly a Passover meal, possibly not) with his disciples, during which he warned them of the danger he was in. He infused the foods with new symbolism.

1. The "Last Supper" is multiply attested by Mark (14:22–25; 1 Cor. 11:23–26; see also Matt. 26:26–29; Luke 22:15–20).
2. Some of what Jesus says may pass the criterion of dissimilarity; e.g., that he would not drink wine again until he drank it in the kingdom, which assumes that the kingdom would come right away—even though the Gospel writers knew it hadn't come decades later.
3. Jesus' realization of his impending arrest is not implausible.
4. It is difficult to know exactly how Jesus phrased his words at the Last Supper, because the passion predictions in the Gospels are so similar to early Christian preaching about Jesus that the words may have been put on his lips.

Essential Reading:

Mark 11–15; Matthew 21–27; Luke 19–23.

Ehrman, *Jesus: Apocalyptic Prophet*, chap. 12.

Sanders, *The Historical Figure of Jesus*, chap. 11.

Suggested Reading:

Sanders, *Jesus and Judaism*, chap. 16.

Questions to Consider:

1. Is it possible to think that Jesus was opposed to the Temple of God in Jerusalem (which God himself had ordered to be built and maintained) without thinking that he was opposed to Judaism itself? That is to say, how could he oppose the central institution of the Jewish religion without being anti-Jewish?
2. Explain the significance of the timing of Jesus' arrival in Jerusalem for an understanding of his arrest. Why does it matter, in particular, that he arrived in time for the Passover festival?

Lecture Twenty—Transcript
The Last Days of Jesus

We saw in the last lecture that Jesus was not well received during his public ministry. He was rejected by some of the villages and towns he visited during his preaching. He was spurned by people from his hometown, and he was rejected even by his own family. Moreover, he entered into a number of hard-hitting disputes with other Jewish teachers of the law, especially those who were Pharisees. As I've indicated, though, it was not these disputes that ultimately led to Jesus' demise. Instead, it was the controversy that he stirred up when he went to Jerusalem during the last week of his life, during a Passover celebration, where he raised the ire of the power players among his people, who decided to have him removed from the public eye as a troublemaker.

As we'll see, the historical events surrounding Jesus' last days are best understood in light of his own apocalyptic message. It's important to any reconstruction of the historical Jesus to make sense of the connection between the content of his message and the reason for his death. This is a major principle that one needs to apply in thinking about reconstructions of the historical Jesus. Some hypotheses of what Jesus ultimately stood for run aground on just this connection. They often sound completely plausible in their reconstruction of what Jesus said and did, but they can't make sense of his execution by the Romans. There needs to be a plausible connection between what Jesus did in his ministry and what happened to him at the end.

If, for example, Jesus is to be understood as, say, a Jewish rabbi, who simply taught that everyone should love God, and be good to one another, why did the Romans crucify him? It wasn't a crime to teach love and kindness. If Jesus was mainly interested in opposing the materialistic world that he found himself in, urging his followers to give up their possessions, to live simple, natural lives, apart from the trappings of society, why would he be sentenced to death? It wasn't a capital offense to share your goods with others.

Let me explain, here at the outset of this lecture, in a nutshell how I understand the connection between Jesus' life and his death. In this lecture, then, and the next one, I'll unpack some of the details. What is the connection, though, between how I've portrayed Jesus in his public ministry and the reasons for his execution by the Romans? In a nutshell: At the end of his life, Jesus brought his apocalyptic message of the coming judgment to Jerusalem. This judgment, he declared, would be inflicted by the Son of Man, who would destroy all those who were opposed to God, before establishing God's kingdom. Those who refused to accept this message were to be condemned, even if they, like the Pharisees, followed the Torah of God to the "T," or maintained the purity regulations of the Essenes, or remained faithful to the sacrificial cult of the Temple promoted by the Sadducees. In fact, religious leaders among these various groups and the institutions they represented would be destroyed at the coming of the Son of Man. So, too, would the Temple itself.

Jesus not only preached this message upon arriving in Jerusalem, he acted it out, entering into the Temple and engaging in a kind of symbolic action of destruction, as a warning of what was to come, overturning some of the tables, and causing a mild ruckus. This public display, and its accompanying message, angered some of the chief priests on the scene, who recognized how explosive the situation could become during the Passover, given the tendency of the celebration to become a silent protest that could always erupt into something far worse, as we've seen in a previous lecture. Fearing a possible uprising, the priests conferred with one another, had Jesus arrested, and questioned him about his words against the Temple. Realizing that it would be dangerous to let him run loose, they decided to have him taken out of the way. They could not handle the matter themselves, however, because the Romans did not allow Jewish authorities to execute criminals. Thus, they delivered him over to the governor, Pontius Pilate, who had no qualms at all about disposing of one more troublemaker who might cause a major disturbance. Jesus was then executed by the Romans on political charges.

For such information about Jesus' last days, we're better informed than for any other period of his life. For the Gospel writers, Jesus' life was by and large a preparation for his death. Thus the focus of these earliest surviving accounts, our canonical Gospels, is on Jesus' last days. We have more information about this than anything else. The Gospel of Mark devotes five of his 16 chapters just to the final week of Jesus' life. The Gospel of John devotes ten out of 21 chapters to this last week. It's no stretch to say that the Gospels are concerned principally with Jesus' Passion, that is, the accounts of his suffering and death. As some scholars have put it, the Gospels are Passion narratives with long introductions, and so we have a lot more information.

I've now given you kind of the brief overview of how I understand the connection between Jesus' life and his death, with the emphasis that you need to see whether someone else makes the connection, or else the reconstruction itself won't be plausible. I want to enter into more detail in the play-by-play in the rest of this lecture and then the one to come.

First, there can be no doubt historically that for the last week of Jesus' life, he left the place of his public ministry, rural Galilee, and went with his disciples to the capital city of Judea in Jerusalem. This is the only reliable account we have of Jesus going to a major urban setting, Jerusalem. What's not particularly clear or obvious is why Jesus did so, why he went to Jerusalem for the last week of his life.

A theologian, of course, might say he did this because he knew it was time for him to die for the sins of the world. This view, though, that a theologian might have, is based on Gospel sayings that cannot pass our criterion of dissimilarity, namely, the predictions that Jesus gives that he must go to Jerusalem because he has to be rejected by the scribes and elders, and be crucified and then raised from the dead. He makes this prediction three times, for example, in the Gospel of Mark, but the prediction clearly cannot pass our criterion of dissimilarity, since it portrays Jesus as being fully cognizant of the details of his own fate. Jesus may have anticipated what was going to happen to him, as we'll see later, but these specific Passion predictions simply can't pass our criteria.

Are there historical reasons for thinking Jesus might have gone to Jerusalem apart from the theological perspective, restricting ourselves to what we can show just on historical grounds? We should remember that the Passover feast was an enormously popular festival among the Jews. Celebrated annually, it was a time for Jews from all over the world to come to Jerusalem to commemorate the exodus under Moses, that God had accomplished as recounted in the book Exodus. Maybe Jesus, like so many other Jews went to Jerusalem simply to celebrate the Passover feast. I think that's a plausible explanation. He was a pilgrim, like so many others.

On the other hand, Jesus' actions in Jerusalem, once he arrives, appear to have been well thought out. It appears that he had something else going on. When he arrived, he entered into the Temple and caused a disturbance. He then spent several days in the Temple teaching his message of the coming kingdom, according to our earliest accounts, and we'll talk in a little more detail later. Given Jesus' understanding that the kingdom was imminent, perhaps it's best to conclude that he went to Jerusalem as part of his mission of proclamation, precisely in order to proclaim this message in the heart of Israel itself, in the Temple in Jerusalem, on the Passover. In other words, Jesus came to the Temple to tell his people how the future salvation would occur and to urge them to prepare for it, by repenting their sins and accepting his teachings. That would explain why he went to Jerusalem, not just to celebrate the Passover, but in order to bring his urgent message to the heart of Israel.

The account of Jesus' so-called triumphal entry into Jerusalem is hard to accept historically. The account is multiply attested, but it does not pass the criterion of dissimilarity. The earliest account we have of Jesus entering into Jerusalem for the Passover feast is, of course, found in the Gospel of Mark. According to Mark's account, Jesus sends out a couple of his disciples to find a colt for him to ride into Jerusalem on, and they get a colt that he directed them towards. They bring it to Jesus, and then they throw their cloaks on this colt, and Jesus sits on it. Then he rides into Jerusalem. Many people spread their cloaks on the road; others spread leafy branches they've cut down in the field. You get the image of people kind of lining the streets and laying down their garments and palm branches in front of Jesus, so that he can tread on them, going into Jerusalem: "Then those who went ahead, and those who followed were shouting, 'Hosanna! Blessed is the one who comes in the name of the Lord. Blessed is the coming kingdom of our ancestor David. Hosanna in the highest heaven.'" The grand triumphal entry of the king into Jerusalem.

It's a spectacular scene, but it's really hard to accept, because it seems to presuppose faith in Jesus as the Messiah by the Jewish crowds, a faith that the later Gospel writers, of course, would want to highlight. In other words, it would be quite similar to what Christians would want to say about Jesus' entry into Jerusalem. In one of the early accounts that is found in the Gospel of Matthew, this coming into Jerusalem actually fulfills a prophecy. Matthew tells us:

This took place to fulfill what had been spoken through the prophets, saying, "Tell the daughter of Zion, 'Look, your king is coming to you, humble and mounted on a donkey, and on a colt, the foal of a donkey.'"

This is a quotation of Zechariah chapter 9.

It's interesting, by the way, in Matthew's Gospel, who quotes this verse that "the king will come on a donkey, and on a colt, the foal of a donkey"—this is a Hebrew parallelism. In the Hebrew Bible, in the Psalms and other poetry, the way they write the poetry is so that it will have one line that will say something, then the second line will say the same thing in different words: "a donkey, and on a colt, the foal of a donkey." Matthew apparently didn't understand that that's what was going on in this prophecy in Zechariah. According to Matthew, what happens is that there are actually two animals, a donkey and a colt. The disciples bring both of them to Jesus; they spread their coats over them, and Jesus kind of straddles the two of them. He rides into Jerusalem, then, kind of straddling these so as to literally fulfill this prophecy of Zechariah, which sounds even somewhat more implausible.

One of the reasons for thinking this account didn't really happen is because of the issue of contextual credibility. What we know of the political situation in Jerusalem during the Passover makes it very difficult to accept that Jesus entered into Jerusalem this way. As we've seen, the week before Passover was tense, and a dangerous time in view of the Roman authorities. As we've seen, this was the one time of year when the Roman governor would bring troops from Caesarea and station them around town, especially around the Temple, in order to quell any possible uprisings of the people. If Jesus actually did enter into the city with such fanfare, with crowds shouting their support for him, as the new ruler of the Jews, the king who fulfills all prophecies, who would therefore have to overthrow the present ruler and hiss armies in order for himself to rule, it's nearly impossible to understand why the authorities didn't have him arrested on the spot and immediately taken away, if this really happened.

Probably the most we can say historically is that Jesus did actually enter into Jerusalem, he was one of the pilgrims, coming for the feast, and it may be that he, like others, rode into town on a donkey. It's also possible that later, people looking back on this thought of it as the triumphal entry of the king into his city, but at the time it didn't really look that way to most people. It's possible, though, that some people in the crowds in Jerusalem had already heard about this teacher from Galilee. Possibly, they had hopes; maybe this will be somebody who will be able to do something for us. Maybe even wondered aloud: "Could this be our future deliverer?" That's possible. There would have been nothing implausible about people speculating such things. We know of Jews, both before Jesus' day and afterwards, who were thought to be some kind of future leader of the nation of Israel. Typically, such people who were thought to be future leaders were handled rather harshly by the Roman authorities. In the instances we know about, these people were executed, as, of course, was Jesus.

One of the most solidly established traditions about Jesus deals with what happened after he arrived in Jerusalem, namely, that he caused a disturbance in the temple, driving out those who sold animals and overturning the tables of the moneychangers. Again, the earliest account is found in the Gospel of Mark, right after the scene of the triumphal entry, Mark chapter 11. We're told that he comes into Jerusalem, he enters into the Temple, he drives out those who sell and those who are buying in the temple, he overturns the tables of the moneychangers and the seats of those who sold doves. He would not allow anyone to carry anything through the Temple. He was teaching and saying, "Is it not written, 'My house should be called a house of prayer for all nations,' but you have made it a den of robbers." We're told then that the chief priests and the scribes heard it, and they started looking for a way to kill him.

It's a very interesting account: Jesus causing a ruckus in the Temple. To understand the account, we need a little bit of background information. Let me say a few words about what was going on in the Temple at the time. First, the Temple itself. The Temple was an enormous place, as I indicated earlier. The walls around the Temple were ten stories high. They encompassed a space that was large enough to hold 25 American football fields. We're talking about an enormous place. It was a glorious place, built with the finest materials available, much of it overlaid with gold. This was the one place where Jews from around the world could come to sacrifice animals to God, as prescribed by the Torah. Jews believed that God Himself dwelt in the Temple. There was an inner room, the Holy of Holies, a room that was completely empty, except that God's presence was believed to dwell there in the Temple. The sacrifices were made there, in close proximity to God Himself.

Jews were commanded to sacrifice animals to God; the Passover feast, as we've seen, required Jews to sacrifice lambs at the Temple. They couldn't sacrifice them in their homes, or someplace else, they had to be sacrificed in the Temple. The problem is that Jews were coming from all over the world to the Temple, to make these sacrifices. They obviously couldn't bring their lambs with them, traveling from Alexandria, Egypt, or Asia Minor, or from Rome, or something. They can't just load the animals up on their shoulders and start walking, so obviously for the Temple to work, people had to be able to purchase animals on the spot. It wouldn't make sense, though, for people to purchase animals using imperial coinage, because the imperial coinage had an image of Caesar on it. Thus, there was a kind of currency exchange set up, where people could exchange their imperial money for Temple currency that didn't have images on it, and use the Temple money, then, to buy the animals that they were going to sacrifice. It's hard to see how the Temple could function without some kind of system like this. Jews had to sacrifice, and so there was really no alternative that one could think of.

Our early accounts, though, indicate that Jesus entered into the Temple, he drove out those who were selling sacrificial animals, and he overturned the tables of the moneychangers. It's hard to know historically what Jesus actually did when he entered the Temple, and what he meant by it. Most scholars recognize that some aspects of our accounts—even though something like this must have happened because it's so widely attested in our sources—most scholars recognize that some aspects of it appear to have been exaggerated. This is particularly true, for example, of Mark's claim, where Mark says Jesus did not allow anyone to carry anything through the temple. How, exactly, did Jesus do that? Recall the size of this place. How could Jesus shut down the operation of the Temple? You can't be sacrificing animals, by the way, if you can't be carrying implements through the temple, sacrificial knives, for example, bowls to capture the blood in, or vessels to carry the skins of the animals in. You can't function as a temple without carrying vessels. This says that Jesus stopped the whole thing. Maybe it's a miracle, although the account doesn't claim it's a miracle. Maybe, then, it's just an exaggeration.

Moreover, another reason for thinking it's an exaggeration is just the historical realities. If Jesus had actually created an enormous stir in the Temple, it's nearly impossible, again, to explain why he wasn't arrested on the spot, and taken out of the way before he could stir up the crowds. We know that soldiers are there. Why didn't they arrest him if he caused such a huge disturbance?

Exaggerations aside, it's almost certain that Jesus did something that caused at least a minor disturbance in the Temple. For example, maybe overturned some tables, and made at least a bit of a ruckus, that then was exaggerated by later Christians recounting the event. As I've pointed out, the event is multiply attested in our independent sources. Moreover, the account coincides with the predictions that Jesus makes about the Temple, that it's going to be destroyed, that we looked at in an earlier lecture.

What's really going on here? A number of years ago, back in the 1970s, a prominent New Testament scholar named E.P. Sanders wrote an influential book on Jesus and Judaism, in which he took a stand on this issue that's become influential among scholars ever since. Sanders claimed that what was going on is that Jesus' actions in the Temple represented a kind of symbolic expression of his proclamation. A symbolic expression of his proclamation. Jesus, of course, sometimes engaged in symbolic acts that illustrated his apocalyptic message. He associates with tax collectors and sinners. Why? To illustrate that such people will enter into the kingdom. In view of Jesus' overarching message of the coming destruction when the Son of Man arrives, perhaps it's best, then, to see Jesus' action in the Temple as a kind of prophetic gesture, an enacted parable, in which he demonstrates on a small scale what was soon going to happen in a big way on the coming day of judgment. The Temple is going to be destroyed, and Jesus, then, kind of showed this through a small act of some kind.

If that's what's going on, it's still hard to know exactly what Jesus found to be offensive about the temple; for example, whether he thought the priests who operated in the temple were corrupt. In the words I quoted from Mark, he seems to indicate that the Temple itself had grown corrupt, but this may be a Christianization of what Jesus said by his later followers who were telling the stories. On the other hand, we do have accounts of other Jews before Jesus and afterward who believed that the Temple had grown corrupt. For example, the Essenes in the Dead Sea Scroll community thought this; in the Hebrew Bible the prophet Jeremiah thought this. It may simply be that Jesus thought the Temple was corrupt, or maybe that Jesus, as a country fellow from rural Galilee, who had been preaching against wealth and power, saw the Temple and the sheer opulence of the place made his blood boil on principle. It's possible.

There are a couple of ways to understand the significance of Jesus' prediction that the Temple was going to be destroyed, in light of his broader apocalyptic message. What is Jesus exactly thinking? You see, the problem is, since God commanded there be a Temple, and told Jews what to sacrifice there, and that's what the Jews are doing, why is Jesus opposing it?

There are a couple of ways to understand it. One way: It may be that Jesus believed that in this coming kingdom of God that he's proclaiming, there would be a new Temple, one that was totally sanctified for the worship of God. In other words, he may have thought that this Temple had become corrupt because of the wicked priests who had been running it, but that in the kingdom of God coming there'd be a new Temple after the old one was destroyed. That kind of view is represented by other Jews we know about from the day; apocalyptically-minded Essenes of the Dead Sea Scroll community thought something very similar to that. Another option is that Jesus may have believed that in the future coming kingdom there'd be no need of a Temple at all. In this future kingdom, there'd be no more evil, no more sin, and therefore there'd be no need for the cultic sacrifice of animals to bring atonement for sins. This was a point of view that was later embraced by some of Jesus' own followers, including the author of the Book of Revelation, in the New Testament; Revelation chapter 1, verse 22. There'd be no need for a future Temple in the coming kingdom. In either case, the implication of Jesus' actions would have been clear. For Jesus, the temple cult, and the officials in charge of it, were a temporary measure at best, a corruption of God's plan at worst. They would soon be done away with when the kingdom of God arrived.

Mark's account is clear that Jesus' actions against the Temple, and his predictions, didn't escape the notice of those who were in charge of the Temple. The priests—who not only had jurisdiction over local affairs of the people of Jerusalem, but also were the principal liaisons with the Roman officials—these priests were, by and large, members of the Sadducaic party. After Jesus does this, in Mark's Gospel, at least, he begins to enter into controversy with Sadducees, the chief priests, and as we saw, they start looking for ways to have him removed from the public eye. Jesus appears to have spent the week prior to Passover there teaching and engaging with his opponents in the Temple. It's striking that his most explicitly apocalyptic message is said to have been delivered there in all three of our earliest Gospels. The Jewish authorities begin to be concerned about an uprising in these accounts, as the crowds start swelling and Jesus begins to attract more attention. For their part, Roman authorities were armed and ready to act. It was decided, then, to have Jesus taken out of the public eye by stealth, so as to avoid any problems.

We're told in our accounts that, prior to being arrested, Jesus had some kind of last meal with his disciples. According to the earliest accounts of Mark, Matthew, and Luke, this was a Passover meal. Jesus at this meal took the symbolic foods that represented the struggles of the children of Israel against the Egyptians—unleavened bread, they would also eat herbs, the lamb, they'd have several cups of wine—Jesus took the symbolic foods and brought new symbolism to them, taking the bread, and saying, "The bread is my body that is broken." Taking the cup, saying, "This is the new covenant in my blood." It's hard to say that the precise words at the "Last Supper" are authentic. It's hard to say that, because they don't pass the criterion of dissimilarity. Jesus is saying that his own death is going to bring in the "new covenant," with God. That's something certainly the Christians believed after the fact. It's striking that these words are multiply attested. They're found also in the writings of the apostle Paul, who says that Jesus said something like this.

There's one thing that Jesus says in the passage in Mark, though, that does seem to pass the criterion of dissimilarity. Jesus says in Mark's Gospel, after he gives the cup and says, "This is the new covenant in my blood," he says that he would not drink wine again until he drinks it anew in the kingdom. That seems to assume that the kingdom is going to come right away. In other words, the next time Jesus drinks isn't going to be 3000 years later, but it's going to be very soon, and it seems to presuppose the nearness of the kingdom, even though the Gospel writers knew that decades later it hadn't come yet. That would suggest that Jesus actually said something like that, which might suggest that Jesus knew what was going to happen.

There'd be nothing implausible at all about his realizing that he was going to be arrested, and that he was in trouble. He probably knew that the authorities were against him, and he probably knew what happened to prophets in Jerusalem who opposed the ruling authorities. They were, in virtually every instance, arrested and either punished in other ways or executed. It's difficult to know, though, how Jesus actually phrased his coming arrest, since as we've seen, his Passion predictions in the Gospels are so much the early Christian preaching about Jesus, that Christians may have put those predictions on his lips.

In conclusion, we can say that Jesus' apocalyptic message can make sense of what happened to him at the end. He brought his message of the impending judgment of God and the imminent arrival of the Son of Man to the heart of Jerusalem during the Passover. He acted out his message of coming destruction by causing a disturbance in the Temple, and this attracted the attention of the authorities in charge of the Temple. After a few days, when Jesus was starting to draw more crowds to hear him preach, the authorities decided that they needed to remove him from the public eye.

Lecture Twenty-One
The Last Hours of Jesus

Scope:

Jesus was almost certainly betrayed by one of his own followers, Judas Iscariot. What is not clear, though, is what it was that Judas betrayed or why he acted as he did. It seems unlikely that he was hired simply to inform the authorities of Jesus' whereabouts, because they could have obtained that information without paying for it. The surviving traditions contain hints that Judas may have divulged insider information that was available to him as one of the twelve disciples and that was used against Jesus at his trial. We do not have good sources for what happened at the trial of Jesus, as we shall see in this lecture. But it is clear that the high priest and his council, the Sanhedrin, considered Jesus a threat and therefore turned him over to Pilate.

Outline

I. In this lecture, we will pick up at the point where the Jewish leaders in Jerusalem decided that Jesus had to be removed.

  A. Jesus was almost certainly betrayed by one of his disciples, Judas Iscariot.

   1. The event is multiply attested (Mark 14:10–11, 43–45; John 18:2–3; Acts 1:16; possibly 1 Cor. 11:23) and is not the sort of thing that a later Christian would probably make up.

   2. Some question exists about the meaning of the Greek word for "betray." One interpretation is that God is "giving him over" to his suffering.

  B. What is not clear is what it was that Judas betrayed.

   1. The common notion that Judas simply told the authorities where they could locate Jesus apart from the crowds may be right, but why would they need an insider for that kind of information?

   2. Judas may have divulged something else, some information that the authorities could use to bring Jesus up on charges.

   3. It is striking that in the reports of Jesus' trials, he is charged with calling himself such things as the Messiah,

©2000 The Teaching Company Limited Partnership

the Son of God, and the King of the Jews (Mark 14:61, 15:2; John 18:33, 19:19).

4. In the public teachings of Jesus that we have established as historically reliable, Jesus never calls himself such things. In our earliest source, when someone does call him the messiah, he hushes it up (Mark 8:30). Where did the authorities get the idea that he called himself such things?

5. This may have been what Judas betrayed. We know that Jesus taught his disciples privately things that he didn't say in public.

6. Did Judas betray insider information? If so, we might have a clue about what Jesus told his disciples about himself.

II. We have several hints about what Jesus taught the disciples about himself that Judas may have divulged to the authorities.

A. The hints come by way of several curious pieces of information that look to be historically reliable.

1. Almost certainly, the charge leveled against Jesus by the Roman governor Pontius Pilate was that he considered himself to be the King of the Jews (Mark 15:2; John 18:33, 19:19).

2. Jesus never calls himself this in any of the Gospels. Why would he be executed for a claim he never made?

3. In addition, during his hearing before the Jewish authorities, who held a kind of preliminary investigation before turning him over for prosecution, Jesus was evidently charged with calling himself the Messiah (Mark 14:62)—a figure of grandeur and power, widely thought to be the future ruler of the people Israel.

B. Jesus spurned the title "Messiah" in reference to himself in public, but it is possible that in one sense he did think that he was the messiah?

1. Jesus taught that after the Son of Man executed judgment on the earth, the kingdom would arrive.

2. Kingdoms, by their nature, have kings. Who would be the king?

3. Ultimately, of course, it would be God—hence, Jesus' common reference to the "Kingdom of God." But he

probably didn't think that God would physically sit on the throne in Jerusalem. Who then would?

4. The earliest traditions also indicate that Jesus thought that he himself would be enthroned. For one thing, only those who accepted his message would be accepted into the kingdom.

5. Jesus also told his disciples that they would be seated on twelve thrones to rule the twelve tribes of Israel. Who would be over them? It was Jesus who called them to be the Twelve. Moreover, his disciples asked him for permission to sit at his right hand and his left in the coming kingdom (see, for example, Mark 10:37). They evidently understood that he would be the ruler in the kingdom, just as he was their "ruler" now.

C. Finally, at least some people during his life almost certainly believed that Jesus would be the future ruler of Israel. If they didn't, we can't explain why these followers thought he was the messiah after he died.

1. Jesus' followers would not have started to believe this on the basis of their later conviction that he had been raised from the dead.

2. Before Christianity, as far as we know, Jews did not expect that the messiah would be raised from the dead. In no surviving Jewish text—whether in the Hebrew Bible or later, up to Christianity—is the messiah said to be one who would die and be raised up.

3. If Jesus' followers called him messiah later, after his death, they must have thought of him as messiah earlier, while he was alive.

4. Yet in our earliest accounts, Jesus doesn't teach that he's the messiah and discourages his disciples from noising it about.

D. The best way to explain all these data is to say that Jesus' teachings about himself were intimately related to his apocalyptic proclamations.

1. Those who heeded his words would enter that kingdom.

2. This would be God's kingdom, ruled by his chosen ones—the twelve disciples on twelve thrones.

3. Jesus would rule over the disciples. He, in effect, would be the king of God's coming kingdom.

4. In that apocalyptic sense (and I would say, only in that sense) did Jesus think of himself as the messiah. He wasn't a cosmic judge, an authoritative priest, or a military leader. He was the one sent from God to proclaim the good news of the coming kingdom, who would be the ultimate ruler when the end arrived.

E. Judas, then, betrayed this private teaching of Jesus to the authorities.
  1. That's why they could level the charges against Jesus that he called himself the Messiah, the King of the Jews.
  2. He meant it, of course, in the apocalyptic sense. They meant it in a this-worldly sense. But he couldn't deny the charge when asked about it ("are you the King of the Jews?"), because that was how he understood himself, and the twelve disciples all knew it.

III. It is also difficult to know why Judas decided to betray this information.

A. Some people have thought that he did it for the money (see Matt. 26:14–15; John 12:4–6).
  1. This is possible, but the "thirty pieces of silver" is a reference to a fulfillment of prophecy in the Hebrew Bible (Zech. 11:12); that is, the tradition doesn't pass the criterion of dissimilarity.
  2. Some argue that Judas grew disillusioned when he realized that Jesus had no intention of becoming a political–military messiah.
  3. Others have reasoned that he wanted to force Jesus' hand, thinking that if he were arrested he would call out for support and start an uprising that would overthrow the Romans.

B. Each of these explanations has merit, but in the end, we'll never know.
  1. Judas cast the money back at the Jewish leaders. Because priests were not allowed to use "blood money," they bought a potter's field with the silver.
  2. Judas died, either by suicide or some other cause.

IV. The early sources all agree that after a last meal with his disciples, Jesus was arrested by Jewish authorities (multiply attested in Mark 14:43 and John 18:3) who conducted a preliminary investigation against him.

A. As local aristocrats, the Jewish high priests were allowed by the Romans to conduct and control their own internal affairs.

    1. The head of the group would have been the high priest, who during this time (A.D. 26–36), was a man named Caiaphas.

    2. There is nothing implausible in a local offender being brought before local authorities. In Jesus' case, the authorities were Caiaphas and his ruling "council," called the Sanhedrin (this also explains why Jewish police arrested Jesus, rather than Roman).

B. Unfortunately, we have no reliable way of knowing what happened when Jesus appeared before Caiaphas.

    1. In part, we are hampered by our sources. According to the accounts, the only persons present were Jesus and the Jewish rulers. Apparently, none of Jesus' disciples was present.

    2. The real problem, though, is that it is difficult to understand the trial proceeding, if it actually happened as narrated, because the charge of "blasphemy" leveled against Jesus cannot be rooted in anything he is actually claimed to have said (Mark 14:61–62).

    3. It wasn't blasphemous to call oneself the messiah (as Jesus allegedly did)—this simply meant that you understood yourself to be the deliverer/ruler of your people. Nor was it blasphemous to say that the Son of Man was soon to arrive—this was simply to acknowledge that the Book of Daniel had predicted something that would happen in your own day.

    4. Yet the high priest accused Jesus of blasphemy. Because no blasphemy was committed, it seems unlikely that the trial proceeded the way that it's described in Mark, our earliest source. (One could conceive of his statement as blasphemous only by assuming, with Mark, that Jesus was the Son of Man, because then Jesus would be saying that he had a standing equal with God. The high priest would have had no reasons to think that Jesus was referring to himself when he mentioned the Son of Man.)

V. We can say a good deal about Jesus' final hours before his appearance before the Roman governor Pontius Pilate.

    A. He was almost certainly betrayed by one of his followers, Judas Iscariot, who may have divulged to the authorities some of Jesus' secret teachings that he had given to the inner circle of twelve.

    B. These teachings concerned his own identity—something he was loathe to discuss publicly. Jesus seems to have thought that he himself would be appointed the ruler of the coming kingdom by God.

    C. Once the local Jewish authorities learned this, they had all the grounds they needed to make a quick arrest to get Jesus out of the public eye.

    D. Working stealthily, the authorities had Jesus arrested at night and brought him into an informal interrogation. We don't know exactly what happened there, but it clearly was enough to make the authorities to hand him over to the Roman governor for trial.

Essential Reading:

Mark 14–16; Matthew 26–27; Luke 22–23; John 18–19.

Ehrman, *Jesus: Apocalyptic Prophet*, chap. 12.

Sanders, *The Historical Figure of Jesus*, chap. 16.

Suggested Reading:

Brown, *Death of the Messiah*.

Crossan, *Who Killed Jesus?*

Questions to Consider:

1. Consider the various options for why Judas decided to betray Jesus. What do you see as the strengths and weaknesses of each option?

2. Why might some scholars doubt the historicity of the following stories found in the Gospel accounts of Jesus' last hours? What historical arguments can be mounted in their favor? Where do you stand on the issue? (a) The institution of the Last Supper (Mark 14:22–25; Matt 26:26–29; Luke 22:15–20; 1 Cor. 11:23–26), (b) Jesus' washing of the disciples feet (John 13:1–20), and (c) Jesus' prayer in the Garden before his arrest (Mark 14:32–42; Matt 26:36–46; Luke 22:39–46).

Lecture Twenty-One—Transcript
The Last Hours of Jesus

In the last lecture, I stressed that it's important to understand the events of Jesus' last days in light of his overall proclamation. Reconstructions of Jesus' life that cannot connect his death with his life are highly implausible. An apocalyptic understanding of his message, though, makes considerable sense of what happened to him at the end. Jesus came to Jerusalem in order to proclaim his apocalyptic message in the heart of Judaism. He believed that the end was imminent, and people needed to repent before the Son of Man arrived in judgment. When he arrived in Jerusalem, he acted out his message by performing a kind of parabolic action in the Temple, overturning tables, as an illustration of the destruction that was coming. It was this that led, ultimately, to his arrest, as the authorities in charge of the Temple, chief priests connected with the Sadducaic party, decided to have Jesus taken out of the way when he began to attract larger crowds, wanting to nip the problem in the bud rather than allow him to stir up the mob. In this lecture, we'll pick up at this point, seeing what can be established as historically reliable information about Jesus' final hours.

It's almost certain that Jesus was betrayed by one of his twelve disciples, named Judas Iscariot. There are several people in the New Testament who are named Judas; it's the same word as "Jude." In fact, Jesus, according to the Gospel of Mark, has a brother with the same name, Jude. Usually his name is given "Jude," and Judas Iscariot is given "Judas," I think just to differentiate them in English. "Iscariot" is a difficult term. We aren't sure what it means, exactly. Probably "Iscariot" is given to differentiate this Judas from other Judases named in the New Testament. What "Iscariot" actually refers to is hard to say. In Hebrew, *Ish Kerioth* could mean something like "man," *ish*, from the village of Kerioth, or it could be that this is something to do with a family named Iscariot. We aren't sure, exactly, what "Iscariot" means. Most people in this world don't have two names; people just have one name. Jesus didn't have a last name. People who have more than one name usually are people who are in the aristocracy of Rome. They have usually three names. These people just have one.

In any event, it's relatively certain that Jesus was betrayed by one of his own twelve. It appears that this was a man named Judas Iscariot,

The reason for thinking that it's relatively certain is that the event is multiply attested all over the map. We have an account in Mark's Gospel, Mark chapter 14. It's also picked up, then, by Matthew and Luke. Independently of Mark, we have an account in John's Gospel, John 18, of Judas Iscariot turning Jesus in, and also an account in the book of Acts chapter 1, that talks about Judas.

Interestingly, also, the apostle Paul may refer to Jesus' betrayal, 1 Corinthians chapter 11, verse 23. This is a passage where Paul is talking to the Corinthians about their need to celebrate the Lord's Supper in a proper way. The way he gets to explaining how they need to celebrate this meal properly, is by recounting how Jesus himself celebrated it. This is the longest passage in which Paul gives a tradition from Jesus' own life, on account of the Lord's Supper. He begins the account by saying, though: "The night in which he was betrayed, the Lord Jesus took bread." It's an interesting reference, because he doesn't mention Judas Iscariot. Judas' name never occurs in Paul's writings. He does say that this happened on the night Jesus was betrayed, though. Thus, most people have taken this as a reference to the betrayal narrative.

It's somewhat complicated, though, because the term in Paul that is translated "betrayed," the term *paradidomi* in Greek, is a term that Paul more regularly uses to refer not to the act of betrayal, but to the act of God handing Jesus over to his suffering. Therefore, instead of referring to the betrayal narrative, Paul may simply be referring to the night that God handed Jesus over to his death. In other words, this may not be support of the Judas tradition, or it may be; scholars debate. Even without 1 Corinthians 11, though, the account is multiply attested in Mark, John, and Acts. Moreover, as I noted in an earlier lecture, this is not the sort of tradition that Christians would be inclined to make up: That Jesus was turned over by one of his twelve? That he had no more power or authority over his closest followers than that? Given that it passes both independent attestation and dissimilarity, it looks like this is something that actually happened.

What's not clear, though, is what it was that Judas betrayed. What was it that he betrayed? The common notion is that Judas simply told the authorities where they could find Jesus apart from the crowds. So Judas told them, "He goes out regularly to pray in Gethsemane, so you can go and find him there." It's possible that that's what he told the authorities. I have to say, though, that I've always found that a little bit odd, that the authorities would have to pay an insider to get that kind of information. Why couldn't they simply have him followed? It may be that that's why he betrayed him, but it seems to me that something else might be going on. It's possible that Judas betrayed something else. That is, that he divulged information that the authorities could actually use against Jesus when they wanted to bring him up on charges. I want to explore that possibility, at some length, in the first part, here, of this lecture.

It's striking that in the various accounts of Jesus' trials that we'll be discussing later, Jesus is charged with calling himself such things as the "Messiah," the "Son of God," the "King of the Jews." These are charges leveled against Jesus that are thought either to be religiously blasphemous, or to be politically dangerous—King of the Jews; Messiah. The problem is that in Jesus' public teachings that we've established as historically reliable, Jesus never calls himself these things. In our earliest source, the Gospel of Mark, when someone does call Jesus the Messiah, Jesus hushes it up, Mark chapter 8, verse 30. Jesus asks his disciples: "Who do people say that I am?" "Well, some say you're Elijah, some say you're John the Baptist, some say you're a prophet raised from the dead." Jesus asks, "Well, who do you say that I am?" Peter replies, "You are the Messiah." Jesus says, "Don't tell anybody." Then he goes on to teach that he has to go to Jerusalem and be executed. Jesus isn't exactly propounding the idea that he is the Messiah, and in these early sources, he doesn't go around saying that he's the Messiah. He doesn't ever say that, in fact, until after he's arrested.

Why would he be put on trial for saying something that he didn't say? Is it possible that this is what Judas betrayed? We know that Jesus taught his disciples privately things that he didn't say in public. That's presumably one of the reasons for having an inner circle. Did Judas betray insider information to the authorities about what Jesus was saying about himself? If so, then we might have a clue into Jesus' self-sense, into what Jesus thought about himself, at least as he told his disciples.

I want to explore this possibility in some greater detail. We have several hints in our sources about what Jesus taught his disciples. They're no more than hints, but they're clearly there in our traditions, things that Judas might have divulged to the authorities.

These hints come by way of several curious pieces of information that all look to be historically reliable.

It's almost certain that the charge leveled against Jesus by the Roman governor Pontius Pilate, the thing that ended up getting Jesus executed, was that Jesus considered himself to be the King of the Jews. Mark chapter 15, verse 2; John chapter 18 verse 33; it's multiply attested that Jesus is executed for calling himself the King of the Jews. That's a political offense, of course, because only the Romans can appoint a king. If you're not appointed a king by the Romans, that means you've got to overcome whatever king the Romans have appointed. It's a political charge. Jesus never calls himself this in any of our Gospels, however. Jesus doesn't go around saying, "I'm the King of the Jews." Why would he be executed for a claim he never made?

Moreover, during Jesus' trial before the Jewish authorities; Jesus first appears before Jewish authorities, then they take him to see Pilate; they hold a kind of preliminary investigation before turning him over. Jesus was evidently charged with calling himself the "Messiah." The Messiah, in Jewish circles, as we've seen, could refer to a number of different figures. It could refer to a cosmic judge coming on the clouds of heaven. It could refer to a great priest who's going to be interpreter of the law. More commonly, apparently, it was thought to be some kind of future ruler of the people of Israel, a person of grandeur and power.

We've seen that Jesus appears to have spurned the title of "Messiah" in reference to himself in public. Nonetheless, it's possible that in one sense Jesus may have thought that he was the Messiah. Remember, Jesus taught that the Son of Man was going to execute judgment upon the Earth, and that afterwards the kingdom of heaven, kingdom of God, would arrive. Kingdoms, by their very nature, have kings. Who would be the king of this coming kingdom in the teaching of Jesus? Publicly, he never says. On one level, of course, the ruler's going to be God Himself. That's why Jesus calls it the "kingdom of God." However, he probably didn't think that God Himself was going to physically come down to earth and sit on the throne at Jerusalem. Who, then, is going to be the king of this kingdom?

There are several indications in our earliest traditions that Jesus thought that he, himself, would be the one who would be enthroned.

For one thing, only those who accepted his message would be accepted into the kingdom. In other words, there's an intimate tie between Jesus and this kingdom. You have to accept what he says to be admitted. More importantly, though, he appears to have told his disciples that they would be seated on twelve thrones, ruling the twelve tribes of Israel. Okay, there'll be twelve rulers, but who would be ruling them? Remember, it was Jesus himself who called them to be the twelve. He is their master here on Earth. They are his disciples. Moreover, we have traditions in which the disciples ask him for permission to sit on his right and his left in the coming kingdom, Mark 10, verse 37. Evidently, the disciples understood that he would be the ruler in this kingdom, as he was their ruler now.

As a final piece of the puzzle, it's almost certain that some people during Jesus' lifetime believed that he would be the future ruler of Israel. Not just the disciples, but other disciples—some of the disciples, but not just the disciples—thought that he would be a future ruler. Otherwise, it's virtually impossible to explain why, after his death, people came to call Jesus the Messiah.

Let me explain what I mean. I think the common assumption that people have is that if anyone came to think that Jesus was raised from the dead, they would naturally say, "He must be the Messiah." That's faulty logic, though, because there weren't any Jews who thought that the Messiah was going to be raised from the dead, so far as we know. We have lots of sources of early Judaism, lots of accounts that talk about a future ruler of some kind, a future Messiah figure. In no Jewish text of any kind that survives from antiquity is there any statement at all that the Messiah is going to be one who dies and then is raised from the dead. This kind of idea is not found in the Hebrew Bible; it's not found in Jewish writings during the first century.

That means, though, that if Jesus' followers called him the Messiah after his death, it couldn't have been because they believed he was raised, because the Messiah wasn't supposed to be raised. They wouldn't have called him the Messiah later unless they were calling him the Messiah earlier. In other words, they may have thought that he was the Messiah; he gets crucified, and that disconfirms their belief, but then when he's raised from the dead, they think, "Oh, God has vindicated him. He really is the Messiah." It wouldn't lead them to think that he was the Messiah, but it might confirm something they had earlier thought. If that construct of things is right—I think that part is pretty certain—then some of Jesus' followers, not just his disciples, may have thought that he was the Messiah prior to his death. Yet, in the early accounts, Jesus doesn't teach that he is the Messiah. He also discourages people who do think so from noising it about.

How do we tie together all of these data? I think the best way to explain all of these data together is to say that Jesus' teachings about himself intimately related to his apocalyptic proclamation that the end of the age was coming soon, that the arrival of the Son of Man was imminent, that the kingdom of God was almost here. Those who heeded his words would enter into that kingdom. This would be God's kingdom, ruled by his chosen ones, the twelve disciples on twelve thrones, and Jesus himself—as he must have taught the twelve, I think—Jesus himself would have ruled over them in this kingdom. In effect, Jesus would be the king of God's coming kingdom. In that apocalyptic sense, that Jesus is the ruler of the future kingdom—and I would say only in that apocalyptic sense— did Jesus think of himself as the Messiah. He wasn't a cosmic judge, he wasn't an authoritative priest, and he wasn't a military leader that was going to drive out the Romans. He was the one sent from God to proclaim the good news of the coming kingdom, and he would be the one who would be its ultimate ruler when the end arrived.

In this reconstruction of things, then, Judas betrayed this private teaching of Jesus to the authorities. Judas told the authorities what Jesus had been teaching them about his role in this coming kingdom. That's why they could level the charges against Jesus that he called himself the Messiah, the King of the Jews. He didn't teach this publicly, he did it privately; but they could charge him with it, because Judas told them, and then Jesus couldn't deny it. Jesus meant it in the apocalyptic sense: "Yes, I'm the King of the Jews in the future kingdom." They meant it, though, in a kind of "this worldly" sense. You know, "Are you the Messiah, the King of the Jews?" He has to, at his trials then, admit that he thinks that he is, and that's what leads, then, to his execution. In this reconstruction of things, then, Judas didn't just betray where they could find Jesus, but what they charged him with. Understanding this ties together all sorts of things, including this problem that they end up executing Jesus for calling himself something that he never calls himself.

It's difficult to know why Judas might have gone about betraying this sort of information to the authorities. What motivated Judas? Some people thought that he did it for the money. Matthew chapter 26 indicates this, that the authorities had agreed to pay Judas 30 pieces of silver. Unfortunately for this idea, this reference in Matthew is actually an allusion to a prophecy in the Hebrew Bible: Zechariah chapter 11, verse 12, where a person receives 30 pieces of silver and casts it over to the potter. Remember Judas ends up killing himself, in this field of blood that is a "potter's field." It looks like, in other words, that this tradition of 30 pieces of silver is used to show that this is a fulfillment of a prophecy. In other words, it can't pass the criterion of dissimilarity.

Thus, people have come up with other reasons for thinking that Judas did it. Some have argued, reasonably, I think, that Judas had grown disillusioned when he realized that Jesus was not the person he thought he was. In other words, Judas may have thought that Jesus really was going to be some kind of political, military Messiah, who was going to rouse the forces up and drive out the Romans, and when that didn't happen, out of disillusionment he turned Jesus in. That's possible. Others have reasoned that Judas wanted to force Jesus' hand, thinking that if Jesus were arrested, he would call out for support, and start an uprising, that would overthrow the Romans, in order to compel Jesus to do what Judas wanted him to do. That again is plausible, I think. Each of these explanations has some merit. In the end, I'm afraid we're never really going to know what it was that motivated Judas to do what he did.

We have two accounts, by the way, of what ended up happening to Judas. In the Gospel of Matthew, we're told that Judas went out and hanged himself afterwards out of regret. What happens, then, is he casts the money back into the temple out of regret; he hangs himself; and the priests who have given him the money, then, can't put the money back in the treasury because it's blood money—money that's been used to betray innocent blood—so they use it to buy a potter's field, the "field of blood," because it's bought with blood money. The Book of Acts has an account of Judas dying, but it doesn't say that Judas hanged himself. In fact, it doesn't say he committed suicide. It says that he "burst forth in the midst, and his bowels gushed out on the earth." It's not clear what that's referring to. What people have tried to do over the years is to reconcile the two accounts, saying Judas hanged himself, and maybe the rope broke, and he kind of gushed out over the earth, or some other way of reconciling it. If you didn't know about the account in Matthew of him hanging himself, it would sound like Judas kind of spontaneously burst. There are traditions in the second century that that's what happened to Judas; he actually swelled up, sort of a supernatural thing, and just became so immense, he finally just kind of split open and died. In the Book of Acts, that happens in a field, and it's called the "field of blood" because it's where Judas kind of spilled forth his blood. It looks like, historically, somehow Judas must have died in this field, and it was associated with his death. It may have been a field that was composed of red clay. It was a "potter's field" and people called it the "field of blood" because it has red clay, but then somehow it got associated with Judas' death.

All right, back to Jesus' last hours. Our early sources all agree that after having a last meal with his disciples, Jesus was arrested by Jewish authorities. I think it's pretty clear that Jesus was arrested by the Jewish authorities. It's led, of course, over the years to claims that Jews were responsible for Jesus' death, but these accounts are pretty clear that it's not the Jews who are responsible for Jesus' death, it's the Jewish authorities, the leaders. Jesus had enemies in the hierarchy of the Temple authorities, and these are the ones who are responsible for arresting Jesus, and then to conducting a kind of preliminary investigation against him. As local aristocrats, the Jewish high priests were allowed by the Romans to conduct and control their own internal affairs. The head of the group of the chief priests was the high priest. He was the head officer, as it were, of the temple, who was given jurisdiction by the Romans to conduct basic internal affairs among the Jews.

During this time, the high priest was a man named Caiaphas, who was the high priest throughout the governorship of Pontius Pilate. There are some things to suggest that Caiaphas and Pontius Pilate were closely linked to one another. When Pontius Pilate was removed from his duties by the Romans—his behavior became too atrocious for even the Romans to handle him; he was a brutal governor, it appears—when they removed him from office in the year 36, Caiaphas also was removed from the high priesthood, and so it looks like he was in cahoots with Pilate during his governorship. The high priest, Caiaphas, and the chief priest were responsible for having Jesus arrested. There's nothing implausible about a local offender being brought before the local authorities. In this case, Jesus is brought before the council of Jews, called the Sanhedrin. It's hard to know much about the Sanhedrin during Jesus' own day. We know a lot more about what later Jews though the Sanhedrin should be like, but in Jesus' day, it's hard to say exactly what the Sanhedrin was. It appears to have been a kind of council that provided advice for the high priest.

Jesus, then, appears before this council, the Sanhedrin, and has a kind of preliminary trial before them. Unfortunately, there's no way of knowing what happened in this hearing of Jesus, before this council, in part because we're hampered by our sources. According to the early Gospels themselves, the only people present—in this trial of Jesus before the Jewish authorities—the only people present were Jesus, who was going to be executed the next day, and the Jewish rulers, who presumably weren't available for interviews later by Christians who wanted to know what happened. The followers of Jesus themselves weren't there. Sources indicate that they had all fled, gone into hiding, probably fearing for their own skins; if they've arrested Jesus, then they're probably going to get the followers next. The disciples have all fled.

It's hard to know what happened in this trial, because the only people there are people who won't be able to give us the information. The real problem, though, is that it's difficult to understand trial proceeding, as it's narrated in our earliest source, because it doesn't actually make sense in the earliest source. What happens is that the high priest asks Jesus, this is in Mark chapter 14, verses 61-62, the priest asks Jesus: "Are you the Messiah, the Son of the Blessed?" Jesus says, "I am, and you will see the Son of Man coming on the clouds of heaven." The high priest screams out, "Blasphemy!" tears his garments, and they say that Jesus then deserves to die. The problem is that the account, as narrated, doesn't include a blasphemy of any kind. For Jesus to say, "Yes, I am the Messiah," is not a blasphemy. There's nothing blasphemous about calling oneself the Messiah, anymore than it's blasphemous to say, "Yes, I am the President of the United States," or "I am the president of the Southern Baptist Convention." I may not be, but it's not a blasphemy to say that I am; there's nothing illegal about it.

There were Jews that we know about who called themselves "Messiah," and there were Jews that we know about that the leading religious leaders of the Jews called the "Messiah." "Messiah" simply means "a future ruler of the people;" it's not blasphemous to say so. It's also not blasphemous to say "You'll see the Son of Man coming on the clouds of heaven." That's simply to say, "Yes, Daniel was right, in the Hebrew Bible, that it's going to happen, and we'll be alive when it comes." There are other prophets saying the same thing. To say so is not a blasphemy.

What, then, was the blasphemy? Some people have thought that since Jesus answered, "Are you the Messiah, the Son of the Blessed?" and Jesus answered, "I am," that that was a blasphemy, that Jesus was taking the name of God—"I am" is the name of God. That's a common explanation for this, but I think it's completely wrong, because in fact that's simply how you answer a question in the affirmative throughout the New Testament. In the Gospel of John, there's a man who's born blind that Jesus heals. He's brought before the authorities, and they say, "Are you the one who was blind that Jesus healed?" The man replies, "I am." Same words. He's not claiming to be God, he's just answering the question. Jesus is asked, "Are you the Messiah?" He says, "I am." I don't think that's what's going on.

I think the only way to explain what's going on is to assume what Mark, the author of the Gospel, assumes about Jesus—namely, that Jesus is the Son of Man. That's what Mark assumes. If you assume that Jesus is the Son of Man, and he says, "You will see the Son of Man coming on the clouds of heaven," then you would think that Jesus himself is a heavenly being. That would be a blasphemy. In other words, from Mark's perspective, the high priest would think this was blasphemous. If you think about it historically—what would happen in the trial itself—the high priest wouldn't have Mark's perspective that Jesus is the Son of Man. Thus, it doesn't make sense as a historical narrative, because it wouldn't work, there wouldn't be a blasphemy committed. It would make sense as a theological narrative, though. Mark, in other words, has written this account in order to show you that the Jewish authorities found Jesus guilty of blasphemy, even though blasphemy does not appear to have occurred. In short, we really can't know what happened at Jesus' trial before these Jewish authorities.

In conclusion, let me tie together what I think we can say about Jesus' final hours before he appears before the governor, Pontius Pilate. Jesus was almost certainly betrayed by one of his followers,

Judas Iscariot, who appears to have divulged to the authorities some of Jesus' secret teachings that he had been giving to his inner circle of the twelve. These teachings concerned Jesus' own identity, something he was loathe to discuss publicly, but Jesus appears to have thought that he himself would have a place of prominence and importance in this coming kingdom that he was proclaiming, that he would be appointed by God to be the ruler of this kingdom. He taught his disciples this privately, evidently. Once the local Jewish authority learned of this, they had all the grounds they needed to make a quick arrest, to get Jesus out of the public eye. Working stealthily, they had him arrested at night and brought him into an informal interrogation. We don't know exactly what happened at this interrogation, but it clearly was enough to make the authorities hand Jesus over to the Roman governor for trial. That's where we'll pick up the story in the next lecture.

Lecture Twenty-Two
The Death and Resurrection of Jesus

Scope:

One of the most certain facts of history is that Jesus was crucified on orders of the Roman prefect of Judea, Pontius Pilate. As a provincial governor, Pilate had free rein to handle difficult situations; trial by jury or due process were not required. We don't know why the Jewish authorities handed Jesus over to Pilate; they may have done so out of deference to Pilate, or because they did not want the responsibility, or because they wanted Jesus permanently taken out of the way and were not allowed under Roman law to perform capital punishment. In this lecture, we will try to determine what we can from the historical record about the trial and death of Jesus. We will also discuss the contradictory reports of Jesus' resurrection.

Outline

I. We are not well informed about what happened at Jesus' trial before Pilate.

    A. In an earlier lecture, I discussed Pilate's position—and power—as governor of the Roman province of Judea.

    B. It is not completely clear why the Jewish authorities didn't handle the problem posed by Jesus themselves.

        1. They may have wanted to show deference to the Pilate, who was in town to take care of such problems during the Passover.

        2. The authorities may have been concerned about the large following Jesus was acquiring (if, in fact, he was acquiring a large following; it's hard to know). If so, they may not have wanted to incur any animosity among the masses.

        3. They may also have wanted Jesus taken out of the way—that is, they wanted him executed. Most historians believe that although the Romans allowed the local aristocracies to run their own affairs, they reserved the right of capital punishment for themselves.

    C. It is difficult to know what actually transpired when Jesus appeared before Pilate.

1. His followers who later told stories about it were not there, and the principal participants, Pilate and the chief priests, would not have been likely to release details to inquiring Christians later.

2. The Gospel accounts of the crowds at the trial do not pass the criterion of contextual credibility. We know from Josephus that Pilate was a brutal ruler who did not cater to the whim of the populace.

3. The idea of the crowds calling for Jesus' blood does not pass the criterion of dissimilarity; later Christians telling the story may have wanted to emphasize the culpability of the Jewish people.

4. We can trace this tendency through the Gospels in chronological order (Mark, Luke, Matthew, John, and the non-canonical Peter). This trend was carried out in church traditions in the second century, including accounts of Pilate's conversion. In other words, Pilate and the Romans became more innocent, and the Jews became more guilty as time passed. This overlooks the important fact that the Jewish leaders, not the Jewish people, instigated the arrest of Jesus.

D. What is virtually certain is that the point at issue in Jesus' trial was, again, his own claims about himself.

1. Pilate would not have cared one bit about whether Jesus kept the Sabbath, or told people to love one another, or urged his followers to give away their wealth.

2. He would have cared about things that related to his rule as a representative of Rome. Independent sources attest that the ground for execution was that Jesus called himself the King of the Jews (Mark 15:26; John 19:19).

3. This tradition also passes the criterion of dissimilarity. "King of the Jews" is not a title that Christians themselves used of Jesus, insofar as we can tell from our surviving sources.

4. Mark's account is not an eyewitness report, but it may not be far off in the essentials. Pilate, having heard from the Jewish chief priests that Jesus was known to speak of himself as the messiah (= "king" in this context), queried him about it. Jesus either admitted the charge or did little or nothing to defend himself against it.

5. Pilate needed to hear no more. Jesus was a potential troublemaker who was stirring up the crowds and who thought of himself as a political usurper of the prerogatives of Rome. Without further ado, Pilate ordered him executed as an enemy of the state.

E. The trial was probably short. It may not have lasted more than a couple of minutes and was probably one of several items on a crowded morning agenda. Two others were charged with sedition the same morning. All three were taken outside the city gates to be crucified.

II. Crucifixion was a horribly slow and torturous death reserved by the Romans for the lowest of criminals.

A. Romans did not think that death sentences should be carried out in a humane and private manner.
1. They used public torture as a deterrent, a way to show to that the power of the Empire could be brutally brought to bear against the body of anyone who dared to defy it.
2. Jesus was not the only person crucified in the ancient world. This mode of execution was common for slaves, common criminals, rabble-rousers, people accused of sedition. When the Roman general Titus overthrew Jerusalem after a two-year siege in A.D. 70, he crucified so many people that he ran out of lumber.

B. According to the Gospel traditions, before being led off to his execution, Jesus was flogged (Mark 15:15; John 19:1).
1. Flogging, too, was a horrific punishment; the Romans used leather thongs with little pieces of glass or bone tied to the ends to rip off the skin and the inner muscle.
2. The account of Jesus' flogging may be a Christian addition to show how much he suffered, or it may be historically true.
3. Given that public torture of criminals from the lower classes was the rule of the day, the accounts are completely plausible.

C. Jesus and the others would have been taken by soldiers outside the city gates, carrying their crossbeams to the upright stakes kept at the site of execution. We don't know the actual site.

    1. The uprights were reused, maybe every day. There the condemned would have been nailed to the crossbeams, or to the uprights themselves, through the wrists and possibly the ankles.

    2. A small ledge may have been attached to the upright on which the condemned could sit to rest.

D. We know a bit more about crucifixion now than we used to, largely because of an archaeological discovery made some thirty years ago.

    1. The discovery was the partial remains of a crucified man, named Yehochanan, his ankle bone still attached to a piece of olive wood through which a stake had been driven. The nail had been driven into a knot in the wood and couldn't be removed.

    2. Yehochanan appears to have been tied to the cross by the arms; more commonly, a person was nailed through the wrists.

E. Death by crucifixion was slow and painful.

    1. It came not by loss of blood, but by suffocation, as the lung cavity distended and the person could no longer breathe.

    2. Death came only when the victim lacked the strength to pull up on his arms to relieve the pressure on his chest; sometimes it took days.

    3. In Jesus' case, death came quickly, within several hours—possibly because he had been so badly abused already.

    4. Jesus' disciples were not there with him, though some of the women who had accompanied him from Galilee reportedly looked on from a distance (Mark 15:40). None was close enough, though, to hear what, if anything, he said at the end.

    5. By mid-afternoon, on the day before Sabbath, he was dead.

III. In several independent accounts, we are told that Jesus' body was buried by an influential but secret follower, Joseph of Arimathea (Mark 15:42; John 19:38; G. Pet. 23).

    A. Some scholars have called this tradition into question on the grounds of contextual credibility.

        1. Crucified criminals were usually not allowed decent burials, but were left on their crosses to rot and be devoured by scavengers or tossed into a common grave as part of their humiliation.

        2. At least one recent scholar, John Dominic Crossan, has argued that Jesus' body was eaten by dogs—which is admittedly possible, but there is really no way, historically, to know.

        3. It does seem improbable that Jesus' corpse was left hanging on the cross. If it had been, his followers would presumably have seen it there later and been somewhat less inclined to maintain that it had been raised from the dead on the third day following.

    B. We can say, then, that Jesus' body was probably buried somewhere by someone, either by the soldiers in a common tomb or, as the tradition says, by someone other than his family and closest followers.

    C. The important thing, of course, is what his followers claimed happened next.

IV. Christianity is rooted in the belief that God raised Jesus from the dead.

    A. Historians cannot claim that the resurrection of Jesus "probably" happened.

        1. Even if it did happen, historians would have no way of demonstrating it, given the limitations of what can be appealed to as historical evidence. Because historians can establish only what probably happened, and a miracle of this nature is highly improbable, the historian cannot say it probably occurred.

        2. Moreover, the sources are hopelessly contradictory, as we can see by doing a detailed comparison of the accounts in the Gospels. Who went to the tomb? How many people went? What were their names? What did they see when they got there? Whom did they meet? What were they told? What did they do as a result?

    3.   Answers to each of these questions are not only different among the Gospels but also completely divergent.

B. As a result of these limitations, there are some things that we really cannot affirm as historians.

    1.   We cannot affirm that Jesus really was raised (though we aren't required to deny this either).

    2.   We cannot say even that he was buried in a private tomb.

    3.   We cannot say that three days later that tomb was empty.

    4.   Nor can we say that three days later the disciples *claimed* it was empty and that he had appeared to them (we only know that later they claimed it was empty and that he had appeared to them).

    5.   Nor do we know that all of the remaining disciples (Judas having killed himself) actually became believers.

C. What we do know, though, is also important.

    1.   We know that some (all? most? a few?) of his disciples who knew Jesus had been killed claimed at a later time (three days? three months? three years?) that his tomb was visited by some of his women followers three days later and was found to be empty.

    2.   They also claimed to have seen him alive afterwards.

    3.   They came to believe that he had been raised from the dead.

    4.   This claim completely changed their lives and the history of our world ever since.

Essential Reading:

Mark 15–16; Matthew 27–28; Luke 23–24; John 19–20.

Ehrman, *Jesus: Apocalyptic Prophet*, chaps. 12–13.

Sanders, *The Historical Figure of Jesus*, chap. 16.

Suggested Reading:

Brown, *The Death of the Messiah.*

Crossan, *Jesus: A Revolutionary Biography.*

Crossan, *Who Killed Jesus?*

Questions to Consider:

1. Throughout the Gospels, words are attributed to Jesus from the cross. Explain why historians would have difficulty establishing these words as historically authentic.

2. Try to formulate what you see as the responsibility of the Jewish authorities and the responsibility of the Roman authorities in Jesus' death. Throughout the ages, Christians have charged Jews with the responsibility for Jesus' death; in more recent times, this charge is seen as an instance of anti-Semitism. Do you think it is? Why or why not?

Lecture Twenty-Two—Transcript
The Death and Resurrection of Jesus

In the past two lectures, we've seen how Jesus' apocalyptic message led to his execution in Jerusalem. It happened at the time of the Passover, when thousands of Jews would come to the holy city to commemorate the great act of salvation God had performed on their behalf in the distant past, when he saved their ancestors from the oppression of a foreign power. Many of these worshipping Jews, of course, hoped that God would do so again. This made the Passover feast a particularly incendiary time during the Roman period. We know from Josephus of riots that had broken out during the festival, in which thousands of people were killed, and we know of other years in which prophets came to Jerusalem during the celebration to announce that God was going to intervene on behalf of his people. In no instance did these prophetic declarations end happily. Inevitably, prophets were seen as a threat to the stability of the social order, and were punished. So, too, with Jesus, arrested by the authorities as a potential troublemaker, possibly on suspicion that his apocalyptic predictions might cause a riot, or even foment an uprising; they had him turned over to the Roman governor, Pontius Pilate, for punishment.

We're not well informed about what actually happened at Jesus' trial before Pilate. In an earlier lecture, I discussed Pilate's position as governor of the Roman province of Judea. Provincial governors were Roman aristocrats who were appointed to govern the various lands Rome had conquered. Pilate himself was not in the very upper crust of the Roman aristocracy; he was of what was called the equestrian rank, rather than senatorial. He wasn't a Roman senator sent out to be a governor; he was of the economic class right below the senators, the equestrian, or the knight class. As with all governors, Pontius Pilate had two major responsibilities; to bring in the tribute, and to keep the peace. The central imperial government in Rome accorded its governors virtually free reign to do what was necessary in order to fulfill these obligations.

Among other things, this meant that Pilate had the power of life and death, with no requirement of trial by jury, careful cross-examination of witnesses, the possibility of judicial appeal, or anything else that might strike us today as due process. Pilate's job was to conduct a trial quickly and fairly, in order to accomplish his goals of making sure that there were no riots. In most cases, governors in situations like this decided a case quickly and efficiently, and the sentence was carried out immediately. There were no long waits on death row while an appeal was made. If a governor found an offender guilty, he was simply taken off and punished on the spot. If it were a particularly problematic case, then the execution might be ordered to be slow and painful.

It's not completely clear why the Jewish authorities who had Jesus arrested in the first place didn't handle the problem posed by Jesus themselves. It doesn't look to me that the Romans are the ones who went out and arrested Jesus. It appears from our earliest sources—they all agree—that in fact it was the Jewish authorities who had Jesus arrested, probably because they found his teachings about the Temple and his stirring up the crowds problematic. The Romans would have been happy to comply with what the Jewish authorities wanted in this case, but the Romans weren't the ones who went out and arrested Jesus, it appears.

Why didn't the Jewish authorities, who had Jesus arrested, take care of the problem themselves? There are several possibilities. It's possible that the Jewish authorities simply wanted to show deference to the Roan prefect, who was, after all, in town precisely in order to take care of such problems during the Passover. Maybe it was just simply out of deference to Pontius Pilate that the Jewish Sanhedrin had Jesus delivered over to him. It's also possible that the authorities really were concerned about the large following Jesus was acquiring, if in fact he was acquiring a large following; it's somewhat hard to know how large the following was. If they were concerned about it, they may not have wanted to incur any animosity among the masses. They didn't want the crowds to be angry with them. It's also possible that the Jewish authorities wanted Jesus to be taken out of the way completely. That is, that they wanted him to be executed.

Most historians believe that even though the Romans allowed the local aristocracies to run their own affairs, they reserved the right of capital punishment for themselves. In other words, if Caiaphas wanted Jesus to be executed, he simply couldn't order that he be stoned to death, or that he be crucified, because the Jewish authorities didn't have that right under the Roman governance of their province. Thus, if Caiaphas did want Jesus taken out of the way permanently, he would have had to have Pilate do so for him.

It's difficult to know what transpired, then, when Jesus did appear before Pontius Pilate. His followers, who later told stories about this trial, were not there to see it happen. The principal participants, Pilate and the chief priests, would not have been likely to release details to inquiring Christians later. Where do the stories come from that we have in the Gospels? We have accounts of Jesus appearing before Pilate. There's an interrogation that takes place, but the people who were recording the events weren't there, and the people participating in the events probably didn't give them the information, so where did they get their information from?

These stories may be the result of simply oral traditions. As people told the tales of Jesus' trial before Pilate, they added some of the details that we now have in the Gospels. In particular, the Gospel accounts that there were large crowds at the trial who were participating in it simply do not pass the criterion of contextual credibility. I pointed out in an earlier lecture that we know something about Pilate's rule as the governor of Judea. Our information comes from our principal source of knowledge of first-century Palestine, the historian Josephus. He tells us a few things about Pilate. What little he tells us makes it fairly clear that Pilate was a brutal ruler who did not cater at all to the whim of the populace. In fact, Pilate more frequently butted heads with the populace in Jerusalem, and in other places in Palestine, because he refused to cater to their whim. Only on rare occasion was he actually backed down by Jews in Palestine. The idea that you have in the Gospels, that Pilate is asking the crowds, "What do you want me to do? I'll do whatever you wish;" that doesn't sound like the Pilate we knew about from our other sources.

Moreover, the idea of the crowds calling for Jesus' blood does not pass the criterion of dissimilarity. The way it works in our earliest account, is that Pilate is asking Jesus, "Are you the King of the Jews?" and Jesus replies, "You say so." Pilate then turns to the crowds and says, "Should I release for you the King of the Jews?" The crowds cry out, "No, release for us instead Barabbas." Barabbas, it turns out, was a criminal who was in jail for an instigation against Rome. Evidently, according to the Gospels at least, it was Pilate's custom during the feast to release one criminal that the crowds desired. Rather than desiring Jesus, then, the crowds want to have this person Barabbas released to them, the one who's in jail for some kind of uprising against the Romans. Pilate then agrees to release

Barabbas. He then asks the crowd, "What should I do with this person, Jesus?" They say, "Crucify him." In order to give into the crowds, then, Pilate orders Jesus to be crucified.

This doesn't pass the criterion of dissimilarity, precisely because we know that Christians who are later telling the story may have wanted to emphasize the culpability of the Jewish people in the death of Jesus. As you trace the tradition of Jesus' execution through our sources, it becomes clear with the passing of time, the Christians who are telling the stories, place more and more blame on the Jewish people for the death of Jesus, and less and less blame on the Romans for his death. In fact, you can trace this movement through the Gospels themselves; it's very interesting to do so. The earliest Gospel, Mark, has Pilate asking the crowds, "What do you want me to do with Jesus?" "Crucify him," and to give into the whim of the crowd, he crucifies him. About ten or 15 years later, we have the Gospel of Luke, who tells the same story, but puts a different slant on it. In Luke's Gospel, on three separate occasions, Pilate declares that Jesus is innocent, and tries to release him, but the Jewish crowds refuse. In this account, the reason Jesus gets crucified is because the Jewish people really want him crucified, even though Pilate, the Roman governor, doesn't.

The Gospel of Matthew, from about the same time, tells the same story. In Matthew's Gospel, Pilate not only declares that Jesus is innocent; when the crowds insist on Jesus' being executed, Pilate calls for a basin of water, and they bring water to him, and he washes his hands in front of the crowds, and says, "I am innocent. I wash my hands of this man's blood. I'm innocent of this blood." The crowd cries out, this is only in Matthew's Gospel, "His blood be upon us and our children." In other words, the Jewish people are taking responsibility for Jesus' death, and passing that responsibility on to their own descendants. This verse, found only in Matthew's Gospel, is used, of course, through the ages in order to show that the Jews were Christ-killers. It's found only in Matthew, though; it's a later development. You see, what's happening is the Jews are becoming more guilty. The Roman's are becoming more innocent.

It becomes even clearer in the Gospel of John, our last Gospel. In John's Gospel, Pilate three times tries to release Jesus. The crowds won't let him. They finally say to Pilate, that "If you release Jesus, you are not a friend of Caesar." They threaten to take his case before the Roman Emperor. Then it says in John's Gospel that Pilate handed Jesus over to them to be executed. That's usually translated out of the English translations you read because it doesn't make any sense. Pilate hands Jesus over to the Jews so that they're going to execute him. That's what the text says.

Even later, in the Gospel of Peter, as we've seen, the Jews are fully responsible. It's not even Pilate who orders his execution, in the Gospel of Peter. Instead, it's Herod, the Jewish king who orders Jesus executed, and it's Jews who kill him. This tradition, in which Pilate gets increasingly exonerated, and the Jews become increasingly guilty, gets carried out into the second century in some very intriguing traditions. In some parts of the Christian church in the second century, Pilate was thought to be completely innocent. In some traditions that circulated at the end of the second century, it was alleged that Pilate later regretted what had happened, and himself converted to be a Christian after Jesus' death. We have an account cited in an early church father, it's a legendary account, that the next week or so, Pilate is really upset about what happened, and he wrote a letter to the Roman Emperor, saying, "You won't believe what I did. I crucified the Son of God, we're in trouble here," and he's going on like this. In parts of the Christian church, the Ethiopian church, Pilate was eventually canonized as a Christian saint.

What's this all about? Why is Pilate made to look more innocent? The more you make Pilate look innocent, the more you make the Jews look guilty. As Christians and Jews start fighting it out more and more, Christians start attacking Jews for the killing of Jesus. This in part also, as the story gets told later on in the tradition, is to show that in fact the Romans never were opposed to Jesus. This is a way of Christians saying, "Romans shouldn't be opposed to us." Christians who were being persecuted by the state could say, "We've never done anything wrong," all the way back to Jesus himself. In fact, the Roman prefect, Pilate himself, declared Jesus innocent.

In point of fact, we don't really know much about what happened at this trial before Pilate. It is pretty clear though, I think, that it was not the Jewish crowds that were ultimately responsible for Jesus being killed. The Jewish leaders deliver Jesus over to Pilate, and Pilate, after a short trial, ordered Jesus to be crucified.

It is pretty certain what the point at issue was at Jesus' trial before Pilate, even if we don't know all the specifics. The point at issue was

Jesus' own claims about himself. Pilate would not have cared a bit about whether Jesus, for example, kept the Sabbath, something that some Jewish Pharisees were offended by. Pilate wouldn't have cared whether Jesus told people that they ought to love one another, or whether he urged his followers to give up their wealth. What he would have cared about were the things related to his rule as a representative of Rome. It's independently attested that the ground of execution for Jesus was that he called himself "King of the Jews." It's independently attested in Mark, and in John. Moreover, it's not only multiply attested that this is the case, and it's not only contextually credible that that would be a charge to have Jesus crucified for, the charge also passes the criterion of dissimilarity.

Christians who were telling the stories about Jesus called him a number of things. They called him the Son of God, the Son of Man, the Lord of All; they eventually called him God. It's interesting that throughout the New Testament, no Christian author calls Jesus the King of the Jews. In other words, Christians didn't think about Jesus that way, so that they wouldn't have modified the traditions about his death and had him being killed for claiming to be the King of the Jews, because they didn't call him King of the Jews. Why then, is our tradition filled with this idea that he's killed for calling himself the King of the Jews? That's probably why he really was killed. It passes the criterion of dissimilarity.

Mark's account of the trial was not an eyewitness report. It's probably not far off, though, in its essentials. Pilate, having heard from the Jewish chief priest that Jesus was known to speak of himself as the Messiah—that's the King, the future King—asked Jesus about it. Jesus either admitted to the charge, or he did little or nothing to defend himself against it. That would make sense of all of these data. Pilate, then, needed to hear no more. Jesus was a potential troublemaker, who was stirring up the crowds, and thought of himself as a political usurper of the prerogatives of Rome. Without further ado, Pilate ordered him executed as an enemy of the state. The trial of Jesus itself was probably short and to the point. It may not have lasted more than a couple of minutes. It was probably one of several items on a crowded morning agenda that the governor had. Two other persons were charged with sedition the same morning. All three people were taken outside of the city gates to be crucified.

Crucifixion was a horribly slow and torturous death, reserved by the Romans for the lowest of criminals. Unlike modern Western societies, Romans did not think that death sentences should be carried out in as humane and private a manner as possible. In our system of justice, we think that if somebody is going to be executed, it should be done privately; you should figure out a humane way to do it. That's the way we look at things. The Romans had a completely different way of thinking about it. Romans used public torture as a deterrent for crime, a way to show everyone who could see that the power of the Empire could be brutally brought to bear against the body of anyone who dared defy it. If the Romans had problems with things like car-jacking, they wouldn't deal with these things kind of privately in some court out of the way. The Roman approach was, "If you have somebody who's committed a car-jacking, you crucify the person in public after humiliating and torturing the person, and everybody will walk by, see the person crucified in the public square—and then see how much car-jacking takes place." That was their logic of punishment.

Jesus, of course, was not the only person crucified in the ancient world. This was a common mode of execution, for slaves, common criminals, rabble-rousers, people causing sedition. When the Roman general, Titus, overthrew Jerusalem during the first uprising—Jerusalem fell in the year 70 A.D.—Titus crucified so many people that he ran out of lumber. This was a common mode of execution.

According to the Gospel traditions, before Jesus was led off to be executed, he was flogged. This is multiply attested in both Mark 15 and John 19. Flogging was, itself, a horrible punishment. The Romans would use leather thongs that had little pieces of glass or bone tied to the ends, so when they would flog a person, they would drag it across his back, and rip off the skin, then the inner muscle. It's hard to say whether this account of Jesus being flogged is a Christian addition to the story, in order to show how much he suffered, or if it's an historical account. This kind of flogging itself, of course, could practically kill a person. Since public torture of criminals from the lower classes was the rule of the day in the Empire, then the accounts in general terms are completely plausible. It may well be that Jesus was flogged before being crucified.

Jesus and the others, then, would have been taken by soldiers outside the city gates. We don't know the place of Jesus' crucifixion. If you visit Jerusalem, you'll have people tell you that it was this place, or that place; in fact, we don't know where it would have taken place. It does appear that the person who was going to be crucified was made to carry the cross beam to the upright stakes that were kept at the site of execution, which apparently was outside of the city walls. The uprights for the crosses were reused, possibly reused every day. At the place of execution, the condemned would have been nailed to the crossbeams, or possibly to the uprights themselves, through the wrists, and possibly through the ankles.

The way the crucifixion worked, then, is they would not nail the crucified person through the hands, the way it's normally portrayed in art, because if the person's nailed through the hands, then when he's hanging up, the nails would actually rip out. They would nail them between the two large bones in the wrist. Often, it appears, they would also nail them through the ankles. There might have been—there sometimes was, apparently—a small ledge that was attached to the upright that would allow the person to sit while he was dying.

We know a little bit more about crucifixion now than we used to. We used to know only on the basis of what was said in literary sources. Sources were not completely forthcoming about the process, because it was thought to be such a horrible thing. People didn't describe it. They probably didn't need to describe it, because everybody knew what it involved. We're a little bit better informed now, because of an archaeological discovery made 30 years ago. They discovered a partial skeleton of a crucified man named Yehochanan, whose ankle bones were still attached to a piece of olive wood through which a stake had been driven. The nail that had been used to crucify this person had been driven into a knot in the wood, so that they had trouble removing it. He was buried; his skeleton was still partially there, but the nail was still through the ankle. Yehochanan appears to have been, in his case, to have been tied to the cross by his arms, then nailed through the ankles. It appears, though, that more commonly, a person would have been nailed through the wrists as I've indicated.

The death by crucifixion was slow and painful. It didn't come by loss of blood, but by suffocation. The person would be hanging on the cross, and the lung cavity would distend as the weight of the body bore down upon it. The only way the person could survive was by pulling up on his arms, tied or nailed to the crossbeam, pushing up on the nails that were through the ankles. The death would then be prolonged, as long as the person had strength to continue pulling up to relive the pressure on his chest. Sometimes, in fact, this took days. In Jesus' case, death came quickly, within several hours, possibly because he had been so badly abused already. Jesus' disciples weren't there with him to see these things happen, although we do have an account that some of the women who had come with him from Galilee were looking on from a distance. None of them would have been close enough to hear what, if anything he said at the end. Thus, the seven last words of the dying Jesus are not things that anybody was there, probably, to have heard. By mid-afternoon, on the day before the Sabbath—so it's a Friday, apparently—Jesus was dead.

In several accounts, we're told that Jesus' body was buried by an influential but secret follower, a man named Joseph of Arimathea. Mark, John, Gospel of Peter all say this. Some scholars have called into question Jesus' burial by Joseph, on the grounds of contextual credibility. Normally, Romans did not allow crucified criminals to be buried properly. They either left their carcasses on the crosses to rot, as further humiliation, and to be devoured by scavengers there, or they tossed them into a common grave. At least one recent scholar, John Dominic Crossan, whom I've mentioned before, has argued that in fact Jesus' body was eaten by dogs. That admittedly is possible, but of course there's no way historically to establish anything like that as a fact. It does, though, seem improbable, to me at least, that Jesus' corpse was simply left hanging on the cross. If it had been, then it would be a little bit harder for his followers a little bit later to claim that it'd been raised from the dead the third day afterwards. We can say, then, that probably Jesus' body was buried somewhere by someone, either by the soldiers in a common tomb, as was a common practice, or by someone who was close to him, his family, or a close follower, in a private tomb, as the tradition says. The really important thing, of course, is what his followers claimed happened next.

Christianity is rooted in the belief that God raised Jesus from the dead. I've already pointed out why historians can't claim that that the resurrection of Jesus probably happened. Even if it did happen, historians would have no way of demonstrating it, given the limitations of what can be appealed to as historical evidence. Historians can only establish what probably happened in the past, and a miracle of this nature is so highly improbable—that's why we call it a miracle—that a historian just can't say that it probably happened. Moreover, the sources concerning the resurrection of Jesus are hopelessly contradictory, as you'll see if you simply read all of the accounts and compare what they say with one another; it's almost impossible to straighten out what happened. Who went to Jesus' tomb? How many people went? What were their names? What did they see when they got there? Whom did they meet? What were they told? What was the result? All of these things are different among our various accounts.

If you wanted to do a simple comparison, just compare Matthew and Luke about what the disciples are supposed to do. Matthew's disciples are told, "Go to Galilee to meet Jesus," and they go, and they meet him. In Luke, the disciples are told, "Don't leave Jerusalem," and they stay in Jerusalem, and meet Jesus. Which is it? In Luke's Gospel, they stay there until the day of Pentecost, 50 days later. Which is it? These Gospels have contradictions about what happened at the resurrection.

As a result of the limitations of our discipline, and the problems posed by our sources, there are some things that we simply cannot affirm as historians about the resurrection. We can't, first of all, affirm that Jesus was really raised, as I've indicated. I'm not saying that you have to deny that he was raised; I'm saying as a historian, you just can't say. Secondly, we can't say that he was buried in a private tomb; we don't know that. We can't, third, say that three days later, that the tomb was empty. Nor can we say that three days later the disciples claimed it was empty. We only know that at a later time, they said that they had said three days later the tomb was empty, if you see what I mean. Nor do we even know that all of the remaining disciples, apart from Judas, actually became believers. We don't actually know that.

What we do know, though, is important. We do know for a fact that some of Jesus' disciples, maybe all of them, maybe most of them, at least a few of them, disciples who knew that Jesus had been killed, at some later time claimed that his tomb was visited by some of his women followers three days later and they found it empty. These people also claim to have seen him alive afterwards. These people came to believe that Jesus had been raised from the dead, and this claim completely changed their lives, and the history of our world ever since.

Lecture Twenty-Three
The Afterlife of Jesus

Scope:

The religion of Christianity is probably best understood as having begun not with Jesus' ministry, his death, or his resurrection, but with the belief in his resurrection among some of his followers. These first Christians were themselves Jewish apocalypticists, who believed that God would raise the dead at the end of time. Once they came to think that Jesus had been raised, they drew the logical conclusion: With Jesus' resurrection, the end had already begun. Moreover, because Jesus was the first to be raised, he was obviously a significant figure in God's plan to destroy the forces of evil. Christians who held such views had difficulty convincing non-Christian Jews who were expecting a person of grandeur, not a weak, crucified criminal. Jews and Christians engaged in heated debates over these passages. Even then, not every Christian understood Jesus in the same way. In most instances, the beliefs about Jesus that emerged were far removed from what the man himself was really like.

Outline

I. We can't really say that Christianity began with Jesus' preaching, because Christianity is rooted in a belief in Jesus' death for the sins of the world and his resurrection from the dead.

   A. Whereas Jesus preached about the Son of Man, who was soon to come in judgment against the earth, the early Christians preached about Jesus, who had died and been raised from the dead. Or, to use an old formula, the early Christians appear to have taken the religion *of* Jesus and made it into a religion *about* Jesus.

   B. Nor can we say that the new religion began with Jesus' death, because without a resurrection, Jesus' death is just another tragic death among thousands, even millions, of tragic deaths throughout history.

   C. Nor can we say, at least as historians, that the new religion began with Jesus' resurrection, both because historians are unable to affirm on historical grounds that the resurrection happened (i.e., it's a matter of faith, not historical demonstration) and because if Jesus had been raised and no one believed it, Christianity still wouldn't have started.

D. Christianity, then, began with the belief in Jesus' resurrection. How did belief in the resurrection affect how Jesus' followers understood who he was and what he taught?

II. It is important to remember who Jesus' followers were. We know some of them by name: Simon Peter, James, John, and some other disciples, along with several women, such as Mary Magdalene.

   A. We can assume that they were followers of Jesus precisely because they agreed with or were persuaded by his message. This means, then, that even before Jesus died, his closest followers—the ones who later came to believe that he had been raised from the dead—were Jewish apocalypticists.

   B. Now comes the key question: What would a Jewish apocalypticist think about the resurrection of a great man of God?

      1. Recall: Apocalypticists believed that the dead would be resurrected when God came in judgment. Such a person who came to believe that Jesus was raised from the dead would draw an obvious conclusion: The end of the age has begun (cf. 1Cor. 15–20).

      2. It is also significant that Jesus was the first raised: He is the one who has inaugurated the beginning of the end.

      3. The early disciples concluded that the end had started and that God had chosen Jesus to defeat the cosmic forces of evil aligned against him. Jesus had been exalted to heaven, but he was soon to return in judgment on the earth.

   E. Thus, belief in Jesus began to affect how people understood who he was in relation to God, the world, and the salvation of the human race.

      1. During Jesus' life, he had talked about God as father and likened him to a kindly parent. His followers came to think that Jesus was the one and only Son of God.

      2. During Jesus' life, he had talked about the coming Son of Man who would arrive on the clouds of heaven in a mighty act of judgment against God's enemies. His followers came to think that he himself had been raised up into heaven and began to speak of him as the coming judge of earth, the Son of Man.

3. During Jesus' life, he talked about the kingdom of God that was soon to arrive and evidently maintained that he would have a place of prominence in it. His followers came to think that that was precisely what would happen; Jesus would reign as the future ruler, the King of the Jews, the Messiah.

4. During Jesus' life, he talked about implementing the ethics of the kingdom. His followers came to think that the kingdom had already begun and that he was already its ruler. In fact, he was ruler of all things in heaven and earth—the Lord of all.

F. In a relatively brief time, the disciples shifted their attention away from the imminent arrival of the Son of Man and the kingdom of God onto Jesus himself, whose resurrection revealed that he was the Son of God, the Son of Man, the Messiah, and the Lord.

III. Jesus' early followers, though, had considerable difficulty trying to convince other Jews of their claims. We have seen that Jews at the time had a range of expectations of what the future messiah would be like.

A. Some saw him as a great warrior figure like King David, one who would take up arms against the foreign oppressor, drive him out of the land, and reestablish Israel as a sovereign state.

B. Others saw the messiah as: a cosmic figure of power who would come from heaven to destroy God's enemies or a mighty priest who was authorized by God to deliver divinely inspired interpretations of God's law. In every case, the messiah was a figure of power and grandeur.

C. Jesus, of course, was none of these things, but an itinerant preacher from rural Galilee who was crucified as a common criminal. Jesus' death showed most Jews that he was *not* the messiah. Most considered the idea that he was the messiah to be blasphemous.

1. Christians today tend to think that Jesus was crucified, because that was what the messiah was supposed to do.

2. Before Christianity, we have no indication that any Jew anywhere thought that the messiah would suffer and die, even for the sins of the world. Not a single reference exists to any such idea in any Jewish text—including the Hebrew Bible—before Christianity.
4. Why then do Christians assume that that is what the Jewish messiah *was* supposed to do? Because that's what the early Christians concluded based on what they already knew about Jesus.

C. Early Christians began searching their Scriptures to see how these things could be.
1. The Hebrew Bible did not discuss the messiah's suffering. Some passages refer to the suffering of a righteous man (cf. Isaiah 53), who feels abandoned by God, but whose suffering is accepted as a sacrifice for others.
2. Some passages, such as the Psalms of Lament (e.g., Pss. 22, 35, 69) and the songs of the Suffering Servant of the Lord in the book of Isaiah (Isaiah 53), were taken to refer not just to *any* person who was suffering, or even to Israel as a whole (cf. Isaiah 49:3), but to the future messiah of Israel.
4. Jews and Christians began to debate the meanings of these texts, and the debates continue to this day.

D. The point is that early Christians began to interpret Jesus differently once they came to believe that he had been raised from the dead, and they soon began to make exalted claims about him that they then went to their Scriptures to try to support.

IV. Different Christian communities developed different understandings of who Jesus was. For the early Jewish followers of Jesus, it made perfect sense to call Jesus the Son of Man.
A. That meant that he was the cosmic judge coming from heaven referred to in Dan. 7:13–14.
B. But what would the term mean to later communities of Christians made
up of converted pagans who didn't know Dan. 7:13–14? It would probably mean not that Jesus was some kind of divine figure, but that he was a human—the Son of Man.

C. The early Jewish followers of Jesus would have had a clear view of what it meant to call Jesus the Son of God.

    1. In the Hebrew Bible, the Son of God refers to any human being who was specially chosen by God to mediate his will on earth—like King Solomon of old (2 Sam. 7:14).

    2. To Christians who were converted pagans, it would probably mean not that Jesus was a human who was in close standing with God, but that he was actually divine—the Son of God!

D. Eventually, Christians proclaimed both things about Jesus—that he was the Son of Man and the Son of God, both human and divine.

    1. By the end of the first century, with the Gospel of John, we know of Christians who called Jesus "God."

    2. This was obviously far removed from what Jesus himself said. Jesus was an apocalyptic prophet of the coming kingdom; the Christians came to think of him as the creator of the universe. It's an astounding difference.

E. The various notions of who Jesus was affected the way each Christian community told its stories about Jesus. This seems to be a certain fact of history; otherwise, one could never explain why the stories were changed so frequently and in such different ways.

    1. Christians who continued to be convinced that Jesus was a righteous man, but nothing more than a man, would obviously remember his sayings far differently from Christians who believed that Jesus was God himself.

    2. The Gospels we have inherited reflect these differences. They do not really all say the same thing.

    3. As historians, we cannot take any one of these accounts at face value as preserving a portrait of Jesus as he really was. Instead, we need to sift through each of these portraits carefully and cautiously, seeking to determine the words and deeds of the man who stands behind them all.

Essential Reading:

Ehrman, *Jesus: Apocalyptic Prophet*, chap. 13.

Frederiksen, *From Jesus to Christ.*

Hurtado, *One God, One Lord.*

Suggested Reading:

Brown, *Death of the Messiah.*

Dunn, *Christology in the Making.*

Questions to Consider:

1. Take a passage such as Psalm 22 or Isaiah 52:13–53:12 and try to explain how an early Christian might interpret it to support the view that the messiah had to suffer and be raised from the dead. Then try to explain how an early Jew might interpret it in a completely different way.

2. Imagine an early debate between a non-Jewish Christian and a non-Christian Jew over whether Jesus was the messiah. What would be the strongest arguments on both sides?

For further background on the development of early Christian thought on Jesus, as reflected in Scripture, non-canonical writings, and other sources, we recommend the course *The New Testament,* also by Professor Ehrman.

Lecture Twenty-Three—Transcript
The Afterlife of Jesus

In the last lecture, we saw that even though historians are relatively well informed about Jesus' last days and hours, including his death, they're handicapped when it comes to talking about his resurrection. For one thing, our sources are full of discrepancies on almost every point in their accounts of what happened when Jesus was raised from the dead. Even if they weren't full of discrepancies, however, we'd have to take seriously the fact that these accounts were produced by people who believed that Jesus had been raised, who were retelling stories about that event that had been in circulation for several decades among believers, who were using the stories, in numerous instances, in order to get other people also to believe. In other words, these are not disinterested accounts by outside observers. These are accounts by people who have a vested interest in the stories themselves.

Even more seriously, since the resurrection of Jesus involves a miracle, that is, an event that by its very nature defies all probability, the historian, given the limits of the discipline, can never say that it "probably" happened. I should stress that I'm not saying that historians have to say, "It didn't happen." Historians simply don't have access to miraculous events of the past. If the miracles did happen, the historian has no way to demonstrate that they happened. One thing that historians probably can say did happen, though, and can say it, in fact, with utmost certainty, is that sometime after Jesus' death, whether three days, three months, or three years, sometime after Jesus' death, some of his followers began to claim that he had been raised from the dead. That much is certain. That claim transformed our world.

It might be useful to take a moment to reflect on the question of when Christianity actually began as a religion. When did Christianity as a religion come into being? We can't really say that Christianity began with Jesus' preaching, because Christianity is a religion that's rooted in a belief in Jesus' death for the sins of the world, and his resurrection from the dead. Whereas Jesus preached about the Son of Man, who was soon to come to earth in judgment against all those aligned against God, the early Christians preached about Jesus, who had died and been raised from the dead. There's a difference between what Jesus was preaching in his ministry and what Christians preached about Jesus; or to use an old formula that's been around for a long time, the early Christians appear to have taken the religion of Jesus and made it into a religion about Jesus. They took the religion of Jesus and made it into a religion about Jesus, so that we really can't say that Christianity began with Jesus' own proclamation. Nor can we say that the new religion began with Jesus' death, because without a resurrection, Jesus' death is just another tragic death among thousands, even millions, of tragic deaths throughout the history of the world.

We can't say, though, that the new religion began with Jesus' resurrection, both because historians are unable to affirm on historical grounds that a resurrection happened; that is, belief in resurrection is a matter of faith, not of historical demonstration, and because, if Jesus had been raised from the dead, and no one believed it, Christianity still wouldn't have started. I think what we have to say, then, is that Christianity began not with Jesus' preaching, not with his death, and not with his resurrection, but that Christianity began with the belief in Jesus' resurrection.

The first question I want to pursue in this lecture is how belief in Jesus' resurrection among his followers affected the way that they understood who he was, and what he taught. How did the fact that they believed he was raised from the dead affect what they thought about him and how they understood his teaching? To begin to answer the question, it's important to remember who Jesus' followers were. Who were these people who were Jesus' followers, who later interpreted him and his teachings?

We know some of them by name. We have lists of the twelve disciples in several of our Gospels; Mark and Luke give different lists, but some names are in common among them. We know a few things about a few of these disciples; for example, Simon Peter, James, and John, who were thought to be the three closest disciples to Jesus. We know the names of some of the others of the twelve. We know the names of several women, such as Mary Magdalene, who was a woman who was a close companion with Jesus. By the way, Mary Magdalene in the New Testament is not said to be a prostitute; that's a later tradition that floated round about her. There's nothing about her in the New Testament indicating that she herself was a prostitute. Later traditions indicated that she was a prostitute. Some later traditions actually indicate she and Jesus were very close to one another, so much so that some of the male disciples were somewhat jealous of their relationship. There have always been traditions floating around that Jesus and Mary had some kind of an intimate personal relationship, too. All of those are legendary materials. We know very little about her except that she was one of Jesus' close followers.

We can assume that all of these people were Jesus' followers, precisely because they agreed with, or were persuaded by, his message. That's why they followed him. This means, then, that even before Jesus died, his closest followers, the ones who later came to believe that he had been raised from the dead, his closest followers during his lifetime, were Jewish apocalypticists. If they weren't Jewish apocalypticists, they wouldn't have had as their master Jesus, who was preaching a Jewish apocalyptic message. If we want to know how belief in Jesus' resurrection affected his followers, it's significant that they were apocalypticists prior to their belief in the resurrection. The key question is, how would a Jewish apocalypticist think about the resurrection of a great man of God? They think Jesus is a great man of God. They came to think he got raised from the dead. What conclusions would they draw?

I find it interesting that many Christians today, probably most Christians I run into, my undergraduate students, have extremely fuzzy notions about what it means to say that Jesus was raised from the dead. If you try and press one of my undergraduates, for example, on their belief in this, though they believe Jesus was raised, if you ask them "What does it mean, exactly?" they'll have very unclear, unfocused ideas about it. Everything from "It must mean that Jesus is God"—you're never sure why; what's the logic? If Jesus is raised, why does that make him God? When Lazarus was raised from the dead, does it mean that Lazarus was God? Well … . When you start pressing people, they haven't thought about it much. Everything from Baptists saying, "It's hard to keep a good man down" kind of thing, Jesus was good and so God raised him from the dead, but they don't have very clear notions about what it might mean. If they were Jewish apocalypticists, there wouldn't be any fuzzy notion at all about it. It'd be crystal-clear, what it would mean for a man to be raised from the dead.

Remember what Jewish apocalypticists believed. They believed that this was an evil age, that God was soon going to intervene, overthrow the forces of evil, and bring in a day of judgment. On that day of judgment, at the end of this age, when the time had been fulfilled for this age to end, there was going to be a resurrection of dead people. If that's what a person believes, and they come to think that Jesus was raised from the dead, they would draw an obvious conclusion. The resurrection of Jesus shows that the end of our age has begun already.

This in fact was the conclusion that the early Christians drew. We know this because we have some of their writings. The earliest author we have in the New Testament is the apostle Paul. He's writing about 20 years after Jesus' death, but he's our earliest author. It's striking what he thinks of Jesus' resurrection. In 1 Corinthians 15, he tries to convince his Corinthian readers that there's going to be a future resurrection; people by this time had already begun to deny that that was going to happen. Paul wants to show that it will happen, and he does so by showing them that since they think Jesus was raised from the dead, they necessarily have to think that there is a resurrection of the dead. In that context, Paul calls Jesus "the first fruits of the resurrection" (1 Corinthians chapter 15).

"The first fruits of the resurrection." What does that mean? In fact, it's an agricultural image. When farmers harvest their crops, the first day of the harvest, they go out, they bring in the crops, and that night, they have a festival, a party. They celebrate the first fruits. The next day, of course, they go out and collect the rest of the harvest. By calling Jesus the "first fruits," Paul is saying that he's the first to rise from the dead; the rest is going to come soon. These apocalyptic Jews naturally thought they were living at the end of time. This was confirmation of Jesus' message that the end was imminent.

In addition, though, these early followers of Jesus must have found it to be supremely significant that it was Jesus who was the first one raised. Jesus, then, was thought to have inaugurated the beginning of the end. The early disciples concluded on these grounds that the end had started, and that God had chosen Jesus to defeat the cosmic forces of evil that were aligned against him. They thought, in fact, that Jesus had been exalted to heaven, but that he was soon to return in judgment on the Earth. For these people, the resurrection of Jesus just didn't mean that his body got reanimated. It meant that God had reversed Jesus' death. Death was destroyed. Jesus was brought back to life, not to die again, like Lazarus, or Jairus' daughter, the people in the Bible who get raised from the dead. For the early Christians, Jesus was raised from the dead, and he's not going to die again. He's in heaven now with God, and he's going to come back in judgment on the Earth.

In other words, the belief in Jesus began significantly to affect how people understood—people began to understand—his relationship to God, to the world, and to the salvation of the human race. Because he was raised changed everything these people thought about Jesus. I want to consider the changes of their views of Jesus several ways, by showing you how people began to think differently about Jesus once they thought that he was resurrected.

His followers, of course, knew during his lifetime that Jesus had talked about God as a father, likening God to a kindly parent who'll give his children what they need. Once his followers came to think that Jesus got raised from the dead, they began to think that God really was Jesus' father, in a unique way; that in fact Jesus was the one and only "Son of God." During Jesus' lifetime, he talked about the coming Son of Man, who would arrive on the clouds of heaven in a mighty act of judgment against God's enemies. His followers thought, once they came to believe he had been raised, that he himself was coming back from heaven; in other words, that Jesus was the Son of Man. During his lifetime, Jesus talked about the kingdom of God that was soon to arrive, and he evidently maintained that he would have a place of prominence in it. After they began believing in his resurrection, his followers came to think that that was precisely what would happen, that Jesus would reign as the future ruler, King of the Jews, the Messiah. During Jesus' lifetime, he talked about the need to implement the ethics of the kingdom, instructing his followers that if they followed his teachings, they would already begin to experience a foretaste of the kingdom in the present. His followers came to think that the kingdom had already begun with his resurrection, that he was already its ruler now, in fact. His followers after the resurrection started thinking that he was

the ruler of all things on heaven and earth; he was the Lord of all.

What I'm trying to show is that within a relatively brief time, when the disciples of Jesus began thinking he was raised from the dead, they started shifting the focus of their attention away from the imminent arrival of the Son of Man and the kingdom of God that was to appear, onto Jesus himself, whose resurrection revealed to them that he was the Son of God, the Son of Man, the Messiah, and the Lord of all.

These things being said about Jesus were fairly different from what Jesus, evidently, himself was proclaiming, at least in public. Jesus' early followers found that it was rather difficult to convince other people about these claims concerning Jesus. These followers were themselves Jews. They lived as Jews. They lived among Jews. Thus, the first people they tried to convince about Jesus were their fellow Jews. They wanted to convince their fellow Jews that Jesus was all these things; the Son of God, the Son of Man, the Messiah, Lord. They found it rather difficult.

We've seen already that Jews at that time had a range of expectations of what the future Messiah would be like. These expectations are what made it difficult for most Jews to accept that Jesus was the Messiah. Some Jews thought of the future Messiah as a great warrior figure, like King David, who would take up arms against the foreign oppressor, drive them out of the land, and reestablish Israel as a sovereign state. This is a future political messiah figure. Others saw a future Messiah as being a cosmic figure of power, who would come from heaven to destroy God's enemies. Others saw the future Messiah as a mighty priest, who was authorized by God to deliver his divinely inspired interpretation of the law. In all of these cases, the future Messiah was a figure of grandeur and power. Jesus, of course, was none of these things. Jesus was widely known, insofar as he was known, to be an itinerant preacher from rural Galilee, who offended the authorities, and so was crucified as a common criminal. To say that this preacher, crucified for crimes against the state, was the Messiah struck most Jews as completely ludicrous. It struck many Jews, in fact, as being beyond ludicrous, as being blasphemous against God.

Christians today tend to think that, of course, Jesus got crucified, because that's what was supposed to happen to the Messiah. I need to re-emphasize, though, that prior to Christianity, we have no indication that any Jew, anywhere, at any time, thought that the Messiah was going to suffer and die, not even suffer and die for the sins of the world. There's not a solitary reference to any such idea, in any pre-Christian Jewish text, including the Hebrew Bible. Why, then, do Christians assume that this is what the Jewish Messiah was supposed to do? Why do Christians assume that the Messiah was supposed to suffer and die? Many Christians have difficulty understanding why Jews don't accept Jesus as the Messiah. Many of my undergraduates don't understand. Jews can be so blind. Their thinking is that the Messiah was supposed to suffer and be raised from the dead; Jesus did suffer and was raised from the dead; why are they so blind as not to accept it? What they don't realize is that Jews weren't expecting a Messiah who was going to suffer and be raised from the dead.

Why did Christians in the early church say that that's what the Messiah was supposed to do, if no Jews prior to that time had said so themselves? It's because the early Christians believed that Jesus was the Messiah, and they knew that he suffered and died. They concluded, therefore, that the Messiah had to suffer and die. It's because they believed this was the Messiah. That's why they began passing around the idea that the Messiah had to suffer, even though there weren't Jews prior to that time who thought so. Early Christians, then, were in a bind when they were trying to convince Jews that Jesus was the Messiah, because Jesus wasn't at all what a Messiah was supposed to be like. How did Christians deal with this problem?

They did what you would expect Jews to do. They started looking at their sacred scriptures to try and find evidence that what had happened was in fact predicted in the prophets. They couldn't find passages that said the Messiah was going to suffer and die because these passages don't exist. Christians today appeal to certain passages, such as Isaiah chapter 53, in support of the idea that the Messiah has to suffer and die, a passage that talks about "the suffering servant of the Lord." Isaiah 53, which says, "He was wounded for our transgressions, bruised for our iniquities. The chastisement for our peace was upon him. By his wounds we were healed."

"That sounds like what Jesus did; he suffered for us." Yes, but Isaiah 53 does not talk about the Messiah. Read the passage carefully. The term Messiah never appears there. It's not talking about the Messiah, it's talking about somebody called "the servant of the Lord." "Well, yeah, but that was the Messiah." Maybe. Jews prior to Christianity never interpreted Isaiah 53 as referring to the Messiah, who was going to suffer. In fact, the Book of Isaiah itself tells you who this servant of the Lord is, who suffers for the sake of the people. Isaiah chapter 49, verse 3; Who is the servant? "'You are my servant, oh Israel,' says the Lord." Israel, who suffers its exile during the Babylonians; those who are taken into exile suffer for the sake of the people. That's at least how most Jews interpreted Isaiah 53. Christians came along, though, early Christians, and wanted to find scriptural support for their belief that the Messiah must suffer. They turned to passages like Isaiah 53 and said, "This isn't referring to Israel; this is referring to Israel's Messiah." Jews would look at this passage and say, "No, it's not." This is where the arguments emerged.

Isaiah 53 wasn't the only passage that Jewish Christians would look at. There are a number of passages in the Hebrew Bible that refer to the suffering of a righteous man, who feels abandoned by God, but whose suffering is accepted as a sacrifice for others; for example, Psalm 22. Let me quote some of the verses from Psalm 22. They'll sound familiar to people who know only the New Testament: "My God, my God, why have you forsaken me?" Psalm 22, verse 1.

> All who see me, mock me. They make mouths at me, they shake their heads.
>
> I am poured out like water, and all my bones are out of joint.
>
> My mouth is dried up like a potsherd, and my tongue sticks to my jaw.
>
> A company of evil-doers encircles me. My hands and feet have shriveled.
>
> I can count all my bones. They stare and gloat over me.
>
> They divide my garments among them, and for my clothing they cast lots.

This is a psalm written by a person who's describing the suffering of a righteous man, whose sufferings ultimately are vindicated. Even though the passage doesn't mention any future Messiah—these are all things talked about in the past or the present tense—Christians would read these passages and say, "Aha! These are referring to what the Messiah was going to be like."

In fact, when Christians thought about these texts, they started thinking about them in light of Jesus' crucifixion and suffering, that these passages are referring to Jesus. As a result, when they started thinking about Jesus' crucifixion, and his suffering, they started thinking about that in light of these passages. These passages helped them make sense of what had happened to Jesus, and so when they told stories about Jesus, they took phrases from these passages and put them into the account. It's no surprise, for example, hanging on the cross, our earliest source, Mark. Jesus cries out the words of Psalm 22: "My God, my God, why have you forsaken me?" It's an allusion to the suffering of the righteous man in the Psalm. They divide his clothes by taking lots. Why do they do that? Because that's what the Psalm said.

In other words, Christians read the events of Jesus' death in light of their knowledge of scripture. Jews, though, who didn't accept these interpretations of these passages as referring to a future Messiah disagreed with the interpretations and disagreed, then, that Jesus was the one. These debates between Jews and Christians have gone on for centuries, over the meaning of the Jewish scriptures. They are debates that continue to go on today.

My point is that the early Christians began to interpret Jesus differently once they came to believe that he was raised from the dead, and very soon they began to make exalted claims about him; that they then went back to their scriptures in order to try to support. Moreover, different Christian communities developed different understandings of who Jesus was. For the early Jewish followers of Jesus, it made perfect sense to say that Jesus was the Son of Man. Jesus had preached about the coming Son of Man based on this passage that we saw in Daniel chapter 7, a cosmic judge who's coming from heaven, in order to bring in the kingdom. What happens, though, when people talk about Jesus the Son of Man and start telling non-Jews this? What happens when they start telling pagans that Jesus was the Son of Man, especially pagans who don't know what Daniel chapter 7, verses 13 and 14 say? What do pagans think it means to call Jesus the Son of Man? They'd probably think it would mean not that Jesus was some kind of divine cosmic judge, but that he was the son of a human being, in other words, that he himself is human. That's how Gentiles came to understand the term "Son of Man." It means he's human.

What would Jewish followers of Jesus mean when they called him the Son of God? In the Hebrew Bible, "Son of God" refers to human beings, who are chosen by God to mediate His will on Earth; for example: King Solomon. In 2 Samuel chapter 7, verse 14. He's the

"Son of God." It doesn't mean he's divine, it means that he's a human who mediates God's will. Jews, then, would mean something like that by "Son of God." What would Gentiles think if you called somebody the Son of God? They'd probably think that this is somebody who's half divine. He's God's actual son. "Son of God" for Gentiles means that Jesus is divine.

You see, what's happened is, for Jewish communities to say Jesus is the "Son of Man" means he's divine, "Son of God" means he's human. For Gentile communities it's just the opposite. "Son of Man" means he's human. "Son of God" means he's divine. The meanings end up getting reversed. Eventually, the Christians came to proclaim both things about Jesus. He's both "Son of Man" and "Son of God;" by that, they meant that he's both human and divine.

Already by the end of the first century, from the Gospel of John, we know that Christians are actually calling Jesus not some kind of divine being; they're actually calling Jesus "God." By the end of the first century, Christians are calling Jesus "God." This is obviously far removed from what Jesus himself ever said. Jesus was an apocalyptic prophet of the coming kingdom. The Christians came to think of him as the creator of the Universe. It's an astounding difference.

The various notions of who Jesus was in these various Christian communities, some mainly Jewish, some mainly Gentile, first-century, affected the way each community told its stories about Jesus. This seems to be a certain fact of history, that these different communities are telling stories differently about Jesus, depending on who's in the community and how they've interpreted Jesus in light of the resurrection. It's almost certain that this is happening. Otherwise, you can't explain why the stories of Jesus were changed so frequently and in so many ways. Christians who continue to be convinced that Jesus was a righteous man, nothing more than a man, who proclaimed the imminent end of the world, would obviously remember his own sayings far differently from Christians who thought that Jesus was God Himself, who could provide eternal life in the here and now.

The Gospels we've inherited reflect these differences among these different communities, believe different things about Jesus. When these different Gospels with different perspectives are embodied into a solitary canon of Scripture, it causes people to overlook their distinctive perspectives and to assume these Gospels are all basically saying the same thing. By putting the different Gospels into one canon, it leads people to think the Gospels are all saying the same thing. A historical perspective shows, though, that with the Gospels, each has its own take on who Jesus was. This historical perspective also shows that we are unable simply to take any one of these accounts at face value, as preserving a portrait of Jesus as he really was. Instead, we need to sift through each of these portraits carefully and cautiously, seeking to determine the actual words and deeds of the man who stands behind them all.

Lecture Twenty-Four
The Prophet of the New Millennium

Scope:

Ever since Jesus' day, some of his followers have continued to insist that his proclamation of the imminent end of the age is literally true, and some have set dates for when it will happen. One such case is Edgar Whisenant, whose book, *88 Reasons Why the Rapture Will Occur in 1988*, made an impact on parts of American Christendom. Another is one of the best-selling authors of all time, Hal Lindsey, whose descriptions of the end times have been read by millions. This phenomenon is not recent; nearly every generation from the beginning of Christianity until today has had its doomsday prophets, who have declared that their own generations would be the last. Two things can be said about every single one of these predictors of doom: every single one of them has been incontrovertibly wrong, and they all have been able to base their predictions, in part, on the words of Jesus. In this lecture, we will investigate such prophecies and argue that Jesus' message must be understood in its context to be fully understood. It cannot be moved to our context to predict the end times.

Outline

I.   We have now completed our study of the historical Jesus. We have covered all the available sources for reconstructing his life and have discussed historical criteria that can be used to get behind the later portrayals of his life in the Gospels to see what the man himself was really like.

   A. We have used these criteria to try to paint a coherent picture of what he said, what he did, and why he died.

   1. My thesis for the second half of the course has been that Jesus was an apocalypticist who expected the imminent end of the age with the coming of a cosmic figure of judgment from heaven.

   2. I've tried to show that all the sayings and deeds of Jesus that can be accepted as historically reliable fit well into this apocalyptic framework.

   3. I have begun to show, in the last lecture, how Jesus' own religion was transformed by his followers as soon as they came to believe that he had been raised from the dead.

B. In this lecture, I want to talk about a different kind of transformation of Jesus' teaching, one whose impact is still with us today.

    1. This transformation involves adhering literally to some of his teachings when the situation has drastically changed.

    2. Since Jesus' time, some people have continued to believe that the world will end soon. Most of them have based their beliefs on the teachings of Jesus. Even though every single one of these prophets of doom, from the second century to the 20th century, has been incontrovertibly wrong about their predictions, the business of predicting the end of the age continues to be alive and well.

    3. I would like to mention a couple of the more interesting figures, starting closer to our own time.

II. The year 1988 was supposed to be the year the world ended. Proof was given in a widely distributed and remarkably influential booklet entitled *88 Reasons Why the Rapture Will Occur in 1988* by Edgar Whisenant, a former NASA rocket engineer.

    A. True to its title, the book enumerated biblical and logical reasons why 1988 would be the year that history would begin to end, and how.

        1. Sometime during the Jewish festival of Rosh Hashanah, Sept. 11–13, 1988, Jesus Christ would return from heaven to remove his followers from earth (the "rapture"), before a seven-year period of cataclysmic disaster on earth (the "tribulation").

        2. The tribulation would begin at "sunset 3 October 1988," when the Soviet Union invaded Israel and began World War III. The crises that ensued would lead to the rise of an agent of Satan who would lead millions away from God and declare himself to be divine.

        3. He would then try to take over the world's governments, leading to a thermonuclear war on Oct. 4, 1995, which would devastate the United States ("you can walk from

Little Rock to Dallas over ashes only"). The world would be thrown into nuclear winter (temperatures would never rise above −150° F), and the food and water supply would be eliminated.

D. Even though the book may sound like a quaint bit of Christian science fiction, it was read as Gospel truth by a surprising number of sincere and devout Christians. Within months, over 2 million copies were sold.

    1. Many Christians pointed out that such precision is unbiblical, because Jesus is recorded as saying, "But of that day and hour no one knows, not even the angels of heaven, nor the Son, but the Father only" (Matt. 24:36).

    2. Whisenant was unfazed. After all, he had not predicted "the day and hour" of the end, just the week.

E. To buttress his "88 Reasons," Whisenant used biblical quotations that co-literalists had a hard time refuting, e.g.:

From the fig tree learn its lesson: as soon as its branch becomes tender and puts forth its leaves, you know that summer is near. So also, when you see all these things, you know that he is near, at the very gates. Truly I say to you, this generation will not pass away until all these things take place. (Matt. 24:32–34)

    1. Whisenant pointed out that in the Bible, the "fig tree" is often used of the nation of Israel. The fig tree "putting forth its leaves" is a reference to Israel's coming back to life after a long hiatus.

    2. Because the modern state of Israel was established in 1948 and because a generation in the Bible is forty years—*voilà!*—1988 must be the year of the end time.

F. Whisenant claimed that many other biblical predictions, most of them highly complex, pointed to exactly the same time. One of the simpler examples was in Leviticus 26:28. God tells the people of Israel that if they are disobedient, they will be punished "sevenfold" for their sins.

    1. Whisenant takes this to mean a punishment lasting seven "years," and he notes that in the Jewish lunar calendar, a year consists of 360 days. Moreover, in a number of biblical texts (for example, Numbers 14:34), God reckons one day as a year. This means that the punishment was to last 7 x 360 years, or 2,520 years in all.

3. According to the book of Daniel, Israel's punishment was to begin with the seventy-year oppression of Israel by the Babylonians, which started, according to Whisenant, with the reign of the monarch Nebuchadnezzar in 602 B.C. and ended in 532 B.C.

4. If the time of Israel's punishment is to last an additional 2,520 years, that happens to bring us up to ... surprise!—1988.

G. When 1988 came and went, Whisenant did not retract his views, but simply argued that he had made a slight miscalculation. In a second book published soon after his predictions had failed, he urged that 1989 would be the year!

III. The end never did come, of course. But the constant and inevitable failure of such projects to materialize has never seemed to have the slightest effect on their popularity. A clear case in point comes from one of the best-selling authors of the modern period, an evangelical Christian named Hal Lindsay.

A. Lindsay may well be the most read author of the 20th century. His most famous book, *The Late Great Planet Earth*, was *the* best-selling work of nonfiction of the 1970s, with over 28 million copies in print.

B. Lindsay was a savvy observer of the times with a knack for relating to, even mesmerizing, the average mildly interested reader—especially college students.

1. His book reads like a detective novel and is packed with anecdotes, plausible historical scenarios, and predictions of mass destruction.

2. Writing in 1970, Lindsay saw the world as the stage of God's historical activities and the Bible as the blueprint.

3. Lindsay calculated that a world war would break out in the Middle East in 1989, leading to an invasion of the oil-thirsty Soviet Union, a nuclear counterattack of a ten-nation European commonwealth, and the invasion of an army of 200 million Chinese.

4. At the end of it all, only the European commonwealth would be left, headed by a charismatic leader who was none other than the anti-Christ. The commonwealth would unleash its nuclear arsenals, destroying the major cities of earth.

5. When there appeared to be no hope, God would intervene once and for all. Christ would appear from heaven to overthrow the forces of evil and set up his kingdom on earth.

C. Lindsey insisted that his portrayal of future events is rooted completely in the Scriptures, which accurately portrayed the future of our planet.

1. The problem, of course, is that this claim has been made by every Christian doomsday prophet from the beginning. As always happens, when the predictions do not occur, the prophets must go back to the drawing board.

2. What is most intriguing is that the evangelistic fervor never dies down with each successive edition.

3 When it appeared to Lindsay that it wasn't going to happen as predicted, he wrote another book, *1980s: Countdown to Armageddon*, arguing that everything was going according to plan. The book was on *The New York Times* bestseller list for 21 weeks.

D. Evidently, Lindsey's reputation has not been tarnished a whit by his failed interpretations or his more recent claims that UFOs are deceptive ruses by demons, who will soon stage a massive UFO landing to mislead earthlings into believing in life on other planets. His books and videos continue to be enormously popular.

IV. If we had more time, we could detail other failed prophecies that have been made throughout the course of Christian history. It is worth noting, at least, that they seem to recur in almost every generation. I'll mention a couple of striking examples, not even dealing with the massive concerns among some believers over the approach of the year 2000.

A. Possibly the most well known American failed prophecy was experienced by the followers of William Miller. Miller was a New York farmer who predicted, on the basis of a careful study of his Bible, that the world would end in a cosmic blaze of glory in 1843. Some among his thousands of followers gave away everything they owned in expectation of the day; some went to court to get everything back later.

B. Even more significant historically were the predictions of the Italian monk, Joachim of Fiore, who demonstrated that the anti-Christ would soon appear and the end of the age would arrive by the year 1260. These predictions played a major role in theological reflections during the later Middle Ages.

C. A thousand years earlier, we find an important group of Christians living in Asia Minor adhering to the teachings of a second-century prophet named Montanus, who claimed that the world was going to end in his own generation. One of the greatest theologians of early Christianity, Tertullian, belonged to this group.

D. Just over a century before that, we find the writings of the apostle Paul, which later came to form part of the New Testament—the earliest Christian writings of any kind that we have. Paul tells his followers that Christ will return from heaven in a mighty act of judgment and remove his followers from the world, both those who had previously died and, in Paul's words, "we who are still alive."

E. These are just a few of the many, many prophets that we know about.

    1. Most of those who have predicted the imminent end of all things are lost in the shrouds of history.

    2. All these predictors of the end have two things in common: Every one of them was completely wrong, and every one of them could cite the words of Jesus in support of his or her views.

V. Let me conclude by telling you my point in making this brief survey.

A. My point is not to stress the fact that Jesus got it wrong.

B. Instead, I think that his earliest followers got something right.

    1. I have to admit to being a bit hesitant to make this point, given the fact that these lectures have been completely based on a historical study of Jesus rather than on any theological set of beliefs—mine, yours, or someone else's.

2. To paraphrase the Hebrew prophet Amos, I myself am neither a theologian nor the son of a theologian. My concerns in these lectures are not theological. If someone were interested in theology, however, he or she might want to take heed of how the early Christians handled their traditions about Jesus.

C. One of the frustrations of the historian of ancient Christianity is that the early Christians did not preserve their traditions about Jesus intact, but modified them for new situations in which they found themselves.

1. As we have seen, Christians had no qualms about making Jesus relevant for new situations, instead of trying to pretend that what was suitable in one context was suitable for another.

2. Their willingness, even eagerness, to do so creates problems for historians who want to know what Jesus actually said and did.

D. But what causes such problems for historians may create great possibilities for theologians—or even believers—who are interested in something more than the plain facts of history.

1. Those who refuse to recognize that every new situation is a new context and that new contexts require a rethinking of old traditions are committing the same error as those who refuse to recognize that Jesus must be understood in his own context.

2. We can't pretend that Jesus lived in our context and interpret his words in light of what they might mean today.

3. We also can't pretend that we live in Jesus' context and that his words are immediately relevant to a different situation.

4. That has always been the downfall of the doomsday predictors: They have taken the words of a first-century Jewish apocalypticist and pretended that they were directed to the context that the predictors themselves were living in. These words may have provided hope for a better day to their original hearers. When they are

removed from their original context and used without remainder in new contexts, they simply become shallow and false.

E. Anyone who is interested in understanding what the words of Jesus might mean in our world cannot apply them directly to the modern situation without seeing how that situation is different from his own.

    1. Applying the teachings of an ancient rabbi to a modern context is not the business of a historian, but of a theologian.

    2. The historian can recognize the dangers in assuming that the context of a person's words and deeds are unimportant either to their meaning or their relevance.

Essential Reading:

Boyer, *When Time Shall Be No More.*

Cohn, *The Pursuit of the Millennium.*

Ehrman, *Jesus: Apocalyptic Prophet*, chaps. 1, 14.

Suggested Reading:

Lindsey, *Late Great Planet Earth.*

Weber, *Living in the Shadow of the Second Coming.*

Wojcik, *The End of the World.*

Questions to Consider:

1. Why do you think so many people are interested in knowing the details of the end? Do the reasons for this modern concern seem to be the same or different from the reasons to be found in an ancient apocalyptic context?

2. For those who do not believe that the end is imminent and who think that Jesus was mistaken to think that it was, is there any relevance to his proclamation of the coming Son of Man? (I do not mean for this question to have an obvious answer.)

Lecture Twenty-Four—Transcript
The Prophet of the New Millennium

We've now completed our study of the historical Jesus. We've covered all of the available sources for reconstructing his life. We've discussed historical criteria that can be used to get behind the later portrayals of his life in the Gospels, to see what the man himself was really like. We've used these criteria to try and paint a coherent picture of what he said, what he did, and why he died.

My overarching thesis for the second half of the course has been that Jesus was an apocalypticist, who expected the imminent end of the age with the coming of a cosmic figure of judgment from heaven. I've tried to show that all of the sayings and deeds of Jesus that can be accepted as historically reliable fit well into that apocalyptic framework. I also began to show, in the last lecture, how Jesus' own religion came to be transformed by his followers as soon as they came to believe that he had been raised from the dead. In this lecture, I want to talk about a different kind of transformation of Jesus' teaching, one whose impact is still with us today. This transformation, interestingly enough, does not involve altering Jesus' teachings in light of a new situation, so much as adhering literally to some of his teachings when the situation itself has drastically changed.

Since Jesus' time, there have continued to be people who believe the world will end soon. Most of them have based their beliefs on the teachings of Jesus, and even though every single one of these prophets of doom, from the second century to the twentieth, has been incontrovertibly wrong about their predictions, the business of predicting the end of the age continues to be alive and well among us today. I won't be able to provide anything like a comprehensive account of all those who have predicted the time of the end, but I would like to mention a couple of the more interesting figures, starting closer to our own time.

I'll begin with 1988, a year that will not go down in the history books as the most significant year of the twentieth century, or even of the 1980s, but it was supposed to be. In fact, it was supposed to be the year of all time. 1988 was to be the year the world ended. Proof was given in a widely distributed and remarkably influential booklet entitled *88 Reasons Why the Rapture Will Occur in 1988*. It was written by a man named Edgar Whisenant, who was a former NASA rocket engineer.

True to its title, the book enumerated biblical and logical reasons why 1988 would be the year that history would begin to end. The scenario that Whisenant painted was remarkably detailed. Sometime during the Jewish festival of Rosh Hashanah, September 11-13, 1988, Jesus Christ would return from heaven to remove his followers from earth. The technical term for this in theological circles is the "rapture." The rapture is when Jesus comes from heaven to return for his followers, and then they are caught up with him, to meet him in the air. The term "rapture", by the way, never occurs in the New Testament, but it's a term that evangelical Christians have long used for this event.

According to Whisenant, Jesus would return from heaven during Rosh Hashanah, 1988, for the rapture. This would lead to a seven-year-period of cataclysmic disaster on the earth, a period that is called, in these same circles, the period of the "tribulation." The tribulation would begin at sunset, on October 3, 1988, when the Soviet Union would invade Israel and so inaugurate World War III. The crises that ensued would lead to the rise of a personal agent of Satan, the anti-Christ, who would lead millions away from God, and, in the midst of worldwide ruin and despair, declare himself to be divine. The anti-Christ would then try to take over the world's government. This would lead, ultimately, to a thermonuclear war on October 4, 1995, a war that would devastate the United States. In Whisenant's words: "You'll be able to walk from Little Rock to Dallas over ashes only." It would also throw the world into nuclear winter, in which temperatures would never rise above 150 degrees below zero. It would also, obviously, eliminate the world's food and water supply. Obviously, it wouldn't be a pretty picture.

Even though this book by Whisenant may sound like a quaint bit of science fiction, it was read as gospel truth by a surprising number of sincere and devout Christians. Within months of its production, over two million copies were in circulation. Numerous Christians, as you might expect, pointed out that the precision Whisenant used to pinpoint the dates, the precision itself was unbiblical. After all, had not Jesus himself recorded a saying, from Matthew's Gospel, chapter 24, "But of that day and hour, no one knows, not even the angels of heaven, nor the Son, but the Father only"? Whisenant, though, was unfazed. He pointed out that he had not predicted the day and hour of the end, only the week.

The 88 reasons that Whisenant provides for his readers are presented, for the most part, as biblically certain prophecies that many co-literalists had difficulty disputing. As just one example, from the same chapter of Matthew, before detailing the cosmic disasters that would happen at the end of time, with the arrival of the kingdom, Jesus gives the following saying. He says:

> From the fig tree learn its lesson: as soon as its branch becomes tender and puts forth its leaves, you know that summer is near. Also, when you see all these things, you know that it is near, at the very gates.

How does one interpret this passage? Whisenant points out that in the Bible, "fig tree" is commonly used to refer to the nation of Israel. What does it mean when the fig tree, then, puts forth its leaves? This is obviously a reference to a fig tree that appears to be dead over the winter period, but then in the springtime, it appears to come back to life. When does Israel, the fig tree, come back to life? It obviously comes back to life when Israel once again begins to be a sovereign state in the land. When was that? In fact, it happened already, 1948, with the establishment of the modern state of Israel. That's when the fig tree puts forth its leaves. "Truly I tell you, this generation will not pass away until all these things take place." How long is a generation in the Bible? 40 years. The end of the age has to happen 40 years after 1948, 1988. This must be the year.

Whisenant claimed that dozens of other biblical predictions all pointed to exactly the same time. Let me just give you one of the other simpler examples. Most of the examples are highly complicated. He loves to crunch these numbers; I guess with his engineering background his is what he liked to do. He was able to do it quite effectively. Let me give you one of the more simple examples. Leviticus chapter 26, verse 28; God tells the people of Israel that if they are disobedient, they will be punished sevenfold for their sins. What does this mean? Whisenant takes it to mean that a punishment of Israel will last seven years—"sevenfold." He also notes that in the Jewish lunar calendar, a year consists of 360 days. In other words, the punishment will last seven times 360. In the Bible, in a number of texts, such as in Numbers 14 verse 34, God reckons one day as a year. This means, then, that the punishment of

Israel, before it can inherit its reward, is to last seven times 360 years, or 2,520 years, all told.

According to the book of Daniel, Israel's punishment was to begin with the 70-year oppression of Israel by the Babylonians, which started, according to Whisenant, with the reign of the monarch Nebuchadnezzar in 602 B.C. It begins in 602 B.C., lasts for 70 years, the Babylonian Captivity; it ends in 532, that's when the punishment of Israel is to last—if the punishment of Israel is to last an additional 2520 years, well, you do the math. From the year 532 B.C., you add 2520 years, and, surprise. 1988. Those are two of his reasons. He gives 86 more that I won't try to detail for you here.

What's particularly striking about this example of Edgar Whisenant, is in fact one of the most common features of the entire phenomenon of date-setting among modern predictors of the end. When 1988 came and went, Whisenant did not at all retract his views. Instead, he argued that he had made a slight miscalculation. He had forgotten, in the midst of all of this number-crunching that he had been doing, that when our modern calendars were established in the sixth century A.D., by Dionysius Exiguus, this monk who set our modern calendars, that he didn't begin our present era with the year zero. He began it with the year one, which means, according to Whisenant, that the first decade of this era only had nine years in it, from one to ten. As a result, his calculations were off by a year. He published another book, arguing that instead of 1988, 1989 was going to be the time of he end.

The end never did come, of course; but the constant and inevitable failure of such projects to materialize has never seemed to have even the slightest effect on their popularity. A clear case in point comes not from an obscure author like Edgar Whisenant, but from one of the best-selling authors of the entire modern period, an evangelical Christian named Hal Lindsay. Even though many people today haven't heard of Hal Lindsay—I asked a class just last week of undergraduates how many of them had heard of Hal Lindsay, and none of them had out of 50 students. If I had asked a class that 15 years ago, half of them would have heard of him. They would have heard of him, because in fact Hal Lindsay may well be, as odd as this might sound, he may well be the most read author of the twentieth century. His most famous book is called *The Late Great Planet Earth*. This book was the best-selling work of non-fiction—I'm using the term loosely, in this case—the best-selling work of non-fiction in the 1970's. It sold more books than anything except for the Bible. Today there are 28 million copies of this book in print.

Lindsay was no number cruncher like Whisenant. He was a savvy observer of the times with an unusual knack for relating to, or even mesmerizing, the average mildly interested reader, especially college students, as it turns out. His book, *The Late Great Planet Earth*, reads like a detective novel. It's filled with anecdotes, plausible historical scenarios, and predictions of mass destruction that was soon to come. Writing in 1970, Lindsay saw the world as the stage of God's historical activities, and the Bible as the blueprint. Using this divinely inspired blueprint, Lindsay could make a precise calculation of what would happen at the end of world history, when a world war would break out in the Middle East, leading to an invasion by the oil-thirsty Soviet Union, a nuclear counter-attack by a ten-nation European commonwealth, and the invasion of a 200 million-strong army of Chinese.

The cataclysm was to commence in the 1980s, and Lindsay was able to provide a precise, blow-by-blow account of troop movements, attacks, counterattacks. At the end of it all, there would be left only the European commonwealth, headed by a charismatic leader who in fact was none other than the anti-Christ, which would unleash its nuclear arsenals, destroying the major cities of earth, and then, when there appears to be absolutely no hope, God would intervene once and for all. Christ will come from heaven, to overthrow the forces of evil and to set up his good kingdom on Earth.

Part of Lindsay's persuasive power lay in his insistence that the portrayal of future events is rooted completely in the scriptural texts, which accurately portrayed the future of our planet as it was to materialize in our own time. The problem, of course, is that this has been the claim of every Christian doomsday prophet since there have been Christian doomsday prophets. In addition, as always happens, when the predictions offered so confidently do not occur, well, the doomsday prophets need to go back to the drawing board and start again. What's most intriguing, though, is, as I've noted, is that the evangelistic fervor of these people never dies down with each successive edition of their books. What they do is, when the prophecies don't become fulfilled, what they do then is write another book, claiming either that more prophecies have been fulfilled so that the picture now is even clearer, and this is what's going to take place next, or they write a book saying, "There was a slight miscalculation before, of X, Y, and Z, but now we see the following," etc.

This was the case with Hal Lindsay himself. He had predicted with confidence that the end was going to come sometime in the mid-1980s. He also used this parable that Whisenant had used of the fig tree, saying that it must happen by 1988 because of the nation of Israel, 40 years after that, etc. When it appeared that this wasn't going to happen, well, Lindsay wrote another book, called *1980s: Countdown to Armageddon*. "Armageddon" is the code name for the battle that's to happen outside of the plain of Megiddo, in Israel. You talk about the Battle of Armageddon where, according to the book of Revelations, you have these massive troops converging on one another, massive bloodshed, so that the blood actually rises up to the bridles of the horses, and it's going to be this huge war. This book, then, is *1980s: Countdown to Armageddon*, when this thing is going to happen; a book in which Lindsay, true to form, argues that everything is going according to plan.

Some things were going according to plan. This book was on the New York Times' Bestseller List for 21 weeks. Evidently, Lindsay's reputation hasn't been tarnished a whit by his failed interpretations. Some of his interpretations were made particularly problematic when he talked about how the Soviet Union was so oil-thirsty, and was going to invade; when the Soviet Union ended, his initial response was, in fact, that this was a Soviet ploy. His idea was that Mikhail Gorbachev had made it look like the Soviet Union had disbanded, but in fact, what he really was doing was letting the West put down its defenses and stop spending so much on its missile systems, and once that happened, then the Soviet Union was going to re-emerge and take over the world.

Lindsay, by the way—his claims are not, obviously, politically innocent; he was a very strong advocate for Ronald Reagan's defense policies during the 80s. He was actually used by the Reagan administration, and encouraged people to support the idea of building up America's defense in light of threats from overseas. In any event, Lindsay's reputation wasn't tarnished when these predictions didn't come to fulfillment, nor has it been tarnished by his more recent claims that UFO's are deceptive ruses by demons who will soon stage a massive UFO landing so as to mislead earthlings into believing in life on other planets. They're just demons, trying to confuse people. Lindsay's books and videos continue to be enormously popular.

If we had more time, we could detail other failed prophecies that have occurred throughout the course of Christian history. It's worth noting, at least, that these failed prophecies seem to occur in almost every generation. Here I'll just mention a couple of striking examples, not even dealing with the massive concerns that some believers have right now over the approach of the year 2000. Most people listening to these tapes, of course, will be living after the year 2000 has turned, so we'll know for a fact whether in fact these fears are justified or not.

Let me talk, though, not about the future, but about the past. Possibly the best-known American failed prophecy was experienced by the followers of a man named William Miller, a New York farmer, who in the early part of the nineteenth century came to realize, on the basis of a careful study of the Bible, that the world would end in a cosmic blaze of glory in the year 1843. It took him a long time to convince anybody of this. In fact, William Miller himself, unlike his modern-day counterpart, was not in it for any kind of self-advancement; he wasn't making any money off of this deal. In fact, he was reluctant even to tell anybody what he had found in the Bible. He ended up telling some pastors what he had found, and some of them became convinced. Eventually this thing snowballed, then an avalanche occurred. There were hundreds of people who started to believe this, then thousands of people throughout this country. There were tent meetings in which they would talk about the coming of the end, and people became convinced that it was going to happen in 1843, and they actually picked a date. When that date didn't happen, they picked another date, and then another date. The third date was the big one; thousands of people became convinced that Jesus was going to return on that date. Many of these people actually gave away everything they had, in expectation of that day, thinking that they didn't need this stuff, so they quit their jobs, gave their stuff away. Some people afterwards—after the "great disappointment" as it's called, because they were sure it was going to happen tonight, and it didn't happen—some of the people who had given ought all their stuff ended up going to court in order to try and win some of it back.

Miller wasn't all that unusual in the history of Christianity. An even more significant historical event took place long before this, the predictions of the Italian monk Joachim of Fiore, who way back in the twelfth century had demonstrated that the anti-Christ would soon appear, and that the end of the age would arrive by the year 1260. People don't know about these predictions today unless they happen to be medieval historians or are interested in such things. These predictions of Joachim of Fiore played a major role in the theological reflection throughout the Middle Ages. Once again, people were shocked and dismayed when these predictions didn't come true, because, in fact, they were based on biblical prophecies.

Not even Joachim of Fiore was a new event on the Christian theological front. A thousand years before Joachim of Fiore, we can find an important group of Christians living in Asia Minor. This is a group of Christians that adhered to the teaching of a second-century prophet named Montanus. Montanus claimed that the world was going to end in his own generation. He had a large following. One of the greatest theologians of early Christianity belonged to his group, none other than Tertullian, who was famous as an apologist and theologian of the second century; he was a Montanist, who believed that the end was imminent.

You can press this dating of the end about as far back as you can go. Montanus himself, of course, wasn't the first. A century before Montanus, we find the writings of the apostle Paul, which came to form part of the New Testament itself. These are the earliest Christian writings that we have. In Paul's letters, he tells his followers that Christ is going to return from heaven in a mighty act of judgment and remove his followers from the world; 1 Thessalonians chapter 4. Whom would he remove from the world? Both those who had previously died, and, in Paul's words, "We also who are still alive." Paul appears to have expected he himself would be alive, when these things happened.

These are just a few of the many names that we know about, names of those who believed that the world would end in their own generation. In fact, it appears that every generation has had people who claim that their generation was the last. Most of the names of those who predicted the imminent end of all things, of course, are now lost to us in the shroud of history. There are two things that all of these predictors of the end have in common, as we've already

©2000 The Teaching Company Limited Partnership

seen; two things that every one of them has in common. First, every one of them was completely wrong. Second, every one of them could cite the words of Jesus in support of their views.

Let me conclude by telling you my point in making his brief survey. My point is not, as you might have thought, simply to stress the fact that Jesus himself got it wrong. It's instead to say that I think his earlier followers probably got something right. I have to admit to being a bit hesitant to make this point, given the fact that these lectures have been based completely on a historical study of Jesus rather than any theological set of beliefs—my beliefs, your beliefs, or anybody else's beliefs. To paraphrase the Hebrew prophet Amos, I myself am neither a theologian nor the son of a theologian. Ultimately, my concerns in a lecture series like this are not theological. It does seem to me, though, that if someone were interested in theology, they might want to take heed of how the early Christians handled their traditions about Jesus.

One of the frustrations of the historian of ancient Christianity is that the early Christians did not preserve their traditions about Jesus intact, but modified these traditions in order to meet the new situations they, the Christians, found themselves in. They changed their traditions in light of their new situation. As we've seen, Christians had no qualms at all about doing that. They tried to make the traditions fit the situations they themselves were in. More than anything else, it's their willingness, even their eagerness to do so that creates such problems for historians, who want to know what Jesus himself actually said and did.

That which causes such huge problems for historians may create huge possibilities for theologians, or even for simple believers, who are interested in something more than the plain facts of history. Those who refuse to recognize that every new situation is a new context, and that new contexts require a re-thinking of old traditions, are committing the mirror image of the error of those who refuse to recognize that Jesus has to be understood in his own context. We can't pretend that Jesus lived in our context, and so interpret his words in light of what they might mean today. We have to put him in his own context. We also can't pretend that we live in Jesus' context, and pretend that his words are immediately relevant to a different situation. That's always been the downfall of the doomsday predictors of the end. They've taken the words of a first-century

Jewish apocalypticist and pretended that they were directed to the context that they themselves were living in.

These words may have provided hope and vision for a better day to their original hearers. When they're removed from their original context, and used without remainder in new contexts, they simply become shallow and false. Thus, anyone who's interested in understanding what the words of Jesus might mean in the modern world cannot take them at face value and apply them to the present situation without seeing how that situation is different from his own. The business of applying the teachings of an ancient rabbi to a modern context, of course, is not the business of a historian, but of a theologian. At the least, however, the historian can recognize when a context is changed, and see the dangers involved in assuming that the historical context of a person's words and deeds are unimportant, either to their meaning or to their relevance.

Timeline

1800 B.C.? .... Abraham

1400 B.C.? .... Moses

753 B.C. .... Traditional date for founding of Rome

750–500 B.C.? .... Prophets of Hebrew Bible

750 B.C.? .... Homer

587 B.C. .... Babylonian conquest of Jerusalem

510 B.C. .... Beginning of Roman Republic

c. 400 B.C. .... Plato

333–323 B.C. .... Conquests of Alexander the Great

300–198 B.C. .... Palestine under Egyptian rule

198–142 B.C. .... Palestine under Syrian rule

167–142 B.C. .... Maccabean revolt

145 B.C. .... Book of Daniel (final book of Hebrew Bible)

140 B.C. .... Rise of Jewish sects

142–37 B.C. .... Maccabean rule

63 B.C. .... Conquest of Palestine by Romans

44 B.C. .... Assassination of Julius Caesar

40–4 B.C. .... Herod King of the Jews

4 B.C.–A.D. 39 .... Herod Antipas, ruler of Galilee

27 B.C.–A.D. 14 .... Octavian Caesar Augustus as emperor

4 B.C.? .... Jesus' birth

A.D. 14–37 .... Emperor Tiberius

A.D. 18–36 .... Caiaphas, high priest in Jerusalem

A.D. 26–36 .... Pilate as Governor of Judea

A.D. 30?	Jesus' death
A.D. 33?	Conversion of Paul
A.D. 37–100	Josephus (Jewish historian)
A.D. 37–41	Emperor Caligula
A.D. 41–54	Emperor Claudius
A.D. 54–68	Emperor Nero
A.D. 50–60?	Pauline epistles
A.D. 50–60?	"Q" Source
A.D. 56–117?	Tacitus
A.D. 50–70?	"M" and "L" Sources
A.D. 61–113	Pliny the Younger
A.D. 65?	Gospel of Mark
A.D. 69 79	Emperor Vespasian
A.D. 66–70	Jewish Revolt and destruction of Temple
A.D. 79–81	Emperor Titus
A.D. 80–85?	Gospels of Matthew and Luke
A.D. 81–96	Emperor Domitian
A.D. 90–95?	Gospel of John
A.D. 56–120	Tacitus
A.D. 62–113	Pliny the Younger
A.D. 98–117	Emperor Trajan
A.D. 110–130?	Gospels of Peter, Thomas, and Infancy Thomas

Glossary

Alexander the Great: The great military leader of Macedonia (356–323 B.C.) whose armies conquered much of the lands around the Mediterranean, including Egypt, Palestine, and Persia, and who was responsible for the spread of Greek culture (Hellenism) throughout the lands he conquered.

Antiochus IV (= Antiochus Epiphanes): Syrian monarch who compelled the Jews of Palestine to adopt Greek culture, leading to the Maccabean revolt in 167 B.C.E.

Antitheses: Literally, "contrary statements"; used to designate six sayings of Jesus in the Sermon on the Mount (Matt. 5:21–48), in which he states a Jewish Law ("You have heard it said…"), then sets his own interpretation against it ("But I say to you…").

Apocalypticism: A worldview held by many ancient Jews and Christians that maintained that the present age is controlled by forces of evil that God will destroy at the end of time when he intervenes in history to bring in his kingdom, an event thought to be imminent.

Apocrypha: Literally, "hidden things"; used to describe a group of books on the fringe of the Jewish or Christian canons of Scripture. The Jewish Apocrypha contains such books as 1 and 2 Maccabees and 4 Ezra.

Apollonius: A pagan philosopher and holy man of the first century A.D. who could allegedly perform miracles and deliver divinely inspired teachings; a man believed by some of his followers to be a Son of God.

Apostle: Literally, one who is "sent"; used of one who is commissioned to perform a task. In early Christianity, the term designated missionaries who were specially appointed by Christ. See **disciple**.

Beatitudes: Literally, "blessings"; used as a technical term to refer to sayings of Jesus that begin the Sermon on the Mount (e.g., "Blessed are the poor in spirit…" Matt 5:3–12).

Canon: From a Greek word that means "ruler" or "straight edge." The term is used to designate a recognized collection of texts; the canon of the New Testament is thus the collection of books that Christians accept as authoritative.

Christ: See **Messiah**.

Christology: Any teaching or doctrine about the nature of Christ.

Contextual credibility, criterion of: A criterion used by scholars to establish historically reliable material. With respect to the historical Jesus, the criterion maintains that any tradition about Jesus that cannot be credibly fit into his own first-century Palestinian context cannot be regarded as authentic.

Cosmos: Greek term for "world."

Covenant: An agreement or treaty between two social or political parties; used by ancient Jews to refer to the pact that God made to protect and preserve them in exchange for their devotion and adherence to his law.

Cynics: Group of Greco-Roman philosophers known as street preachers who harangued their audiences and urged them to find freedom by becoming liberated from all social conventions. Because they chose to live "according to nature," with none of the niceties of life, their opponents called them "dogs" (Greek = *cynes*).

Daimonia: Category of divine beings in Greco-Roman paganism. *Daimonia* were thought to be less powerful than the gods but far more powerful than humans and capable of influencing human lives.

Dead Sea Scrolls: Ancient Jewish writings discovered in caves to the northwest of the Dead Sea; believed to have been produced by a group of apocalyptically minded Essenes who lived in a monastic community from Maccabean times through the Jewish War of A.D. 66–70. See **Essenes**, **Qumran**.

Disciple: A follower; literally, one who is "taught" (as opposed to an "apostle" = an emissary, one who is "sent").

Dissimilarity, criterion of: Criterion used by scholars to establish historically reliable material; the criterion maintains that any tradition about Jesus that does not coincide with (or that works against) the vested interests of the early Christians is likely to be authentic.

Docetism: From the Greek word *dokeo*, "to seem" or "to appear." Used to describe the view that Jesus was not a human being but only "appeared" to be.

Egyptian, the: A Jewish apocalyptic prophet of the first century A.D., mentioned by Josephus, who predicted the destruction of the walls of Jerusalem.

Equestrian: The second-highest socioeconomic class of ancient Rome (below "Senator"), which was comprised of wealthy aristocrats.

Essenes: A sect of Jews that started during the Maccabean period who stressed maintaining their own ritual purity in the face of the coming apocalypse; its members are generally thought to have produced the Dead Sea Scrolls.

Fourth Philosophy: A group of Jews mentioned by Josephus who insisted on violent opposition to the foreign domination of the Promised Land.

Four-source hypothesis: A solution to the "Synoptic Problem" that maintains that four sources lie behind the Gospels of Matthew, Mark, and Luke: (1) Mark was the source for many of the stories found in Matthew and Luke, (2) Q was the source for the material (mainly sayings) found in Matthew and Luke but not in Mark, (3) M provided material found only in Matthew, and (4) L provided material found only in Luke.

Gentile: A non-Jew.

Gnosticism: A group of ancient religions, some of them closely related to Christianity, that maintained that elements of the divine had become entrapped in this evil world of matter. These divine elements could be released only by acquiring the secret *gnosis* (Greek for "knowledge") of who they were and of how they could escape. This gnosis was generally thought to have been brought by an emissary of the divine realm.

Greco-Roman world: The lands (and culture) around the Mediterranean from the time of Alexander the Great to the Emperor Constantine, roughly 300 B.C. to A.D. 300.

Hasmoneans: An alternative name for the Maccabees, the family of Jewish priests that began the revolt against Syria in 167 B.C. and ruled Israel before the Roman conquest of 63 B.C.

Hellenization: The spread of Greek language and culture throughout the Mediterranean that began with the conquests of Alexander the Great.

High Priest: Before A.D. 70, the highest ranking official in Judaism when there was no Jewish king, in charge of the operation of the Jerusalem Temple and its priests. See **Sadducees** and **Sanhedrin**.

Holy of Holies: The inner part of the Jewish Temple in which God's presence on earth was believed to dwell. No one could enter this room except the High Priest on the Day of Atonement to make a sacrifice for the sins of the people.

Independent attestation, criterion of: Criterion used by scholars to establish historically reliable material. With respect to the historical Jesus, the criterion maintains that any tradition that is attested independently by more than one source is more likely to be authentic.

Josephus: First-century Jewish court historian, appointed by the Roman emperor Vespasian. His works, *The Jewish War* and *The Antiquities of the Jews*, are principal sources for information about life in first-century Palestine.

Judas Maccabeus: Jewish patriot who led the Maccabean revolt in its earliest phases. See **Hasmoneans**.

L: A document (or documents, written or oral) that no longer survives but is believed to have provided Luke with traditions not found in Matthew or Mark. See **four-source hypothesis**.

M: A document (or documents, written or oral) that no longer survives but is believed to have provided Matthew with traditions not found in Mark or Luke. See f**our-source hypothesis**.

Maccabean revolt: The Jewish uprising against the Syrians starting in 167 B.C.; protested the forced imposition of Hellenistic religion and culture and the proscription of Jewish practices, such as circumcision, by the Syrian monarch Antiochus Epiphanes. See **Hasmoneans**.

Manuscript: A hand-written copy of a text.

Markan priority: The view that Mark, the first of the Synoptic Gospels written, was one of the sources used by Matthew and Luke.

Messiah: From a Hebrew word that literally means "anointed one," translated into Greek as "Christos," from which derives our English word "Christ." The first century saw a wide range of expectations of whom this future deliverer might be: a great warrior king, a cosmic judge of the earth, or a mighty priest inspired to interpret God's law.

Mishnah: A collection of oral traditions passed on by Jewish rabbis who saw themselves as the descendants of the Pharisees, put into writing around A.D. 200. See **Talmud**.

Nag Hammadi: Village in upper (south) Egypt, near the place where a Bedouin named Mohammed Ali discovered a collection of Gnostic writings, including the Gospel of Thomas, in 1945.

Paganism: An umbrella term used for ancient polytheistic religions (i.e., other than Judaism and Christianity).

Passion: From the Greek word for "suffering"; refers to the traditions of Jesus' last days, up to and including his crucifixion (hence the "Passion narrative").

Passover: The most important and widely celebrated annual festival of Jews in Roman times, which commemorated the exodus from Egypt.

Pentateuch: Literally, the "five scrolls"; designates the first five books of the Hebrew Bible (Genesis, Exodus, Leviticus, Numbers, and Deuteronomy), also known as the Torah or the Law of Moses.

Pentecost: From the Greek word for fifty (= *pentakosia*); designates the Jewish agricultural festival that was celebrated fifty days after the feast of the Passover.

Pharisees: A Jewish sect that may have originated during the Maccabean period, which emphasized strict adherence to the purity laws of the Torah and developed special oral laws to help them to do so. See **Mishnah**.

Pseudepigrapha: Literally, "false writings"; ancient non-canonical Jewish and Christian literary texts, many of which were written under pseudonyms.

Pseudonimity: The practice of writing under a "false name," evident in a large number of pagan, Jewish, and Christian writings from antiquity.

Q Source: The source used by both Matthew and Luke for the stories they have in common that are not found in Mark (these are mainly sayings); from the German word *Quelle*, "source." The document no longer exists but is reconstructed on the basis of Matthew and Luke.

Qumran: Place near the northwest shore of the Dead Sea where the Dead Sea Scrolls were discovered in 1945; in the first century, home to a group of Essenes who used the Scrolls as part of their library.

Roman Empire: All the lands conquered by Rome and ruled, ultimately, by the Roman emperor, starting with Caesar Augustus in 27 B.C.; before Augustus, Rome was a republic, ruled by the Senate.

Sadducees: A Jewish party closely connected with the Temple cult and the Jewish priests who ran it; comprised mainly of the Jewish aristocracy in Judea, whose leader, the high priest, served as the highest ranking local official and chief liaison with the Roman governor.

Samaritans: Inhabitants of Samaria, located between Galilee and Judea, who were considered by some Jews to be apostates and half-breeds, because their lineage could be traced to intermarriages between Jews and pagans several centuries before the New Testament period.

Sermon on the Mount: The sermon found in Matthew 5–7 that preserves some of the best known sayings of Jesus (including Matthew's form of the Beatitudes, the antitheses, and the Lord's Prayer).

Sanhedrin: A council of Jewish leaders that played an advisory role to the high priest in matters of religious and civil policy.

Scribes, Jewish: Highly educated experts in Jewish law (and possibly its copyists) during the Greco-Roman period.

Senators: The highest ranking members of the Roman aristocracy, comprised of the wealthiest men of Rome, who were responsible for governing the vast Roman bureaucracy during the Republic and were still active and highly visible under the Empire.

Son of God: In most Greco-Roman circles, a term used to designate a person born to the union of a God and a mortal, who was thought to be able to perform miraculous deeds or convey superhuman teachings. In Jewish circles, the term was used to designate a person chosen to stand in a special relationship with the God of Israel, including the ancient Jewish kings.

Son of Man: A much disputed term that is used in some ancient apocalyptic texts to refer to a cosmic judge sent from heaven at the end of time, based, probably, on Daniel 7:13–14.

Synagogue: An ancient place of Jewish worship, prayer, and reading of the Torah, from a Greek word that literally means "being brought together."

Synoptic Gospels: The Gospels of Matthew, Mark, and Luke, which narrate so many of the same stories that they can be placed next to each other and "be seen together" (the literal meaning of "synoptic").

Talmud: The great collection of ancient Jewish traditions containing both the Mishnah and the later commentaries on the Mishnah called the Gemarah. There are two collections of the Talmud, one made in Palestine during the early fifth century A.D. and the other, in Babylon perhaps a century later. The Babylonian Talmud is usually considered the more authoritative.

Theudas: A first-century Jewish apocalyptic prophet mentioned by Josephus who predicted the parting of the Jordan River and, evidently, the reconquest of the Promised Land by the Jewish people.

Torah: A Hebrew word meaning "guidance" or "direction"; usually translated as "Law." As a technical term, it designates either the Law of God given to Moses or the first five books of the Jewish Bible that Moses was thought to have written, Genesis, Exodus, Leviticus, Numbers, and Deuteronomy.

Tradition: Any doctrine, idea, practice, or custom that is handed down from one person to another.

Zealots: A group of Galilean Jews who fled to Jerusalem during the early stages of the Jewish War against Rome in A.D. 66–70, overthrew the reigning aristocracy in the city, and urged violent resistance to the bitter end. See **Fourth Philosophy**.

Biographical Notes

Alexander the Great

Alexander of Macedonia, otherwise known as Alexander the Great, was one of the most influential people in the history of Western civilization. Born in 356 B.C. to King Philip of Macedonia, he succeeded to the throne at the age of 22 when his father was assassinated. Driven by his desire for conquest and using his military genius and a ruthless military policy, Alexander quickly conquered Greece before moving his armies eastward to overcome Asia Minor, Palestine, and Egypt. His major conquest came over Darius, ruler of the Persian Empire, which extended his territories well into modern-day India. Alexander's historical significance stems from his use of military conquest to spread a previously unheard of cultural unity, termed Hellenism, to the lands around the Mediterranean. It played an enormous role in the history of Western civilization and, of course, for the New Testament, which was rooted in Hellenistic culture and written in Greek.

Caesar Augustus (Octavian)

Octavian was the first of the Roman emperors, who transformed Rome from a Republic (ruled by a Senate) to an Empire (ruled, ultimately, by the emperor). He was born in 63 B.C. to the niece of Julius Caesar and was later adopted as the son of his great-uncle. When Caesar was assassinated in 44 B.C., Octavian left Greece (where he was being educated) to avenge the death. In Rome, he joined forces with two other prominent aristocrats, Lepidus and Mark Antony, to form a so-called "triumvirate" of power. There were differences among the three, however, and when Octavian deprived Lepidus of his power and defeated Antony (and Cleopatra) in battle, he emerged as the sole ruler of Rome. The Roman Senate continued to exist, of course, and to exercise real authority. Octavian was bestowed honorific titles—including "Augustus" (= most revered one)—and power as Rome's "first citizen" and, eventually, the "father of the country." Octavian's rule lasted over 40 years (27 B.C.–A.D. 14) and is often referred to as the period of *Pax Romana*, a relatively peaceful time.

Josephus

Josephus was born to an aristocratic Jewish priestly family in A.D. 37 in Palestine. He was highly educated and became an important figure in Judean politics. When the Jewish war against Rome broke out in A.D. 66 (a war that would lead to the catastrophic fall of Jerusalem and the destruction of the Temple in A.D. 70), Josephus was given charge of the Jewish forces in Galilee in the north. His troops were no match for the Roman legions, however, who marched through the region with ease. Josephus later reported that when surrounded at the town of Jopata, his troops made a suicide pact to prevent the Romans from taking any prisoners. When the killing was nearly complete, Josephus and the one other remaining soldier agreed to surrender.

When brought before the conquering Roman general, Vespasian, Josephus revealed a prophecy from God that Vespasian would become emperor. Soon thereafter, when Nero committed suicide in A.D. 68, the imperial government was thrown into serious turmoil, with three different emperors appearing on the stage in less than a year (dispatched through assassinations and suicides). Eventually Vespasian's troops proclaimed him emperor. He marched to Rome, restored order, and settled in for a ten-year reign. As a reward for prophetic insight, Vespasian granted Josephus an annual stipend and appointed him to work as a court historian.

Josephus's literary projects over the course of his stay in Rome are important to posterity. He first produced a detailed account, in seven volumes, of the Jewish Wars. Then, some twenty years later, in the early 90s, he published his twenty-volume history of the Jewish people from the very beginning (Adam and Eve!) up to his own time, called *The Antiquities of the Jews*. Josephus wrote several other books that still survive, including a defense of Judaism against its cultured despisers and an autobiography. These books by a learned Jew from Palestine, produced with a full range of resources at his disposal, provide our fullest and best (and sometimes only) source of information for the history of the Jewish people (especially in Palestine) during the first century.

Heinrich E. G. Paulus

Heinrich Paulus was one of the major figures in German theological circles in the early part of the 19th century. Born in 1761, he developed a keen interest in Semitic languages at a young age. While still in his twenties, he was appointed a professor of "oriental" (i.e., Semitic) languages at the University of Jena; soon thereafter, he became a professor of biblical interpretation and theology. Most of his career was spent at the University of Heidelberg (1811–1844), where he held a chair in exegesis (= interpretation) and church history.

Paulus is best known for his two major studies of Jesus and the Gospels, which have never been translated into English: *Leben Jesu als Grundlage einer reinen Geschichte des Urchristenthums* (=_The *Life of Jesus_as the Foundation of a Pure History of Early Christianity*, 2 vols.) and *Exegetisches Handbuch über die_drei ersten Evangelien* (= *Handbook for the Interpretation of the First Three Gospels*, 3 vols).

In the first of these works, Paulus develops an "enlightened" understanding of the Gospel traditions about Jesus. He maintains that the miracle stories can best be explained by assuming that the disciples of Jesus misconstrued natural events that occurred during Jesus' ministry, thinking that they involved supernatural events. In Paulus's judgment, in no case did miracles actually occur; the disciples mistakenly thought they did.

David Friedrich Strauss

David Friedrich Strauss was one of the pioneers of modern New Testament studies. Born in 1808, he studied theology and philosophy, first in Blaubeuren, then in Tübingen and Berlin. He was particularly trained in, and enamored by, the philosophical views of G. W. F. Hegel. At the remarkably young age of twenty-seven, Strauss wrote his revolutionary and massively influential study *Das Leben Jesu, kritisch_bearbeitet* (= *The Life of Jesus, Critically Examined*) in two volumes. In this detailed and erudite work, Strauss argued that earlier interpreters of the Gospels, whether traditionalists who subscribed to the supernatural or rationalists who did not, had all misperceived the true nature of the early accounts of Jesus' life by thinking that they provided historical documentation for what had really happened. For Strauss, the Gospels do not contain historical narratives but "myths," i.e., history-like stories that evolved in early Christianity to relate the "truth" about who Jesus really was. These stories didn't actually happen but nonetheless proclaim the Christian message.

The book created a storm of protest in the theological and academic communities. As a result of his views, Strauss was relieved of his duties as a professor at Tübingen and from then on, had difficulty landing a regular teaching post. In subsequent editions of the book, Strauss retracted some of his more radical views about Jesus but later returned to them. Embittered by the controversies over his work, he continued to write in philosophy, theology, and early Christianity (as well as politics and biography) until his death in 1874.

Albert Schweitzer

Widely regarded as the greatest humanitarian of the 20th century and awarded the Nobel Peace Prize in 1953, Albert Schweitzer is perhaps best remembered today as a medical missionary in French Equatorial Africa. Even before beginning his medical studies, though, Schweitzer was already renowned both as a prominent theologian and as a concert organist. Born in 1875 in Alsace, he studied at Strassburg, Berlin, and Paris. His area of theological expertise was the New Testament, and he wrote important books on Jesus' preaching of the kingdom (1901) and on the apostle Paul (1911). By far his most important work was *Quest of the Historical Jesus* (German title: *Von Reimarus zu Wrede*; 1906), which discussed, with wit and penetrating insight, all previous attempts to write a life of Jesus. The book also criticized scholars from the beginning of the modern period (the end of the 18th century) to his own day for failing to recognize the importance of certain critical perspectives (e.g., that the Synoptics are better sources than John) and for overlooking the heavily apocalyptic component of Jesus' message and mission. This was the most important early attempt to push for the view that Jesus was an apocalypticist who must be situated in his own first-century Jewish context. In rough outline, this view has dominated scholarly discussion ever since.

Annotated Bibliography

Allison, Dale. *Jesus of Nazareth: Millenarian Prophet*. Minneapolis: Fortress, 1998. The most thorough recent attempt to show that Jesus was an apocalyptic prophet; the book is written at a scholarly level and deals with the issue of the criteria scholars have used to establish historically reliable tradition.

Boyer, Paul. *When Time Shall Be No More: Prophecy Belief in Modern American Culture*. Cambridge, MA: Harvard University, 1992. A fascinating study of different religious leaders, writers, and sects in America that have maintained that the world was going to end in the near future.

Brown, Raymond. *The Birth of the Messiah: A Commentary on the Infancy Narratives in Matthew and Luke*, 2nd ed. Garden City, NY: Doubleday, 1993. A massive and exhaustive (but highly popular) discussion of the accounts of Jesus' birth in both Matthew and Luke; suitable for those who want to know everything about every detail of the passages.

―――. *The Death of the Messiah: From Gethsemane to the Grave*, 2 vols. London: Doubleday, 1994. A detailed and thorough discussion of the accounts of Jesus' last hours found in all four Gospels.

Carter, Warren. *What Are They Saying about Matthew's Sermon on the Mount?* New York: Paulist, 1994. The best introductory sketch of what scholars have said about the Sermon on the Mount from Matthew 5–7, Jesus' best known set of teachings.

Cartlidge, David R., and David L. Dungan, eds. *Documents for the Study of the Gospels*, 2nd ed. Philadelphia: Fortress, 1994. A valuable selection of ancient literary texts that portray "divine men" in ways that sound remarkably like the portrayals of Jesus in the New Testament. Includes portions of Philostratus's *Life of Apollonius*.

Charlesworth, James H., ed. *The Old Testament Pseudepigrapha*, 2 vols. Garden City, NY: Doubleday, 1983, 1985. The most complete collection of non-canonical writings of early Judaism from before and around the time of the New Testament, with full and informative introductions. Included are a number of "apocalypses" from around the time of Jesus.

Chilton, Bruce, and Craig Evans, eds. *Authenticating the Activities of Jesus*. Leiden: Brill, 1999. Essays by prominent scholars, discussing how one can establish the historical probability of the accounts of Jesus' activities. Best suited for advanced readers.

————, eds. *Authenticating the Words of Jesus*. Leiden: Brill, 1999. Essays by prominent scholars, discussing how one can establish the historical probability of the accounts of Jesus' teachings. Best suited for advanced readers.

————, eds., *Studying the Historical Jesus: Evaluations of the Current Stage of Research*. Leiden: Brill, 1994. A number of essays on important aspects of the historical Jesus. Some of these take exception to the view of Jesus as an apocalypticist, preferring instead to see him as a kind of first-century Jewish Cynic. Most suitable for more advanced readers.

Cohen, Shaye. *From the Maccabees to the Mishnah*. Philadelphia: Westminster Press, 1987. Probably the best place to turn for a clear overview of Jewish institutions, practices, and beliefs from roughly the mid-second century B.C. to A.D. 200.

Cohn, Norman. *The Pursuit of the Millennium: Revolutionary Millenarians and Mystical Anarchists of the Middle Ages*, 2nd ed. New York: Oxford University, 1970. A fascinating and well-received study of the major religious movements of the Middle Ages that anticipated the imminent end of the world.

Collins, John. *The Apocalyptic Imagination: An Introduction to the Matrix of Christianity*. New York: Crossroad, 1984. An excellent overview of Jewish apocalypticism as the context for the proclamation of Jesus and his followers based on the surviving literary texts of ancient Judaism.

Crossan, John Dominic. *The Historical Jesus: The Life of a Mediterranean Jewish Peasant*. San Francisco: HarperSanFrancisco, 1991. A massive, learned, and intriguing study of the historical Jesus that goes to great lengths to situate him in his own historical context (in the first-century Roman empire), discusses critical methodology (championing the use of the criterion of independent attestation), and argues that Jesus was not an apocalypticist but a kind of Jewish Cynic philosopher.

————. *Jesus: A Revolutionary Biography*. San Francisco: HarperSanFrancisco, 1994. A much simpler version of the preceding; ideal for those who do not have a great deal of background in the area.

————. *Who Killed Jesus? Exploring the Roots of Anti-Semitism in the Gospel Story of the Death of Jesus.* San Francisco: HarperSanFrancisco, 1995. A popular treatment of the historicity of the accounts of Jesus' crucifixion, conducted in light of the anti-Semitic overtones that the accounts have assumed over the centuries.

Davies, Margaret, and E. P. Sanders. *Studying the Synoptic Gospels.* Philadelphia: Trinity Press International, 1989. A detailed and thorough discussion of the literary relationships among the first three Gospels (i.e., the "Synoptic problem") and of the major scholarly approaches that can be taken toward them. For advanced students.

Dibelius, Martin. *From Tradition to Gospel,* trans. by B. L. Woolf. New York: Scribner, 1934. This was a groundbreaking study that dealt with the oral traditions about Jesus in circulation before being written down in our Gospels.

Dunn, James. *Christology in the Making: A New Testament Inquiry into the Origins of the Doctrine of the Incarnation.* London: SCM Press, 1989. A full discussion of the early developments of Christian understandings of Jesus, which is particularly interested in the question of when and how Christians first began to think about Jesus as divine.

Ehrman, Bart D. *Jesus: Apocalyptic Prophet of the New Millennium.* New York, Oxford University Press, 1999. Written by the instructor of the course, this study considers all of the evidence for the historical Jesus—including recent archaeological discoveries and non-canonical sources—and argues that he is best understood as an apocalyptic prophet who expected God to intervene in history to overthrow the forces of evil and bring in his good kingdom.

————. *The New Testament: A Historical Introduction to the Early Christian Writings,* 2nd ed. New York: Oxford University Press, 1999. A historically oriented introduction to all the issues in the study of the New Testament (not just Jesus and the Gospels). Designed for use as a college-level textbook and as a resource for anyone interested in the New Testament.

————. *The New Testament and Other Early Christian Writings: A Reader.* New York: Oxford, 1998. A collection of all the writings by the early Christians from within the first century after Jesus' death (i.e., those written before A.D. 130), both canonical and non-canonical. It includes the non-canonical Infancy Gospel of Thomas, the Gospel of Peter, and the Coptic Gospel of Thomas discussed in this course.

Elliott, J. K. *The Apocryphal Jesus: Legends of the Early Church*. New York: Oxford, 1998. A more popular and accessible version of the following, which focuses on the tales about Jesus told in the non-canonical Gospels. An excellent book for those not already familiar with the field.

————. *The Apocryphal New Testament: A Collection of Apocryphal Christian Literature in an English Translation*. Oxford: Clarendon, 1993. An excellent one-volume collection that includes all the important non-canonical Gospels, as well as non-canonical Acts, Epistles, and Apocalypses, in a readable English translation with brief introductions.

Evans, Craig A. *Life of Jesus Research: An Annotated Bibliography*, rev. ed. *New Testament Tools and Studies*; 24; Leiden/New York/Köln: E. J. Brill, 1996. A thorough bibliography of the most important books and articles written by scholars and for scholars about the historical Jesus. Includes a 2045 entries.

Ferguson, John. *Religions in the Roman Empire*. Ithaca, NY: Cornell University, 1970. An overview of the wide variety of Roman religions, with some emphasis on archaeological and other nonliterary sources. The assumptions of the book are now a bit dated, but it still provides some valuable background information.

Fitzmyer, Joseph A. *Responses to 101 Questions on the Dead Sea Scrolls*. New York: Paulist, 1992. A terrific book that answers almost every question that someone new to the study of the Dead Sea Scrolls would ask. Probably the easiest way for a beginner in the field to start; written by a renowned and clear-headed expert.

Frederiksen, Paula. *From Jesus to Christ: The Origins of the New Testament Images of Jesus*. New Haven: Yale University Press, 1988. An important study of the earliest Christian views of Jesus and the development of these views as Christianity moved away from its Jewish roots to become an independent religion.

Fuller, Reginald. *Interpreting the Miracles*. London: SCM, 1963. A somewhat older study that examines how early Christians understood miracles and told their accounts of Jesus' deeds in the New Testament Gospels.

Furnish, Victor Paul. *Jesus According to Paul*. Cambridge: University Press, 1993. A concise and insightful discussion of Paul's understanding of Jesus, including reflections on the question of how much Paul actually knew about Jesus' life. An ideal book for those who are not already advanced in the field.

Green, Joel, et al., eds. *Dictionary of Jesus and the Gospels*. Downers Grove, IL: Intervarsity Press, 1994. A "Bible dictionary" that provides in-depth articles on a wide range of topics pertaining to the historical Jesus and the Gospels. Each article was written by a prominent evangelical Christian with an elevated view of Scripture and its historical reliability.

Hennecke, Edgar, and Wilhelm Schneemelcher, eds. *New Testament Apocrypha*, 2 vols., trans. by A. J. B. Higgins, et al., ed. by R. McL. Wilson. Philadelphia: Westminster Press, 1991. An authoritative study of all the early non-canonical writings preserved from Christian antiquity. It includes English translations of all the major texts, along with detailed scholarly introductions. An indispensable resource for advanced students.

Hurtado, Larry. *One God, One Lord. Early Christian Devotion and Ancient Jewish Monotheism*. Philadelphia: Fortress, 1988. This valuable study deals with the emerging views of Jesus in early Christianity, especially the views of his divine status. It argues that the source of conflict between early Christians and non-Christian Jews was not over whether Jesus could be thought of as divine, but whether he was to be worshipped.

Kee, Howard Clark. *Miracle in the Early Christian World*: *A Study in Socio-historical Method*. New Haven: Yale University Press, 1983. This study of "miracles" in early Christianity approaches the matter from a sociological perspective, situating the early accounts of Jesus' miracles in the broader context of the understanding of miracles and miracle workers in the Greco-Roman world. Best suited for more advanced readers.

Koester, Helmut. *Ancient Christian Gospels: Their History and Development*. Philadelphia: Trinity Press International, 1990. A full and erudite discussion of all the ancient Gospels of early Christianity, canonical and non-canonical, which tries to isolate their sources, dates, and relations to one another. Some of the conclusions have been highly controversial, because the author finds that many of the later Gospels preserve traditions that are earlier than those found among the canonical four. Best suited for advanced readers.

Kysar, Robert. *John the Maverick Gospel*. Atlanta: John Knox, 1976. One of the best introductions to the unique features of John's Gospel; pays particular attention to how John's portrayal of Jesus differs from those of the Synoptic Gospels.

Layton, Bentley. *The Gnostic Scriptures: A New Translation with Annotations*. Garden City: Doubleday, 1987. An accessible translation of important Gnostic documents, including those discovered at Nag Hammadi and those quoted by the Church Fathers. Includes a useful introductory sketch of Gnosticism.

Lindsey, Hal, with C. C. Carlson. *The Late Great Planet Earth*. Grand Rapids: Zondervan, 1970. A blockbuster book, with 28 million copies in print. Lindsey, an evangelical Christian, interprets biblical prophecies to indicate that the world was entering a major period of catastrophe, leading to the second coming of Christ sometime before the end of the 1980s.

———. *The 1980's: Countdown to Armageddon*. New York: Bantam, 1980. An updated sketch of Lindsey's views, in which he argues that the stage is now (was now) completely set for the cosmic disasters of the end of time.

Meier, John. *A Marginal Jew: Rethinking the Historical Jesus*, vol 1. New York: Doubleday, 1991. An authoritative discussion of the historical Jesus written by a highly knowledgeable scholar. The first volume provides one of the clearest discussions available of all the sources, including those outside the canon, for Jesus' life and of the methods scholars use to determine which of the surviving traditions about Jesus are historically accurate.

———. *A Marginal Jew: Rethinking the Historical Jesus*, vol 2. New York: Doubleday, 1994. This second volume includes a systematic and careful discussion of the problem posed for the historian by "miracle" and a detailed evaluation of the traditions of Jesus' miracles as found in the New Testament.

Nickle, Keith. *The Synoptic Gospels: Conflict and Consensus*. Atlanta: John Knox, 1980. Now somewhat dated in its approach, this volume remains one of the best introductory discussions of the background and message of the three Synoptic Gospels.

Pagels, Elaine. *The Gnostic Gospels*. New York: Random, 1976. A best-selling and provocative account of the views of some of the Gnostic Gospels, in opposition to the views found in the emerging "orthodox" Christian church.

Perrin, Norman. *Rediscovering the Teachings of Jesus*. London: SCM Press/New York: Harper & Row, 1967. A dated but classic discussion of the criteria used by scholars to ascertain the actual teachings of the historical Jesus.

Robinson, James, ed. *The Nag Hammadi Library in English*, 3rd ed. New York: Harper & Row, 1988. An authoritative English translation of the documents discovered at Nag Hammadi, with insightful introductions to each of the texts.

Rowland, Christopher. *The Open Heaven: A Study of Apocalypticism in Judaism and Early Christianity*. New York: Crossroads, 1982. An insightful study of apocalyptic thinking from before, during, and after the life of Jesus.

Rudolph, Kurt. *Gnosis: The Nature and History of Gnosticism*, trans. R. McL. Wilson. San Francisco: Harper & Row, 1987. The best available book-length introduction to ancient Gnosticism; includes a discussion of the Nag Hammadi finds and the major tenets of Gnostic thought.

Sanders, E. P. *The Historical Figure of Jesus*. London: Penguin, 1993. One of the clearest and most insightful introductions to the life and teachings of the historical Jesus. Well suited for beginning students.

———. *Judaism Practice and Belief, 63 BCE–66 CE*. London and Philadelphia: SCM Press/Trinity Press International, 1992. A detailed and authoritative account of what it meant to practice Judaism immediately before and during the time of the New Testament, by one of the great New Testament scholars of our generation.

Sandmel, Samuel. *Judaism and Christian Beginnings*. New York: Oxford University Press, 1978. A well-written and insightful sketch of the Jewish religion at the beginning of Christianity. Suitable for those who are relatively new to the field.

Schweitzer, Albert. *The Quest of the Historical Jesus*. New York: Macmillan, 1968. The classic study of scholarly attempts to write a biography of Jesus from the end of the 18th century to the beginning of the 20th (the German original appeared in 1906). It is also one of the first—and probably the most important—attempt to show that Jesus is best understood as a Jewish apocalypticist.

Shelton, Jo-Ann. *As the Romans Did: A Sourcebook in Roman Social History*, 2nd ed. New York: Oxford, 1998. A terrific introduction to all aspects of Roman life; includes clear translations of selected primary texts organized according to social history and a useful section on Roman religion.

Stanton, Graham. *The Gospels and Jesus*. New York: Oxford, 1989. A solid and readable introduction to the major critical problems involved in studying the Gospels and the historical Jesus.

Stein, Robert *The Synoptic Problem: An Introduction*. Grand Rapids: Baker Book House, 1987. A treatment of the range of issues involved in the problem of establishing the literary relationships of Matthew, Mark, and Luke, with a discussion of the hypothetical source Q. A good tool for beginning students.

Strauss, David Friedrich. *The Life of Jesus Critically Examined.* Ramsey, NJ: Sigler Press, 1994. Originally published in 1835–36 and translated into English from the fourth edition by novelist George Elliot, this revolutionary book argued that the Gospels are best understood as containing myths of Jesus, not historical accounts.

Tatum, W. Barnes. *In Quest of Jesus: A Guidebook*, 2nd ed. Nashville: Abingdon, 1999. A clear and readable introduction to the sources and methods available for establishing historically reliable traditions in the Gospels.

Turcan, Robert. *The Cults of the Roman Empire*. Oxford: Blackwell, 1996. A superb introduction to some of the major religious cults in the Roman Empire from roughly the time of early Christianity (and before).

Vermes, Geza ed. *The Dead Sea Scrolls in English*, 3rd ed. Baltimore: Penguin Books, 1987. A readable and accessible collection and translation of the Dead Sea Scrolls in English, with a clear and useful introduction.

———. *Jesus the Jew: A Historian's Reading of the Gospels*. New York: Macmillan, 1973. A readable but very learned study of Jesus in light of traditions of other Jewish "holy men" from his time; written by a prominent New Testament scholar at Oxford.

Weber, Timothy P. *Living in the Shadow of the Second Coming: American Premillennialism 1875–1982*, enlarged ed. Grand Rapids: Zondervan, 1983. An authoritative and interesting account of the historical development of American Protestant thinking about the end of the age.

Whisenant, Edgar. *88 Reasons Why the Rapture Will Be in 1988.* Nashville: World Bible Society, 1988. Written by an evangelical Christian who argued from biblical prophecy that Jesus would bodily return to earth in 1988, leading to a set of worldwide catastrophes and the end of the world as we know it.

Wojcik, Daniel. *The End of the World as We Know It: Faith, Fatalism and Apocalypse in America.* New York: New York University Press, 1997. A fascinating account of how apocalyptic beliefs have affected a wide range of aspects of American culture, from religious fundamentalism, to Catholic visions of Mary, to UFO abduction narratives, to punk rock.